Greek

for the
REST of US

Also by William D. Mounce

Basics of Biblical Greek Workbook

Basics of Biblical Greek Vocabulary Cards

Basics of Biblical Greek Audio CD

The Morphology of Biblical Greek

The Analytical Greek Lexicon to the Greek New Testament

A Graded Reader of Biblical Greek

The Zondervan Greek and English Interlinear New Testament (NASB/NIV)

The Zondervan Greek and English Interlinear New Testament (NIV/KJV)

The Zondervan Greek and English Interlinear New Testament (TNIV/NLT)

Greek for the Rest of Us: Using Greek Tools without Mastering Biblical Greek

Interlinear for the Rest of Us: The Reverse Interlinear for New Testament Word Studies

Mounce's Complete Expository Dictionary of Old and New Testament Words

The Pastoral Epistles (Word Biblical Commentary)

The Crossway Comprehensive Concordance of the Holy Bible: English Standard Version

Greek

for the
REST of US

Using Greek Tools
without Mastering Biblical Languages

Using Greek Tools
without Mastering Biblical Languages

WILLIAM D.
MOUNCE

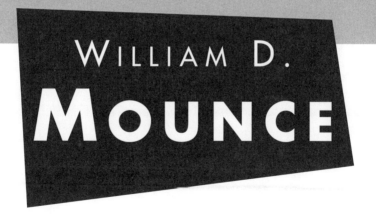

ZONDERVAN®

ZONDERVAN.com/
AUTHORTRACKER
follow your favorite authors

ZONDERVAN

Greek for the Rest of Us
Copyright © 2003 by William D. Mounce

Requests for information should be addressed to:

Zondervan, *Grand Rapids, Michigan* 49530

Library of Congress Cataloging-in-Publication Data

Mounce, William D.
    Greek for the rest of us : using greek tools without mastering biblical greek.
    William D. Mounce.
        p. cm.
    ISBN 978-0-310-28289-1
    1. Greek language, Biblical—Grammar. 2. Bible. N.T.—Language, style. I. Title.
    PA817.M655 2003
    487'.4—dc21   2003002245

Typeset by Teknia Software

Printed in the United States of America

11 12 13 14 15 16 /DCI/ 29 28 27 26 25 24 23 22 21 20 19 18 17 16 15 14 13 12 11 10 9 8 7

for Big Terry

who deeply desires to know God's Word better
but who does not have the time to learn Greek

Table of Contents

Preface

When people learn that I am a Greek teacher, one of the more common responses is, "Oh, I have always wanted to learn Greek." (It may not be the most common, but it has happened a lot.) I always ask them why they want to learn Greek. To date, no one has said they really want to learn the language. What they want is to understand the Bible better, and especially to know what the Greek words behind the English translation mean.

In a perfect world, we would all know Greek and be able to understand the Bible better because we would not rely on translations. But the world is not perfect, and many people are not able to spend the years required to learn Greek properly, even those who have a seminary education.

As I thought about how I might help the situation, I came to the conclusion that if people knew a little about Greek and a lot about how to use the good biblical study tools, they could in fact glean much from the Bible and from other resources that are otherwise beyond their grasp. This includes:

- understanding why translations are different
- finding what the Greek words mean
- seeing the author's flow of thought and his central message
- reading good commentaries and using other biblical tools that make use of Greek

Recently I published *The Interlinear for the Rest of Us* (*IRU*), which helps people get to the Greek behind the English, and now I am writing this text to help you learn how to use *IRU* and other such tools.

Because I spend a lot of time analyzing the biblical author's flow of thought, this book along with one like *How to Read the Bible for All Its Worth* (Fee and Stuart) can also be used in a hermeneutics class where students are learning how to interpret the Bible.

In the Appendix I discuss the basics of Hebrew. I cover the basic areas of the language and the difference between working with Hebrew tools and Greek. However, this is not my area of specialty. Within a few short months, Zondervan hopes to publish *Hebrew for the Rest of Us*, written by Lee Fields.

There are, of course, many dangers in relying on tools rather than actually knowing Greek and Hebrew, and I expressed those concerns in the preface to *IRU*. My fear is that people will think they actually know Greek and Hebrew even though they only know how to use the tools. Alexander Pope once said, a little knowledge is a dangerous thing. But as I indicated in *IRU*, I saw that it is a little bit of *arrogance* that is dangerous. So I offer this text, praying that you will recognize the limits of the approach.

GRU is divided into "weeks," and each week is divided into chapters. The first group of chapters in each week normally discuss Greek grammar, and the final chapter usually takes this new information and shows you how knowing it helps your Bible study.

I suspect this text will be used in many different ways. As I have spoken with those teaching the "Tools" class in different colleges and seminaries, I have found that they have widely different goals. Some will work straight through this text; others will pick and choose individual chapters. I trust that it will help you regardless of your specific class goals.

I am often asked how long it takes to work through the book. When I taught it in seminary, I found that students could easily do one chapter a day, although the last chapter in each "week" could take two days. I lectured once a week, for three hours. This was a comfortable pace and the students were able to get the work done without stress.

The greatest challenge of the book was to find good examples of what I am teaching, especially for the homework assignments. As I continue to find more, they will be posted at my website, www.teknia.com, along with other information you may find helpful.

Lectures over the entire book are available at www.biblicaltraining.org, under "Leadership Training." Click on the link to *Greek Tools for Bible Study* (be sure to register). These are lectures I originally gave for a seminary class and eventually taped when lecturing to a church Bible study group. Most of the emphasis in the lectures is on the final chapter in each "week."

Of the many people I would like to thank, most goes to my Greek assistant Matt Smith for his many hours of help, to my colleagues Lynn Losie, Doug Stuart, and Daniel Wallace for their help, to my editor Verlyn Verbrugge, to many students who patiently endured while I changed my mind on how to teach this material, to Gary Pratico and Miles Van Pelt for their help with the Hebrew, to Steve Yoell, my fellow pastor, for carrying the church load while I finished, to the many laypeople who read the text and helped me see when I was getting too technical, as a Greek teacher has a tendency to do, and to Robin, my wife, who patiently encouraged me to finish the task well.

I trust that you will find this a valuable resource as you work to understand the Word of God better.

Bill Mounce

Abbreviations

Bible Versions

ESV	English Standard Version
KJV	King James Version
NASB	New American Standard Bible (1995)
NET	New English Translation
NIV	New International Version
NIrV	New International Reader's Version
NKJV	New King James Version
NLT	New Living Translation
NRSV	New Revised Standard Version
RSV	Revised Standard Version
TEV	Today's English Version
TNIV	Today's New International Version

Book Abbreviations

BBG	*The Basics of Biblical Greek* (William Mounce, Zondervan)
BDAG	*A Greek-English Lexicon of the New Testament and Other Early Christian Literature* (revised and edited by Frederick Danker, University of Chicago)
ESNT	*Greek Grammar Beyond the Basics: An Exegetical Syntax of the New Testament* (Daniel Wallace, Zondervan)
IRU	*Interlinear for the Rest of Us: The Reverse Interlinear for New Testament Word Studies* (William Mounce, Zondervan)

Other Abbreviations

e.g.	for example
f	one following page
ff	more than one following page
i.e.	that is (used for a restatement)
v	verse
vv	verses

What Would It Look Like If You Knew a Little Greek?

What will you be able to do when you are done working through this text that, perhaps, you cannot do now?

1. You will often be able to understand why translations are different. How many times have you been in a Bible study where the leader is discussing a verse, but your Bible appears to say something considerably different? How can the translations be so different? What does the verse really say? Let me give you a few examples.

Luke 2:14 is one of the better-known verses in the Bible. In the KJV (King James Version) it reads,

> Glory to God in the highest, and on earth peace, good will toward men.

Is there anything in this verse that bothers you? It is a statement of blessing, and God's angels say, "peace and goodwill toward men." Does God's peace extend to all people? "Peace" is a marvelous biblical concept that designates a cessation of hostility between God and us; it's the result of justification (Rom 5:1). The RSV (Revised Standard version) says,

> Glory to God in the highest and on earth peace among men with whom he is pleased.

Here, peace isn't extended to all people, but only to those who are the recipients of God's pleasure. Why are the KJV and the RSV different? The answer is that the Greek manuscripts are different at this verse. Some have *eudokias* with the "*s*" (the Greek sigma), which is followed by the RSV; others have *eudokia*, which is followed by the KJV. The "*s*" completely changes the meaning. (I will discuss the issue of different Greek manuscripts in chapter 30.)

Another example is Mark 16. If you are reading Mark 16 in the RSV, after the women see that the tomb is empty, the Bible says,

> And they went out and fled from the tomb; for trembling and astonishment had come upon them; and they said nothing to any one, for they were afraid.

The gospel ends at verse 8 on a note of fear. But let me tell you a story that is related, although it won't sound like it at first. Have you ever seen those movies they often show in high school sociology class about the snake people of the Appalachians? They handle rattlesnakes as part of their church worship, and they don't die. They also drink poison, and they don't die. Why are these people doing this? Why are my cousins doing this? (They actually are my cousins, by the way. My family is from Gravelswitch, Kentucky.) "Because the Bible says so," they would respond. If you are reading the KJV, it doesn't stop at verse 8 but goes on to verse 20. Verse 18 says, "And these signs shall follow them that believe, they shall take up serpents, and if they drink anything deadly, it will not hurt them and they shall lay hands on the sick and they shall recover." Wouldn't you like to know whether v 18 belongs in the Bible or not?

Here is a more subtle example. In 2 Corinthians 1:15 the ESV (English Standard Version) reads,

> Because I was sure of this, I wanted to come to you first, so that you may have a second experience of grace.

Sounds as if Paul is talking about a second work of grace subsequent to conversion. But see how other translations handle the passage.

> In this confidence I intended at first to come to you, so that you might twice receive a blessing (NASB).

> Because I was sure of this, I wanted to come to you first, so that you might have a double pleasure (RSV).

> Because I was confident of this, I planned to visit you first so that you might benefit twice (NIV).

Since none of the other translations give any suggestion of a second work of grace, it is doubtful that the ESV means to suggest this. (I can say this with full certainty, since I was one of the twelve translators of the ESV.)

So what are we going to do with these differences? First of all, we will work to understand why they are different. Second, we will learn to pull the translations together. So often in Bible study when the translations are different, we seem content to let them say different things. Rather, what we need to do is use the different translations to come together and arrive at a common meaning, a meaning that perhaps has several nuances that the different translations are trying to convey.

2. You will discover the meaning of the Greek and Hebrew that lies beneath the English. This is called doing "word studies." Without knowing Greek or Hebrew or without knowing how to use the study tools, the best you can do is learn what the English word means. But as you will learn in several weeks, words can have a wide range of meanings. Think through all the ways we use the word "of," "can," and "run." Words don't have exact counterparts in different languages. The range of meaning of an English word will almost never be the same as the range of meaning for the Greek word behind the English. We call this the word's "semantic range." So just because an English word can have a certain meaning, it is by no means certain that the Greek or Hebrew behind it has that specific meaning.

A good example of this is the Greek word σάρξ, *sarx*. This word can be translated many different ways because English has no exact counterpart

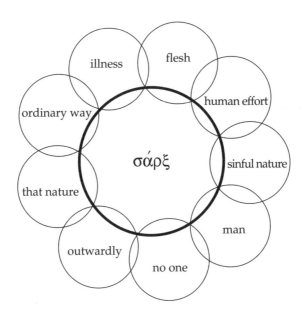

to it. In as short a book as Galatians we find *sarx* translated by the NIV (New International Version) as "flesh," "human effort," "illness," "man," "no one," "ordinary way," "outwardly," "sinful nature," and "that nature." All these English words partially overlap in meaning with *sarx*, but none is an exact equivalent.

Another example is in 1 Corinthians 7:1. The RSV translates, "It is well for a man not to *touch* a woman." Lots of good youth group talks on dating come out of the word "touch." But guess what? The NIV translates 1 Cor 7:1 as, "It is good for a man not to marry." Wait a minute! Are we talking about dating or are we talking about marriage? The fact of the matter is that *haptesthai* can mean "to touch" or it can be understood to be speaking of marriage. Translators have to pick one meaning or the other.

There is another example later on in the same chapter. The RSV translates 1 Corinthians 7:36 as,

> If any one thinks that he is not behaving properly toward his *betrothed*, if his passions are strong, and it has to be, let him do as he wishes: let them marry—it is no sin.

Paul has been encouraging people not to marry in order to be more involved in the gospel ministry, but then he says if that's not your gift, if your passions are strong, then there is nothing wrong with getting married. Go ahead and marry your "betrothed." However, when you read the same verse in the NASB (New American Standard Bible) it reads,

> But if any man thinks that he is acting unbecomingly toward his virgin *daughter*, if she is past her youth, and if it must be so, let him do what he wishes, he does not sin; let her marry.

The italics in the NASB's translation indicate that it has added a word, but the difference is more than that. The question is, who is the "he" who is acting unbecomingly? Is it the husband-to-be (RSV) or her father (NASB)? Either way you look at this verse, it can be confusing.

Another example is John 3:16.

> For God so loved the world that he gave his one and only Son, that whoever believes in him shall not perish but have eternal life (NIV).

What does "so" mean? Most readers think it means "a lot." That's just about the only way someone would read the English. But did you know that the Greek word behind "so" most likely means, "in this way." "For God loved the world *in this way*: he gave ...." The giving of his Son shows *how* God loved the world, not *how much*. (This is why the footnote in the ESV reads, "Or *For this is how God loved the world*.")

My favorite example when it comes to translating words is Matthew 26:27, which talks about the Lord's Supper. The KJV says,

> Drink ye all of it.

My dad tells the story of how, when he was younger, he made sure he drank every last little bit of grape juice in that little cup. He would shake it until every drop was gone; he was going to obey Scripture and drink "all of it." Only one problem: that's not what the verse means. The "all" means "all of you," not "all the liquid." The RSV translates, "Drink of it, all of you."

So as we learn about Greek and translations, we'll see why these types of differences occur and what the Greek really means.

3. You will also learn the basics of exegesis. "Exegesis" is a fancy word for Bible study. Using a methodology I call "phrasing," you will learn to divide a biblical story into smaller, more manageable, pieces, locate the main thought, and see how the other statements in the passage relate to the main point. You will then lay the passage out visually in a way that helps you see the author's flow of thought. This is the best way to help you learn what good commentary writers are trying to do.

For example, below is the salutation from Jude. How many main thoughts are there, and how many descriptions of the recipients does the author include?

> 1:1   Jude,
>   a servant of Jesus Christ and
>   a brother of James,
>   To those
>   who have been   called,
>   who are   loved by God the Father and
>   kept by Jesus Christ:
>
> 1:2   Mercy, peace and love be yours in abundance.

The salutation breaks down into three sections: author; recipients; greeting. Jude tells us three things about the recipients: they have been called; they are loved by God; they are kept by Jesus.

4. The final thing that I am going to help you learn is how to read good commentaries. Let's say you're going to have a Sunday School lesson on Romans 1:17 and you need the help of a commentary. (A commentary is a book that explains what each verse means.) One of the best commentaries on Romans is by C. E. B. Cranfield, so let's say you pick it up and try to read his discussion of the verse. Here is a small part of his discussion (pp. 95-96).

> The other main disagreement concerns the question whether in the phrase δικαιοσύνη θεοῦ in 1.17; 3.21, 22 (cf. 10.3) θεοῦ is to be understood as a subjective genitive or as a genitive of origin, or— to put it differently—whether δικαιοσύνη refers to an activity of God or to a status of man resulting from God's action, righteousness as a gift from God. In support of the view that θεοῦ is a subjective genitive and δικαιοσύνη refers to God's activity, a number of arguments have been advanced: (i) That in 3.5 (θεοῦ δικαιοσύ-

νην) θεοῦ must be a subjective genitive (cf. also 3.25, 26) ....

Does this make sense? Probably not right now. But by the end of this text you will know what a subjective genitive and a genitive of origin are. You'll know what a genitive is. I want you to know enough about English and Greek grammar so that you can pick up an excellent commentary and be able to follow the discussion.

Stated in reverse, I don't want you to make silly mistakes that come from misreading commentaries or misapplying Greek and Hebrew grammar. For example, you probably know the passage, "Are all apostles? Are all prophets? Are all teachers? Do all work miracles? Do all speak in tongues?" (1 Cor 12:29). Have you ever heard anyone claim the answer is "Yes," and insist that a "real" Christian must have spoken in tongues once? I have. But when you get your commentary on 1 Corinthians out, you will read something like this: "Questions preceded by μή expect a negative answer." What does that mean? It means that Greek can indicate whether the person asking the question expects the answer "Yes" or "No." (We do this in English by adding a phrase, like: "All don't speak in tongues, do they?") In 1 Corinthians 12:29, the Greek indicates that Paul's expected answer is, "No."

Limitations

There are limitations to our approach, or what I like to call "baby Greek." You will not be learning the full language, and my concern is that you will forget that you know only a little. I'm going to give you the ability to sound authoritative by citing Greek and Hebrew words and grammar, and perhaps be completely wrong. I actually put off writing this book for several years because of this concern, but I finally came to the conclusion that it's not a little Greek that proves dangerous. It's a little bit of pride that proves dangerous.

If you don't respect this fact, then these tools can become just another way in which you can be wrong. I know a well-known speaker who was talking about how a Christian should not incur debt. I believe in debt-free living, so don't misunderstand me at this point, but the problem was in how he used Romans 13:8: "Owe no one anything except to love one another, for the one who loves another has fulfilled the law." He claimed something like the following.

> Now what's really important in Romans 13:8 is that there are three negations. Unlike in English where if you have two negations they cancel each other out, in Greek when you have double negations they pile up on each other making the statement stronger. Paul has three negations in Rom 13:8 and he's making the point that it's really a sin ever to go into debt.

There are no negatives in this verse in the sense this author speaks of negatives, although you will find μή used once in the idiom εἰ μή, *except*, and twice as parts of words meaning *to no one* and *nothing*. In none of these situations do the rules the speaker was citing apply. He is teaching thousands of people, and he's wrong. So I say as a gentle warning: please remember what we're doing and what we're not doing. We're learning to use the tools; we're trying to follow good commentaries; we're trying to understand what words mean. We're not learning enough Greek to make complicated grammatical pronouncements that aren't supported by the commentaries.

I remember when I was in seminary sitting in the balcony of a large and well-known church listening to the preacher say, "Well, the Greek says this and the Greek says this." And I'm looking at the Greek and I say (I hope to myself), "You're wrong, you're wrong, you're wrong." He didn't really know Greek, but he was using it—it seemed to me—to elevate himself in a position of authority over his people. He should have been more careful, and more humble.

Jehovah's Witnesses are another good example of misusing Greek. They will cite John 1:1—"In the beginning was the Word and the Word was with God and the Word was *a god*" and argue that there is no word "the" before "God." Jesus is not "the" God but "a" god, a created god. But if they really knew Greek, they wouldn't make such a horrible and obvious mistake, for two reasons. (1) There's technically no such thing as the word "the" in Greek. There is a word, ὁ, that can be translated as "the," but it can also be translated as "my," as "your," or as many other words. There is no exact equivalent for the word "the" in Greek. (2) Grammatically the Greek explicitly states that Jesus is, in our language, "the God" (cf. Daniel Wallace, *Greek Grammar Beyond the Basics*, pp. 266-269).

One last illustration. Last year I was sitting at my desk grading papers, minding my own business, and I received a phone call from an elderly gentleman. He started talking and was evidently lonely so I listened, and within ten minutes he had accused every translator of being intentionally deceitful, of not knowing what they were doing, of mistranslating God's Word, and God was going to curse them. I said,

> Well, Sir, do you know any translators?
> No, I've never met any of them.
> Well, I know a lot of them, and they are godly men who would never mistranslate anything on purpose, and they know a lot more Greek than you.
> Well, they don't translate 2 Peter 3:5 properly. The Greek says God created "die-uh" [his mispronunciation of the Greek] water. The earth is formed *through* water. "Die-uh" means "through" and so in this verse Peter is saying that God created the world "through" water and every-

one is translating it "out of" water.

He was absolutely insistent that *dia* meant "through" and he went through a fifteen minute discussion in physics. (I didn't have any idea what he was talking about.) When he finally paused for a breath, I said, "First of all, it's pronounced 'dia.' There's a good chance that if you can't pronounce it, then you probably don't know what it means." (I was a little frustrated.) Then I tried to explain that all words have a range of meaning. *Dia* can mean "through," but it can also mean "out of" or "by," and the translators must make an interpretive decision as to which word they use. (By the way, the ESV did agree on "through," so he should be happy.) I tried to impress upon him the fact of how dangerous it was to slander Christian brothers and sisters and to accuse them of intentionally doing things when he didn't know what he was talking about.

So why should you learn a little Greek, if it is possible to make these types of errors? Because the personal rewards of deepening your biblical study are so great that it is worth the effort. Just remember the importance of humility (Phil 2:1-13) and meekness (Matt 5:5), and that while knowledge puffs up, love builds up (1 Cor 8:1).

WEEK 1

Getting Acquainted with Greek

In this first week we are are going to learn the Greek alphabet. It's fun, and we will need to be able to pronounce Greek if we are going to accomplish our goals. I will also talk to you about the nature of languages and translations. If you have a mistaken view of the relationship between language and the meaning conveyed by words and phrases, studying your Bible will be severely hampered. But don't worry; the discussion is more practical than it is theoretical. So hold on to your hat, and let's go.

CHAPTER 1

The Greek Language

The Greek language has a long and rich history stretching all the way from the thirteenth century B.C. to the present. The earliest form of the language is called "Linear B" (13th century B.C.).

The form of Greek used by writers from Homer (8th century B.C.) through Plato (4th century B.C.) is called "Classical Greek." It was a marvelous form of the language, capable of exact expression and subtle nuances. Its alphabet was derived from the Phoenicians. Classical Greek existed in many dialects of which three were primary: Doric, Aeolic, and Ionic (of which Attic was a branch).

Athens was conquered in the fourth century B.C. by King Philip of Macedonia. Alexander the Great was Philip's son and was tutored by the Greek philosopher Aristotle. He set out to conquer the world and spread Greek culture and language. Because Alexander spoke Attic Greek, it was this dialect that was spread. It was also the dialect spoken by the famous Athenian writers. This was the beginning of the Hellenistic Age.

As the Greek language spread across the world and met other languages, it was altered (which would happen to any language). The dialects also interacted with each other. Eventually this adaptation resulted in what we call Koine Greek. "Koine" (κοινή) means "common" and was the common, everyday form of the language, used by everyday people. It was not considered a polished literary form of the language, and in fact some writers of this era purposefully imitated the older style of Greek (which is like someone today writing in King James English). Koine unfortunately lost many of the subtleties of classical Greek. For example, in classical Greek ἄλλος meant "other" of the same kind while ἕτερος meant "other" of a different kind. If you had an apple and you asked for ἄλλος, you would receive another apple. But if you asked for ἕτερος, you would be given perhaps an orange. Some of these subtleties come through in the New Testament but not often. It is this common, Koine Greek that is used in the Septuagint (the Greek translation of the Old Testament), the New Testament, and the writings of the Apostolic Fathers.

For a long time Koine Greek confused many scholars because it was significantly different from Classical Greek. Some hypothesized that it was a combination of Greek, Hebrew, and Aramaic. Others attempted to explain it as a "Holy Ghost language," meaning that God created a special language just for the Bible. But studies of Greek papyri found in Egypt over the last one hundred years have shown that Koine Greek was the language of the everyday people used in the writings of wills, letters, receipts, shopping lists, etc.

There are two lessons we can learn from this. As Paul says, "In the fullness of time God sent his Son" (Gal 4:4), and part of that fullness was a universal language. No matter where Paul traveled he could be understood.

But there is another lesson here that is perhaps a little closer to the pastor's heart. God used the common language to communicate the Gospel. The Gospel does not belong to the erudite alone; it belongs to all people. It now becomes our task to learn parts of this marvelous language to help us make the grace of God known to all people.

CHAPTER 2

The Greek Alphabet

Introduction

We will learn the twenty-four letters of the Greek alphabet and the transliteration of each.

A transliteration is the equivalent of a letter in another language. For example, the Greek "beta" (β) is transliterated with the English "b." Because they have the same sounds, it is said that the English "b" is the transliteration of the Greek "beta." It is common in modern texts to set off a transliterated word in italics.

> Jesus' last word from the cross was *tetelestai*.

This does not mean that a similar combination of letters in one language has the same meaning as the same combination in another.

> kappa + alpha + tau (κατ) does not mean "cat."

Some word study books and commentaries avoid the Greek form and give only the transliteration. On the next page I have listed the letter's name, its transliteration (in italics), the small and capital Greek form, and its pronunciation. The lectures at www.biblicaltraining.org will help you with the pronunciation of the alphabet and the reading exercises in the following chapters.

Different books may follow slightly different transliteration schemes. Be sure to check the book's scheme before looking up a word.

Alphabet Chart

Alpha	*a*	α	A	a	as in father
Beta	*b*	β	B	b	as in Bible
Gamma	*g*	γ	Γ	g	as in gone
Delta	*d*	δ	Δ	d	as in dog
Epsilon	*e*	ε	E	e	as in met
Zeta	*z*	ζ	Z	z	as in daze
Eta	*ē*	η	H	e	as in obey
Theta	*th*	θ	Θ	th	as in thing
Iota	*i*	ι	I	i	as in intrigue
Kappa	*k*	κ	K	k	as in kitchen
Lambda	*l*	λ	Λ	l	as in law
Mu	*m*	μ	M	m	as in mother
Nu	*n*	ν	N	n	as in new
Xi	*x*	ξ	Ξ	x	as in axiom
Omicron	*o*	ο	O	o	as in not
Pi	*p*	π	Π	p	as in peach
Rho	*r*	ρ	P	r	as in rod
Sigma	*s*	σ/ς	Σ	s	as in study
Tau	*t*	τ	T	t	as in talk
Upsilon	*u/y*	υ	Y	u	as the German ü
Phi	*ph*	φ	Φ	ph	as in phone
Chi	*ch*	χ	X	ch	as in loch
Psi	*ps*	ψ	Ψ	ps	as in lips
Omega	*ō*	ω	Ω	o	as in tone

You may not need to learn the capital letters right away, but you will soon enough.

Helps

The vowels are α, ε, η, ι, ο, υ, ω. The rest are consonants.

Sigma is written as ς when it occurs at the end of the word, and as σ when it occurs elsewhere: ἀπόστολος.

υ is transliterated as "u" if it occurs with another vowel (εὐαγγέλιον ‣ *euangelion*), and "y" if it occurs as a single vowel (μυστήριον ‣ *mystērion*).

Do not confuse the η (eta) with the English "n," ν (nu) with "v," ρ (rho) with "p," χ (chi) with "x," or ω (omega) with "w."

Notice the many similarities among the Greek and English letters, not only in shape and sound but also in their respective order in the alphabet. The Greek alphabet can be broken down into sections. It will parallel the

English for a while, differ, and then begin to parallel again. Try to find these natural divisions.

Pronunciation

In pronouncing the Greek letters, use the first sound of the name of the letter. Alpha is an "a" sound (there is no "pha" sound); lambda is an "l" sound (there is no "ambda" sound).

There is some disagreement among scholars on the pronunciation of a few letters, but I have chosen the most common.

γ usually has a hard "g" sound, as in "get." However, when it is immediately followed by γ, κ, χ, or ξ, it is pronounced as a "v." ἄγγελος is pronounced "angelos" (from which we get our word "angel"). The γ pronounced like a "v" is called a "gamma nasal" and is transliterated as a "n" (*angelos*).

The ι can be either short or long, like the two i's in the English "intrigue." Just listen to how your teacher pronounces the words.

Miscellaneous

Iota subscript. Sometimes an iota is written under the vowels α, η, or ω (ᾳ, ῃ, ῳ). This iota is not pronounced but it does affect the word's meaning. It normally is not transliterated.

Capitals. Originally the Bible was written in all capital letters without punctuation or spaces between the words. For example, John 1:1 began,

ΕΝΑΡΧΗΗΝΟΛΟΓΟΣ

The cursive script was created before the time of Christ but became popular in the ninth century. In cursive the letters are connected, like our present-day handwriting. Spaces were also added between words. In Greek texts today, John 1:1 begins,

Εν αρχη ην ο λογος

In our Greek texts today, capitals are used only for proper names, the first word in a quotation, and the first word in the paragraph.

A **diphthong** is a combination of two vowels that produce only one sound. The second vowel is always an ι or an υ.

αι	as in aisle	αιρω
ει	as in eight	ει
οι	as in oil	οικια

The first capital letters were written with straight lines, which were easier to carve into writing material like rock. In the first century A.D., a modified style of capital letters was created called Uncial. These letters had more curves so they could be more easily written on the newer writing materials such a papyrus and parchment. The earliest New Testament documents are called uncials.

In the 8th to the 9th century, cursive script was written smaller and in a style that could be written faster, saving both time and parchment. This script is known as "minuscule"; there are currently 2,867 New Testament minuscule manuscripts.

αυ	as in sauerkraut	αυτος
ου	as in soup	ουδε
υι	as in suite	υιος
ευ, ηυ	as in feud	ευθυς / ηυξανεν

Greek has two **breathing marks**, "rough" and "smooth." Every word beginning with a vowel or ρ has a breathing mark. (I omitted them in the previous examples.)

The **rough breathing mark** is a ʽ placed over the first vowel and adds an "h" sound to the word.

ὑπερ	▸	*hyper*
ῥαββι	▸	*rhabbi*

The rough breathing mark is transliterated as an *h*, and is placed before the transliterated vowel (but after the initial ρ).

The **smooth breathing mark** is a ʼ placed over the first vowel and is not pronounced or transliterated.

ἀποστολος	▸	*apostolos*

Either breathing mark is placed before an initial capital letter.

Ἰσραηλ	▸	*Israēl*
Ἰεροσόλυμα	▸	*Hierosolyma*

Either breathing mark is placed over the second vowel of an initial diphthong.

αἰτεω ▸ *aiteō*
Αἰτεω ▸ *Aiteō*
Αἱ ▸ *Hai*

John 1:1 looks like this with the breathing marks.

Ἐν ἀρχῃ ἠν ὁ λογος

Summary

1. It is essential that you learn the Greek alphabet and transliterations right away.

2. The vowels in Greek are α, ε, η, ι, ο, υ, and ω.

3. A diphthong consists of two vowels pronounced as a single vowel. The second vowel is always an iota or upsilon.

4. An iota subscript is an iota written under the previous vowel; it is not pronounced.

5. Every word beginning with a vowel or ρ must have a rough or smooth breathing mark.

Exercises

1. Write out the alphabet. The asterisk marks where you start.

2. Write out the following verses from the Lord's Prayer in Greek.

   Πατερ ἡμων ὁ ἐν τοις οὐρανοις

   ἁγιασθητω το ὀνομα σου

   ἐλθετω ἡ βασιλεια σου

   γενηθητω το θελημα σου, ὡς ἐν οὐρανῳ και ἐπι γης

3. Alphabetize all the words in #2 above.

4. Write out the transliteration for each word in the alphabetized list.

5. Pronounce the words in #2 out loud.

6. Make up some English sentences, but write them in Greek script. If Greek doesn't have the necessary sound, use something close: I λικ Γρεεκ.

Advanced Information

In some words we find two vowels that normally form a diphthong, but in a few cases both vowels are pronounced. To show that these two vowels are pronounced as two separate sounds, a **diaeresis** (¨) is placed over the second vowel.

   Ἠσαϊας (Ἠ-σα-ϊ-ας) means Isaiah.

The αι normally forms a diphthong, but in this word the diaeresis indicates that it forms two separate sounds. This is like the French word *naïve* that was brought over into English.

Sometimes the final vowel of a word drops off, and the word is marked for **elison** with an apostrophe (ἀλλα ‣ ἀλλ᾽). English does something similar (e.g., "was not" ‣ "wasn't").

Listening to Bill's Lectures on *www.BiblicalTraining.org*

BiblicalTraining.org is a website committed to bringing the finest in evangelical teaching to the world for free. Its goal is to provide quality education at multiple levels in the home and the church.

My lectures covering *GRU* were recorded when lecturing to a church Bible study group. Most of the emphasis in the lectures is on the final chapter in each "week" in the book. While the nine hours of speaking overlap some with the textbook, I tried to use different examples so that the lectures would fill out the message of the text and not merely repeat it.

The lectures are available in mp3 format (for easy download), Windows Media and QuickTime (complete with graphics).

Here is how you can find the class.

Step one. In your Internet browser, go to *www.BiblicalTraining.org* and register. Registration is free and can be cancelled at any time. After registration, you need to log in.

Step two. Click on "Leadership" under the masthead. This takes you to the index page for all leadership classes. Scroll down until you find the class "Greek Tools for Bible Study." Click there.

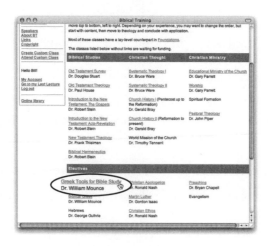

Step three. On the "Class" page you determine which type of audio file to download. If you want to download the audio to an mp3 player, you should choose one of the two mp3 formats. If you want to listen on the web, and especially if you want to see all the graphics that illustrate the lecture, then chose "QuickTime." Then scroll down to the table of contents for the class and select the appropriate lecture.

Step four. If you chose QuickTime or Windows Media, then click the "Start lecture" button. Enjoy the class.

CHAPTER 3

Pronunciation

Syllabification

Just as it is important to learn how to pronounce the letters correctly, it is also important to pronounce the words correctly. But in order to pronounce a Greek word you must be able to break it down into its syllables. This is called "syllabification."

Greek words syllabify basically the same way as English words do. Therefore, if you "go with your feelings," you will syllabify Greek words almost automatically. If you practice reading the examples below you should pick it up. I will mark the syllables below with a space. There is one vowel or diphthong per syllable (just like in English). A single consonant goes with the following vowel (e.g., αὐ - τός, not αὐτ - ός). I included the interlinear translation for the fun of it.

John 3:16	οὕ τως	γαρ	ἠ γα πη σεν	ὁ	θε ος	τον	κο σμον,	ὡ στε
	so	for	he loved	the	God	the	world	so that

	το	υἱ ον	τον	μο νο γε νη	ἐ δω κεν,	ἱ να	πας	ὁ
	the	son	the	only	he gave	so that	each	the

	πι στευ ων		εἰς	αὐ τον	μη	ἀ πο λη ται	ἀλλ'
	one who believes		in	him	not	he might perish	but

	ἐ χῃ	ζω ην	αἰ ω νι ον.
	he might have	life	eternal

1 John 1:9	ἐ αν	ὁ μο λο γω μεν	τας	ἁ μαρ τι ας	ἡ μων,	πι στος	ἐ στιν
	if	we confess	the	sins	our	faithful	he is

	και	δι και ος,	ἱ να	ἀ φη		ἡ μιν	τας	ἁ μαρ τι ας
	and	just	so that	he might forgive		to us	the	sins

	και	κα θα ρι ση	ἡ μας	ἀ πο	πα σης	ἀ δι κι ας.
	and	he might cleanse	us	from	all	unrighteousness

Eph 2:8	τῃ	γαρ	χα ρι τι	ἐ στε	σε σω σμε νοι	δι α	πι στε ως
	by the	for	grace	you are	saved		through	faith

	και	του το	οὐκ	ἐξ	ὑ μων,	θε ου	το	δω ρον.
	and	this	not	of	you	of God	the	gift

Accents

Almost every Greek word has an accent mark. It is placed over a vowel and shows which syllable receives the emphasis when you say the word.

name	*pitch*	*example*
acute	voice rose	αἰτέω
grave	voice stayed level	θεὸς
circumflex	voice rose and dropped	Ἰησοῦς

Originally the accent was a pitch accent, the voice rising, or rising and falling on the accented syllable. A few centuries after the writing of the New Testament, the pitch accent was shifted to stress, like Modern English. Here is John 1:1 as it actually is written in modern texts.

Ἐν ἀρχῇ ἦν ὁ λόγος

Here are the verses we saw earlier but now with accents. Read them, this time paying attention to which syllable receives the stress.

John 3:16   οὕτως γὰρ ἠγάπησεν ὁ θεὸς τὸν κόσμον, ὥστε τὸν υἱὸν τὸν μονογενῆ ἔδωκεν, ἵνα πᾶς ὁ πιστεύων εἰς αὐτὸν μὴ ἀπόληται ἀλλ᾽ ἔχῃ ζωὴν αἰώνιον.

1 John 1:9   ἐὰν ὁμολογῶμεν τὰς ἁμαρτίας ἡμῶν, πιστός ἐστιν καὶ δίκαιος, ἵνα ἀφῇ ἡμῖν τὰς ἁμαρτίας καὶ καθαρίσῃ ἡμᾶς ἀπὸ πάσης ἀδικίας.

Eph 2:8   τῇ γὰρ χάριτί ἐστε σεσῳσμένοι διὰ πίστεως· καὶ τοῦτο οὐκ ἐξ ὑμῶν, θεοῦ τὸ δῶρον.

Punctuation

The comma and period are the same in Greek as they are in English. However, a period above the line is the Greek semicolon, and an English semicolon is the Greek question mark.

Punctuation	*Greek*
θεός,	comma
θεός.	period
θεός·	semicolon
θεός;	question mark

Summary

1. Greek words syllabify basically the same way as English words do.

2. There are three accents: acute, grave, circumflex. When pronouncing the word, place emphasis on the accented syllable.

3. A period above the line is the Greek semicolon, and an English semicolon is the Greek question mark.

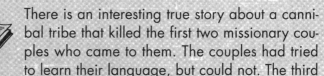

There is an interesting true story about a cannibal tribe that killed the first two missionary couples who came to them. The couples had tried to learn their language, but could not. The third brave couple started experiencing the same problems with the language as had the two previous couples until the wife, who had been a music major in college, recognized that the tribe had a very developed set of pitch accents that were essential in understanding the language. When they learned the significance these accents played in that language, they were able to translate the Bible into that musically-minded language. Luckily for us, while Greek accents were pitch, they are not that important.

Exercises

1. Practice reading the three verses I showed you earlier.

    John 3:16   οὕτως γὰρ ἠγάπησεν ὁ θεὸς τὸν κόσμον, ὥστε τὸν υἱὸν τὸν μονογενῆ
    ἔδωκεν, ἵνα πᾶς ὁ πιστεύων εἰς αὐτὸν μὴ ἀπόληται ἀλλ᾽ ἔχῃ ζωὴν
    αἰώνιον.

    1 John 1:9   ἐὰν ὁμολογῶμεν τὰς ἁμαρτίας ἡμῶν, πιστός ἐστιν καὶ δίκαιος, ἵνα
    ἀφῇ ἡμῖν τὰς ἁμαρτίας καὶ καθαρίσῃ ἡμᾶς ἀπὸ πάσης ἀδικίας.

    Eph 2:8   τῇ γὰρ χάριτί ἐστε σεσῳσμένοι διὰ πίστεως· καὶ τοῦτο οὐκ ἐξ ὑμῶν,
    θεοῦ τὸ δῶρον.

2. Practice reading the Lord's prayer. Identify the punctuation.

    Πάτερ ἡμῶν ὁ   ἐν τοῖς οὐρανοῖς·
    Father our the in the heavens

    ἁγιασθήτω τὸ ὄνομά   σου·
    Be hallowed the name   your

    ἐλθέτω   ἡ   βασιλεία σου·
    Let come the kingdom your

    γενηθήτω τὸ θέλημα   σου,
    Let be done the will   your

        ὡς ἐν οὐρανῷ καὶ ἐπὶ γῆς·
        as in heaven also on   earth

    τὸν ἄρτον ἡμῶν τὸν ἐπιούσιον δὸς ἡμῖν σήμερον·
    the bread our the daily   give to us today

    καὶ ἄφες ἡμῖν τὰ ὀφειλήματα ἡμῶν,
    and forgive us the debts   our

        ὡς καὶ ἡμεῖς ἀφήκαμεν   τοῖς ὀφειλέταις ἡμῶν·
        as also we   have forgiven the debtors   our

    καὶ μὴ εἰσενέγκῃς ἡμᾶς εἰς πειρασμόν,
    and not lead   us   into temptation

        ἀλλὰ ῥῦσαι ἡμᾶς ἀπὸ τοῦ πονηροῦ.
        but deliver us   from the evil

Advanced Information

Punctuation. If the last syllable of a word has an acute accent and that word is not followed by a punctuation mark, the acute becomes a grave.

καί εἰρήνη ‣ καὶ εἰρήνη

Some words can push their accent back on the previous word, which then might have two accents.

τὸ ὄνομά μου
ἰσχυρότερός μού ἐστιν

Syllabification. Some people prefer to learn the actual rules for syllab-ification instead of trusting their instincts. Here are the basic rules.

1. There is one vowel (or diphthong) per syllable. (Therefore, there are as many syllables as there are vowels/diphthongs.)

    ἀ κη κό α μεν   μαρ τυ ροῦ μεν

2. A single consonant goes with the following vowel.

    ἐ ω ρά κα μεν   ἐ θε α σά με θα

    By "single consonant" I mean that the following letter is not a conso-nant. (The τ in αὐτός is a single consonant.) If you find two or more consonants in a row that form a single sound, they are called a "conso-nant cluster." (The γρ in γραφή form a consonant cluster.)

    If the consonant is the final letter in the word, it will go with the pre-ceding vowel.

    ἔμ προ σθεν

3. Two consecutive vowels that do not form a diphthong are divided.

    ἐ θε α σά με θα   Ἡ σα ΐ ας

4. Double consonants are divided. (A "double consonant" is when the same consonant occurs twice in a row.)

    ἀ παγ γέλ λο μεν   παρ ρη σί α

5. A consonant cluster that forms a single sound goes with the following vowel.

    Χρι στός   γρα φή

6. A consonant cluster that does not form a single sound is divided, and the first consonant goes with the preceding vowel.

   ἔμ προ σθεν   ἀρ χῆς

CHAPTER 4

What Are Translations?

Communication isn't as easy as we might think. When was the last time you used plain English words and your friend looked at you with with a deadpan face and said, "What did you say?" You think, "I was crystal clear. Why can't you understand me?" But that's just the nature of communication. Even in speaking the same language in the same culture to someone you know, words don't always convey the meaning that you intend them to.

Let me give you some examples. Getting used to the road signs when we first moved to New England was a treat and a half. I still remember going up Monument Street and seeing the sign, "Thickly Settled," and I thought, "What does that mean?" I stopped the car and turned to Robin (my wife) and said, "This must be where the really stupid people live because they're thick in the head." (I knew that wasn't what the sign meant, but I really had no idea what it did mean.) It turns out that "thickly settled" is a legal designation based on how closely the homes are built, and areas that are "thickly settled" have specific speed limits.

When we drove around Wenham Lake for the first time, we saw the sign "Lightly Salted." We had never seen a sign like that before and really had no idea what it meant until about the fourth time we saw the same sign elsewhere and realized the signs were all located next to lakes, which we later learned are used for reservoirs. They don't salt the roads in winter there so the salt doesn't run off and contaminate the drinking water. Now someone who is from New England might say that I am thick in the head for not understanding what the sign so "obviously" meant. No, not really. For someone who's not from New England, and it's during the summer, and who's never seen a sign like that, its meaning isn't immediately obvious.

What about communicating in the same language but in different countries? I will never forget the time when I first went to Aberdeen in Scotland and was on Princess Street. I was asking for directions to a store and a lady said, "It's at the top of the street." I wanted to say, "Ma'am, the street is level. What do you mean, 'top?'" I knew she didn't mean "on top of the pavement," but how can you have a "top" on a flat street? She was communicating with me, but I didn't have the foggiest idea what she meant.

What if you speak a different language but live in the same century? When I was learning German, I went to school in Germany for a few months. I learned that "Ich" means "I," "bin" means "am," and "kalt" means "cold." So one day I said to my friends, "Ich bin kalt," and they literally rolled on the ground laughing hysterically. When they finally regained some composure, they informed me that I had said, "I am sexually frigid." If I wanted to say, "I am cold," I had to say, "Es ist zu mir kalt,""It is to me cold."

What happens when you get all the way down this progression and you have different languages from different countries separated by the centuries, which is the position we are in with the Bible? Acts 20:37 says, if you translate word for word, "They fell on his neck." What does that mean? It means they were hugging and kissing him, in our terminology. They were falling on his neck and embracing him. How did you get that from "fall on the neck"? I think of my son, hiding around the corner, and when I'm not looking he falls on my neck and any other part of my body that he can hit. (He's in a hitting stage.)

What is the point? The point is that communication is not simple. If there is miscommunication between two people speaking the same language, living in the same culture, looking directly at each other and being able to see body language and all the other clues we use in communication, then how much more difficult it is to understand communication coming from two thousand years ago, through a different language, stemming from a different culture.

Why am I talking about this? It is because one of the first steps toward learning to study your Bible is to understand the nature of language. It is the *meaning* conveyed by the words of Scripture that is so important to us, but to get to that meaning we have to go through *words* and *grammar*. And because you probably do not know Greek or Hebrew, you must rely on the translators' understanding of the words and grammar as they attempt to convey the passage's meaning. But why are the translations so different if they are working with the same words and the same grammar? All the translators I know are good people and highly qualified in their field; but each translation team is working with its own philosophy, and that is what makes all the difference. Each translation has its own answers to a set of questions. (I need to tell you up front that I was the chair of the New Testament committee for the ESV. This may show my bias in the following discussion.)

1. Audience

First of all the translators ask, "To whom am I writing? Who is my audience?"

There are different ways to look at this question. The first is in terms of age. Am I writing for adults or children? This will affect a lot of things, such as word choice. In the RSV, 1 John 2:2 says, "He is the expiation for our sins." What's "expiation"? (The Greek word is ἱλασμός.) The ESV uses the word "propitiation." The NIV tries to simplify it by saying, "He is the atoning sacrifice." Maybe if you are an adult, you could figure out what "atoning sacrifice" means. The NLT (New Living Translation) simplifies it even further and says, "He is a sacrifice." What should the translator do with ἱλασμός? If you're translating for adults, you can say, "I'm going to use the word 'propitiation' and they'll look it up if they want to know what it means; adults can see the difference between 'expiation' and 'propitiation.'" If you're translating for children, they generally can't.

Another issue when it comes to the reader's age is the complexity of the sentence structure. Greek can write long sentences, like German. A good example is Ephesians 1:3-14. It's one sentence in Greek, so what will you do? The answer largely depends upon your audience. If you are translating for children, you're going to divide it into about ten smaller sentences. If you are writing to adults, you will turn it into less. The NIrV (New International Reader's Verion) uses 36 sentences and 7 paragraphs; the NIV uses eight sentences and two paragraphs; the ESV has five sentences and two paragraphs; the KJV I have uses three sentences.

The KJV is written at about a twelfth-grade level. The NIV is written at about the ninth-grade level. The NIrV is written firmly at the third-grade level. So, for example, the word "fort" is considered a fourth grade word and the translators couldn't use it. They could use the word "stronghold," probably because you can look at its two parts and figure out what it means. They couldn't use the word "manure" but could use the word "poop." (There is stuff about poop in the Bible and you have to have a word for it.)

Another issue about the translator's audience is whether they are Christian or non-Christian. Vocabulary can be broken down into two parts, active and passive. Your active vocabulary are words that you use; passive vocabulary are words that you don't use but can understand.

Someone who became a Christian at a young age and was raised in a church has a much larger passive Christian vocabulary (what I call, "translationese") than someone who is a recent Christian or not a Christian at all. That's going to affect how you translate. For example, in Romans 11:16, Paul discusses how Jews and Gentiles relate to each other in the church. The RSV translates,

> If the dough offered as first fruits is holy, so is the whole lump;
> and if the root is holy, so are the branches.

If you were raised in a church and understand the Old Testament background of Abraham and the patriarchs, you could figure it out. The NLT says,

> And since Abraham and the other patriarchs were holy, their children will also be holy. For if the roots of the tree are holy, the branches will be, too.

In other words the NLT interprets the metaphor for you. You might think, "Isn't that being pretty free with their translation?" In one sense, perhaps it is too much. Under inspiration Paul decided to use a metaphor. But on the other hand, the NLT does not assume that its readership is Christian and they're translating with that in mind. I don't think you can fault them for their intent, but it does illustrate why translations can be radically different.

Another example is Luke 2:7. The RSV translates,

> And she gave birth to her first-born son and wrapped him in swaddling cloths, and laid him in a manger, because there was no place for them in the inn.

What are "swaddling cloths"? Whatever it means, I am used to the expression, and when I read other translations of this passage that don't use "swaddling cloths," it feels as if they left something out. The NIV reads, "she wrapped him in cloths." The NLT has a good translation, "She wrapped him snugly in strips of cloth." In other words, the translators are trying to help you understand what swaddling cloths are. Actually I've been wrong on this my whole life. I thought swaddling cloths were diapers, but they're not. When my three children were born, they were cleaned up and wrapped tightly in a blanket. It's like the baby is back in the womb. That's what swaddling clothes are, and that's why the NLT says, "she wrapped him snugly." The translators are trying to help you understand not only the words but what the words mean.

Other issues in terms of audience are whether you want to write a translation that can be used for public readings, perhaps liturgical readings, and whether you want people to be able to memorize it easily. This controls word choice, how many words you use, whether alliteration is helpful, and so on. These and other issues related to audience have a significant impact on how the translator works, and hence one reason why translations are different.

2. Words or Meaning

The second question is, "Am I going to translate *words* or *meaning*?

As a caveat I need to say something about the word "literal," because it is a poor word. It appears to mean one thing, but it means something else. If you ask most evangelical Christians, "What kind of Bible do you want?" they will say, "I want a literal translation." But for some people "literal" means "word for word." If the Greek has eight words, then the English should have eight words. If the first word is a participle in Greek, then the first word should be a participle in English. If the Greek doesn't have a word, then we're not going to add one unless we absolutely have to and then we will italicize it. (So we have the italics in the NASB and the KJV.) The implication is that there's minimal interpretation in this type of translation process.

However, if you look up the word "literal" in Webster's dictionary, its first meaning has to do with *meaning,* not *form.* "Literal" means,

> in accordance with, involving or being the primary or strict meaning of the word or words, not figurative or metaphorical.

In other words, technically, if you say, "I want a literal translation," what you're saying is that you want a translation that *means* the same as what the author meant. We call this "authorial intent," reproducing the intention of the author. I want to hear what was meant for me to hear, not what the translator may want me to hear. When I am reading Matthew, I want to hear Matthew. And yet many people think of "literal" in terms of *form*, of a word-for-word equivalence.

What I would like to do is simply not use the word "literal" because people use it in a way that begs the question. The real question is how do I translate meaning from Greek into English so that to an English American reader, in my case, it means the same as what Matthew wrote to his original audience.

Back to the second question of translating words or meaning. There are two ways to translate. You can either translate words, or you can translate

meaning. The NASB is an example of translating words, or what is technically called "formal equivalence." The "formal" means that there is grammatical formal equivalence: if the Greek has a participle, the English has a
participle; if the Greek has a conjunction, the English has a conjunction;
and if the Greek has ten words, the English tries to have ten words. Again
the assumption is that there's minimal interpretation in this method of
translation. There also is often the desire to use the same English word for
the same Greek word, no matter where the Greek occurs.

The other way to translate is to translate meaning. The technical term
for this is "dynamic equivalence," or what is now called "functional
equivalence." The dynamism has to do with the grammatical forms. In a
dynamic translation you don't care whether the Greek uses a participle or
not. You don't care whether the Greek uses ten or twenty words. That's
not the point. Dynamic translation chooses whatever words the English
requires in order to convey the *same meaning*. This is where the NIV fits.
We often use the word "paraphrase" for this type of translation because
instead of going word for word, it goes thought for thought. The problem
is that the term "paraphrase" has been identified with being overly interpretive, and if you call something a paraphrase, you generally are not
complementing it.

So you can translate words or meaning. There are advantages and
difficulties with both of these approaches, but if you want to understand
why Bibles are different, there are differences with which you must
wrestle.

Problems with Formal Equivalence

Let me give you two problems of the "word-for-word" approach. The
first is that it's interpretive. The very reason that people want a word-for-
word translation is that they believe there's not going to be any interpretation, and that's simply not true. *All translation involves interpretation.* It is
impossible to translate without being interpretive. Anyone who disagrees
with this statement simply does not know Greek, Hebrew, or probably
any other language well.

For example, in John 2:4 the Greek, word for word, reads, "Jesus says
to her, 'What to me and to you?'" Almost no one is going to go word for
word on this one, so they say,

> What do I have to do with you? (NASB)
> What does that have to do with us? (NASB 95)
> What have you to do with me? (RSV)
> What concern is that to you and to me? (NRSV)
> Why do you involve me? (NIV)

> How does that concern you and me? (NLT)
> What does your concern have to do with Me? (NKJV)
> What have I to do with thee? (KJV)
> You must not tell me what to do. (TEV)
> What do you want from me? (NJB)

Even the NASB will not go word for word because it means nothing at all. In John 10:24 the RSV reads,

> So the Jews gathered round him and said to him, "How long will you keep us in suspense? If you are the Christ, tell us plainly."

That sounds pretty straight forward, until you look at each word. Here is a word-for-word translation from the Greek of the phrase, "How long will you keep us in suspense":

> Until when the soul of us will you lift up.

That's what the words say in the Greek. You have to be interpretive. What does it mean to "lift up the soul"? Even the NASB must be interpretive.

The NIV translates Romans 16:1,

> I commend to you our sister Phoebe, a *servant* of the church in Cenchrea.

The RSV translates,

> I commend to you our sister Phoebe, a *deaconess* of the church at Cenchreae.

That's an important difference. Was Pheobe part of the official structure of the church, a deaconess? Was there an official structure of the church? Was there, in the official structure of the church, a place for a woman? How are you going to translate διάκονον? "Servant," "deacon," or "deaconess"? And the interesting thing here is that the noun is masculine, but you can still legitimately translate it "deaconess." The translator must make an interpretive decision.

John 5:6 is about the paralytic at the pool of Bethesda. The RSV translates,

> When Jesus saw him and knew that he'd been lying there for a long time he said to him, "Do you want to be healed?"

One of the more interesting questions in all of Scripture, it seems to me. "No, I've been lying here for thirty-eight years because I like the view! Yes, I want to be healed!" But as we know, Jesus often calls for a public commitment before he heals. The important part for our discussion is that Jesus "knew," which is one of the legitimate translations of the Greek word. But the NIV reads,

> When Jesus saw him lying there and learned that he had been in this condition....

What just happened? We moved from superhuman knowledge (RSV) to Jesus asking for information (NIV). Both are legitimate translations of the same word, but the translator must make a choice. He or she has to make an exegetical decision as to whether Jesus knew that this man had been lying there for a long time, or whether he had asked somebody about him. All translation is interpretive.

1 Corinthians 6:9-10 is another good example. How do you translate μαλακός? If you look up the word in a dictionary, it refers to the passive member in a homosexual relationship. So the RSV says,

> Do you not know that the unrighteous will not inherit the king-dom of God. Do not be deceived neither the immoral nor the idolators nor the adulterers nor *sexual perverts* nor thieves, nor the greedy, nor drunkards, nor revilers, nor robbers will inherit the kingdom of God.

Their translation of μαλακός is *sexual perverts*, which is quite general. The phrase "sexual perverts" can refer to a lot of things. But the NIV translates it as "male prostitutes" and the NASB uses the word "effeminate." "Effeminate" has a lot of meanings other than "homosexual." A person can be effeminate and not be a homosexual. How are you going to trans-late the word? Is it a general word for sexual perversion? Is it a specific word for male prostitutes, or does it refer to effeminate people? It's an issue of interpretation. All translation is interpretive.

So one of the problems of going word for word is that it's interpretive, the very thing that it tries not to be. A second problem of going word for word is that, frankly, word-for-word translations can lose or distort mean-ing. For example, the NASB usually translates πόλις as "city," both Nazareth (Matt 2:23) and Jerusalem (Matt 4:5). But what does the word "city" mean to you? It is a rather large place, isn't it? And while Jerusalem was a large city, Nazareth was a wide spot in the road, perhaps a "village" or a "hamlet." While there are advantages at times to using the same English word for the same Greek or Hebrew word, at times it distorts the meaning of the original word.

The KJV translates Romans 12:16 as, "Mind not high things," which sounds as if we are not to think about important or significant issues. While this may be more word for word, it obscures the fact that Paul is telling the Roman church to not be proud, as most modern translations agree.

Problems with Dynamic Equivalence

There are also significant problems with the dynamic equivalent approach to translation. The first relates to the translators' view of grammatical structure. Because they generally do not view the structure of the language as having much connection with meaning, they often exercise considerable freedom in translating. I certainly agree that many times there is no real significance in structure. What Greek says best with a prepositional phrase may be best said in English with a relative clause.

However, there is one distinction that I think is critical; and because dynamic translations often ignore this distinction, I cannot recommend dynamic translations for serious Bible study. (There, I showed my hand.) The distinction between a dependent and independent clause is critical in exegesis. A dependent clause is one that cannot stand on its own; it is not a complete sentence. An independent clause can stand alone; it contains a subject and finite verb. (I will talk in detail about this in chapter 7.) Usually, we put our main thought in the independent clause and secondary thoughts in dependent clauses. As you will see in chapter 8, finding the main point is the key to Bible study.

For example, if I said, "I want to learn Greek and to study my Bible," what is the main point I am making? Is there a main point? You may infer from your own sense of worth that I want to learn Greek *in order to* study my Bible, but you really can't tell; and when it comes to interpreting Scripture, we shouldn't be guessing if possible. But if I said, "After learning Greek, I can study my Bible better," then you can clearly see my priorities.

Of course, this distinction between dependent and independent clauses does not always hold up. If I say, "I want to learn Greek in order to study my Bible better," "in order to study my Bible better" is a dependent phrase indicating the purpose of my study and is the main point. But as a general rule, the distinction is important to observe.

What if I said, "Go, make disciples." What is the main point? I have heard sermons on the "Great Commission" that placed almost all the weight on the "Go." But "Go" is a dependent construction (a participle), and the only independent verbal form in the verse is "make disciples." The Great Commission is not to go; it is to make disciples. (I will talk more about this in a later chapter.)

This can also be reversed. Sometimes an independent clause will be made dependent. Ephesians 4:26 in the NIV reads, "In your anger do not sin." The problem is that Ephesians 4:26 has two separate commands: "be angry; do not sin." While it is a controversial verse, the NIV has removed one of the two possible meanings. Formal equivalent theory tends to respect this distinction between dependent and independent constructions, and hence (in my opinion) formal equivalent translations are better for serious, in-depth Bible study.

A second problem with dynamic equivalence is that it is often overly interpretive. While it is certainly true that all translation involves interpretation, sometimes I think some translators give up and feel free to be as interpretive as they want. I personally don't feel the need to make something clearer in English than it is in the Greek.

This willingness to be overly (in my opinion) interpretive comes up with gender language. I will discuss gender language in detail below, but a few examples will suffice here. Some translators have concluded that words like "brother," "man," and "he" no longer function as generic terms referring to both men and women (TNIV, Today's New International Version, NLT, and NRSV, New Revised Standard Version). Fair enough, but how do you make this decision? The TNIV translates James 3:1 as "Not many of you should presume to be teachers, my brothers and sisters," interpreting ἀδελφός as "brothers and sisters." Therefore, they have removed from debate whether the early church had women teachers. (My opinion or yours on this issue is not the point. The point is that the TNIV removed the discussion entirely when they translated the one word ἀδελφός not as "brothers" but as the multiple "brothers and sisters," suggesting that James is addressing women and men teachers.)

The TNIV also translates John 19:12 as, "Pilate tried to set Jesus free, but the *Jewish leaders* kept shouting, 'If you let this man go, you are no friend of Caesar,'" despite the fact that the Greek just says "Jews."* The translators' motives are not necessarily bad; they want to keep people from misunderstanding the Bible (see point 6 below). However, because of their willingness to be quite free in translating, they have laid the crucifixion at the feet of the Jewish leaders. Only the Jewish leaders called for Jesus' crucifixion. The point here is not whether they are right or not. The point is that dynamic equivalence lends itself to a type of translation that can be much more interpretive than formal equivalence

---

* V 6 talks about the "chief priests and their officials," and v 15 about the "chief priests" again. The TNIV leaves it "Jews" in v 4 and v 14. In Matthew's account it is the "crowd" (27:20) and "all the people" (27:25) who were persuaded to shout with the leaders.

Thirdly, dynamic equivalence allows English style more sway than does formal equivalence. For example, Greek style does not mind repeating the same word over and over again in the same context; English avoids this, using synonyms if possible. But then in translation you lose the fact that the same word is used throughout a passage and in fact could be the theme that ties the paragraph together.

For example, here is 1 Timothy 2:1-6 in the NLT. The Greek words in parentheses are all forms of the same Greek word. When you see this repeated word, you can understand the flow of Paul's thought.

> [1] I urge you, first of all, to pray for all people (ἀνθρώπων). As you make your requests, plead for God's mercy upon them, and give thanks. [2] Pray this way for kings and all others who are in authority, so that we can live in peace and quietness, in godliness and dignity. [3] This is good and pleases God our Savior, [4] for he wants everyone (ἀνθρώπους) to be saved and to understand the truth. [5] For there is only one God and one Mediator who can reconcile God and people (ἀνθρώπων). He is the man (ἄνθρωπος) Christ Jesus.

Timothy is to pray for all "people" because God wants all "people" to be saved through the one mediator between God and "people," the "human being" Christ Jesus. The NIV more clearly connects the four Greek words.

> [1] I urge, then, first of all, that requests, prayers, intercession and thanksgiving be made for everyone — [2] for kings and all those in authority, that we may live peaceful and quiet lives in all godliness and holiness. [3] This is good, and pleases God our Savior, [4] who wants all men to be saved and to come to a knowledge of the truth. [5] For there is one God and one mediator between God and men, the man Christ Jesus.

Conclusion

Both formal and dynamic equivalent methods of translation suffer from the same problems because of the nature of language and communication; they both are interpretive. The translator's beliefs and knowledge, or lack of knowledge, all come into play in the translation process. In a dynamic equivalent translation the possibility for (mis)interpretation is greater. As you try to write more smoothly and with better English, the only way to do so is to become more and more interpretive. So the NLT is more interpretive than the TNIV, and the TNIV is more interpretive than the NIV, and the NIV is more interpretive than the RSV, and the RSV is more interpretive than the ESV, and the ESV is more interpretive than the NASB, but they're all interpretive, every last one of them.

There is an Italian proverb that says, "Translators are traitors" (*Traddutore, traditore*; "Translators, traitors"), and it's true. All translation loses meaning. All translators are traitors to the actual meaning. There is no such thing as a noninterpretive translation. Anyone who says otherwise probably has a limited exposure to translation theory and it may not be worth discussing the point with them.

That was the second and the biggest of the issues as to how we go about translating. Are you going to translate words and be interpretive, or are you going to translate meaning and be more interpretive?

3. Ambiguity

Translators have to ask themselves, "What am I going to do with ambiguity?" If the Greek or Hebrew isn't clear, when it can mean several different things, what am I going to do? The KJV, NASB, RSV, and ESV generally answer that question, "Leave it alone. If we can reproduce in English the same ambiguity that is present in the Greek, then we will leave it ambiguous. We will not make up the reader's mind." On the other hand, the NIV will not leave any ambiguity. They make up the reader's mind whenever they feel it is necessary, and the NLT goes to even greater lengths than the NIV.

2 Corinthians 5:14 in the RSV reads,

> For the love of Christ controls us.

What does "love of Christ" mean? The same ambiguity in the Greek is present in the English, and there are two possible meanings. It is Christ's love for me that controls, or it is my love for Christ that controls. The RSV says, "I'll keep it 'the love of Christ.' You figure it out for yourself." But the NIV wants to make it clear what they think it means: "For Christ's love compels us." In other words, it's Christ's love for me. The NLT says, "Whatever we do it is because Christ's love controls us." See what they're doing? They are saying that because of their audience, because of their translation philosophy, they want to tell you what they think this ambiguous construction means.

When I started writing this book, I thought I would find many places where the translations differed sharply from each other. To my surprise and delight, this proved not to be the case. Rather, what I found was that some translations leave a verse ambiguous, and others take an interpretive stance and remove the ambiguity; but the majority of the time the latter group of translations take the same interpretive stance. The NIV and NLT are remarkably similar in what they see Scripture meaning.

4. Move Implicit to Explicit

Some translations feel the need to fill out the story. In other words, there will be things that are perhaps *implicit* in the Greek and they'll make it *explicit* in English.

Sometimes this is just necessary. For example, Greek does not always require a direct object; English does, and so the translators must add one in, as in 1 Peter 1:8.

> Though you have not seen him, you love *him*.

Other times, in order to avoid misunderstanding, the translator supplies the antecedent for the pronoun. (Greek has means for the pronoun to connect itself to its antecedent that English does not, so the translator is not "adding to" the Bible.) Romans 6:10 in the NIV reads,

> The *death* he died, he died to sin once for all; but the life he lives,
> he lives to God.

"Death" in Greek is the relative pronoun, whose antecedent is in the previous verse.

Other times the translator will add words to help clarify meaning. For example, Philippians 1:7 says,

> It is right for me to feel thus about you because I hold you in my
> heart, for you are all partakers with me of grace.

The NIV says, "All of you share in *God's grace.*" The NLT writes, "We have shared together the *blessings of God.*" The word "God" is not in the Greek, but the translators felt that the verse was not fully understandable without identifying the source of the grace, and so they included it.

Matthew 10:29 in the RSV reads,

> Are not two sparrows sold for a penny?

The NLT has, "Not even a sparrow, worth only half a penny." They were trying to say it's even less than a penny. In the KJV, it is a "farthing."

5. Fill Out the Story

If you take this a step further, some translations will add to the story. They will add things that are not even implied, and this is where eyebrows should start to be raised, in my opinion. At some point you have to say this is God's Word, and this is how the Holy Spirit inspired the author to say it. If you want to know what it means, study, but don't change the biblical text.

A good example is 1 Peter 1:7b. The RSV writes,

> your faith, more precious than gold which though perishable is
> tested by fire, may redound to praise and glory and honor at the
> revelation of Jesus Christ.

It is not clear about whose "glory" Peter is speaking. The NLT makes the
decision for the reader.

> So if your faith remains strong after being tried by fiery trials, it
> will bring you much praise and glory and honor on the day when
> Jesus Christ is revealed to the whole world.

In Acts 28:11. Paul is leaving Malta and the RSV says,

> After three months we set sail in a ship which had wintered in
> the island, a ship of Alexandria, with the Twin Brothers as figure-
> head.

However, the NIV adds to the end of the verse, "Castor and Pollux," iden-
tifying the twin brothers. (The ESV lists their names in a footnote.) The
Greek word is Διόσκουροι, which is a transliteration of the Latin *Dioscuri*.
The Dioscuri were the twin sons of Zeus (Διός κοῦροι), Castor and Pollux.
You can see why the translators added the names.

6. Possible Misunderstanding

Translators will look at the possibility of misunderstanding. I don't
know how many times in the ESV meetings we would come up with a
good translation, but then somebody would notice that the original was
clear but our translation was open to misunderstanding.

For example, the RSV translates Matthew 5:28,

> But I say to you that every one who looks at a woman lustfully
> has already committed adultery with her in his heart.

The problem with this translation is that it can give the impression that if
a man has a passing lustful thought, that he has sinned. Is temptation to
sin actually sin? However, the Greek explicitly says that if a man looks at
a woman *for the purpose of* lusting, he has committed adultery. I don't
believe that a temptation that shoots through your mind constitutes sin;
it is the intention, the dwelling on it, that is a sin. So when you read the
RSV translation, you don't understand that the Greek is clearly saying,
"looks for the purpose of lusting." But if you read some of the other translations, you can see that they're struggling with this specific issue. The
NASB says "but I say to you, that everyone who looks on a woman *to lust
for her* has committed adultery with her already in his heart." They're trying to make you see that there's intent involved. This is why the ESV
reads, "I say to you that everyone who looks at a woman *with lustful*

intent." We wanted to be as clear as the Greek is and not open up the text to misunderstanding.

7. Sensitivity and Euphemisms

There are passages in Scripture where the Greek is painfully explicit, but because of our culture we cannot say it, and so translators, out of deference perhaps to the fact that children will be listening, turn it into a euphemism.

On the ESV translation committee we called this the "giggle factor." One of the people on the oversight committee was a pastor; we'd come up with a translation that perhaps was more sexually explicit than we were comfortable with and we'd ask him, "Can you preach this?" Often he shook his head and said, "I will not be able to get control of my high school students for at least ten minutes if we put that into the translation."

For example, in Genesis 31:10, the story of Jacob's dream about Laban and the spotted goats, the RSV says,

> In the mating season of the flock I lifted up my eyes, and saw in a dream that the he-goats which leaped upon the flock were striped, spotted, and mottled.

The pastor said, "I can't read that. As soon as my high-school students realize the animals are mating, the euphemism of 'leaping' is so evocative that I will lose their attention." So we came up with "the goats that mated with the flock." We said what was happening.

What do you do with sexually explicit language such as in the Song of Solomon? The Jews knew what they were doing when they prohibited Jewish boys who were under the age of 30 from reading it because the language, the anatomical language, is unbelievably specific.

What about what I call "potty language." In the New Testament the most famous passage is Philippians 3:8,

> Indeed I count everything as loss because of the surpassing worth of knowing Christ Jesus my Lord. For his sake I have suffered the loss of all things, and count them as *refuse.*

The NIV says "rubbish." The NLT says, "garbage." The problem is that the word usually refers to human or animal excrement.

In 1 Kings 18:27, the RSV says,

> And at noon Elijah mocked them, saying, "Cry aloud, for he is a god; either he is musing, or he has *gone aside.*"

The NLT says, "Perhaps he is deep in thought, or he is *relieving* himself." The Hebrew is a sarcastic, rather crude statement, suggesting that Baal has gone to the bathroom and wasn't paying any attention. Everyone I know agrees that you can't translate that literally. Several translations use the metaphor of being asleep and the need to be awakened. So what the translator is doing is massaging Scripture because of what is socially unacceptable, and all translations do it.

8. Theological Biases

Another thing that affects translation are theological biases, and it doesn't matter whether you are liberal or conservative. Your theological assumptions will affect your translation. When the RSV came out, it created a tremendous uproar in evangelical circles; the National Council of Churches (who owned the RSV) was branded the anti-Christ, because if you go to some of the key theological passages, the translators significantly changed the KJV. In the prophecy in Isaiah 7:14, which Matthew applies to Mary and Jesus, they translate, "For behold a *young woman* shall conceive and bear a child," instead of a "virgin." In Romans 9:5, depending upon how you punctuate it, Jesus is or is not called "God."

> to them belong the patriarchs, and of their race, according to the flesh, is the Christ. God who is over all be blessed for ever. Amen (RSV).

> Theirs are the patriarchs, and from them is traced the human ancestry of Christ, who is God over all, forever praised! Amen (NIV).

The same kind of thing happens in the evangelical church. At Acts 13:48, the RSV says,

> And when the Gentiles heard this, they were glad and glorified the word of God; and as many as were *ordained* to eternal life believed.

In the original Living Bible, not the New Living Translation, this is how Kenneth Taylor translates it:

> When the Gentiles heard this they were very glad and rejoiced in Paul's message and as many as *wanted* eternal life believed.

It is impossible to get the word "wanted" out of the Greek. This is an issue of theological disposition. Theological biases are everywhere.

9. Inclusive Language

What is a translator to do with inclusive language? Can "he" mean "he" and "she?" Can the English words "man" and "brother" be used generically of men and women or not?

The ESV committee spent a tremendous amount of its translation time dealing with this issue. The use of "man," and the use of the third person singular "he," are so so pervasive throughout the biblical text that if you cannot use "man" and "he," you must radically alter much of the biblical text, as has been done by the NRSV. They do this by changing third person "he" to second person "you," changing singular "he" to plural "they," or changing active verbs to passive.

The story I like to tell is of my nine-year-old daughter Kiersten. One day I walked into her bedroom and noticed she had xeroxed a verse from the Bible, cut it out, crossed out the "him" and written "her" over it, and stuck it on her bulletin board. I called Robin and said, "Do you know about this?" She said, "I've never seen this before in my life." We called Kiersten in and asked her, "Why did you do this?" She said, "Because I wanted to." "Do you feel, Kiersten, that by saying 'him' it doesn't include you?" "Oh, yes!" Kiersten replied.

So what are we going to do with passages such as, "Blessed are the peacemakers, for they shall be called sons of God" (Matt 5:9). Now I personally believe there are times because of Old Testament backgrounds that you want to keep the word "sons," "sons of Israel," "sons of God," etc. But this particular verse is not one of them. I thought this should have been translated, "children of God." (I lost the vote.)

Kiersten has provided an interesting learning situation for me as she constantly makes me reassess the words I use. I'm trying to change my vocabulary, not because of feminism but because I don't want to offend my daughter, and I don't want to unnecessarily offend any of you. But when it comes to the Bible, it's really hard to remove its patriarchal character, and it is a legitimate question as to whether we should. In fact, the only way to get rid of its patriarchal character is to so radically retranslate it that we are becoming so interpretive that the translation, in my mind, is of limited value. In my opinion, this is the problem with the NRSV, and to a lesser extent the TNIV. The Bible is an ancient, patriarchal book, and if we turn it into a modern inclusive book to get rid of every "he" used in a generic sense, we significantly change what it says.

Perhaps the best illustration is Matthew 18:15. The RSV translates it,

> If your *brother* sins against you, go and tell him his fault, between you and him alone. If he listens to you, you have gained your brother.

The NRSV will not use the word "brother" here so it says,

> If another *member of the church* sins against you, go and point out the fault when the two of you are alone. If the member listens to you, you have regained that one.

First of all, there is no "church," not in the sense that we think of it today, at this stage of Jesus' ministry. Second, it leads to misunderstanding. Does this mean that I have to deal with people who go to the same church (building) that I do, but if the person goes to "that other church" down the road, then Jesus' instructions are not applicable? I am sure some may say this is a silly argument and that obviously it is not true, but I guarantee you that people today are making just that mistake.

The NLT is inclusive, and I think they have done a better job. It reads,

> If another believer sins against you, go privately and point out the fault. If the other person listens and confesses it, you have won that person back.

That's about as good as you can do on that verse if you want to get rid of the "brother." It seems considerably better than the TNIV and its confusing use of the plural "they."

> If a brother or sister sins, go and point out the fault, just between the two of you alone. It they listen to you, you have won them over.

Another example is Philippians 4:21. Paul says,

> The *brethren* who are with me greet you.

In other words, the people who accompanied Paul, who were a part of his inner circle, were sending their greetings to the Philippian church. The TNIV says, "The brothers and sisters who are with me send greetings." They have forced the interpretation. Just about everywhere else the NRSV translates ἀδελφοί as "brothers and sisters," but here they write, "The *friends* who are with me greet you." Even the NRSV isn't willing to say that women were *necessarily* part of Paul's inner traveling circle. They properly left the interpretive issue open for the reader.

Hebrews 2:17 in the RSV reads,

> Therefore he had to be made like his brethren in every respect, so that he might become a merciful and faithful high priest in the service of God, to make expiation for the sins of the people.

But the TNIV writes,

> For this reason he had to be made like his brothers and sisters in every way.

Jesus had to be made like his "sisters" *in every way*? I think the NLT does a better job on this verse:

> Therefore, it was necessary for Jesus to be in every respect like us, his brothers and sisters, so that he could be our merciful and faithful High Priest before God. He then could offer a sacrifice that would take away the sins of the people.

Another problem is what to do with the phrase "son of man?" This is Jesus' main term for himself, and it is deeply Christological, drawing its terminology and theology from Ezekiel and Daniel. The NRSV uses the phrase "son of man" in the New Testament. However, in Ezekiel they translate the phrase, "O mortal," thus losing the possibility of readers seeing the link. Their desire for inclusive translation makes it impossible for the reader of their translation to see the connection. (They kept "a son of man" in Daniel 7:13.)

Fortunately, all these translations I have been discussing have continued to call God "Father" and have not made him our "mother" or "parent."

10. Practical Concerns

Translations are not only done by committees; they're done by human beings, and human beings have practical needs. For example, these committee meetings can become extremely expensive.

In an ESV translation meeting, there was one time in which my dad and I proposed a translation that nobody liked for a verse. We argued for half an hour, and when we finally agreed on a translation, someone pointed out, "Do you realize that we agreed on a translation that Bob and Bill gave thirty minutes ago except for one word." Someone else said,"I wonder how much that word cost?" The publisher, under his breath, said, "$300." This money has to come from somewhere. Translators are generally paid for the work now, you have to pay for what they eat and where they sleep, and you have to finish the project. So on translation committees there generally are goals like finishing a chapter by lunch, and at that point things tend to speed up.

Another practical concern is trying to anticipate the "political" repercussions of a translation. (The ESV never chose a translation because of political repercussions, but we did think about them.) Think of Psalm 1.

> Blessed is the man who walks not in the council of the ungodly.

You can't make everyone happy with this translation. If you say "Blessed is the person," there is a huge contingent, millions of evangelicals, who are used to that verse saying "man" and who still use the word "man" in a generic sense, and they are not going to buy your Bible. But the minute you say "man," you've lost another contingent of people.

The "translation history" of a passage—how it has always been translated—is one thing that blindsided me. I didn't really care how everyone else translates a passage. I'm willing to change anything if I think it makes it more accurate, more understandable, and more readable. And so we came to the Lord's prayer, "Hallowed be thy name."

> I said, "I'm sorry but nobody knows what what the word 'hallowed' means."
> "Yes they do, next verse," was the response.
> "Wait a minute," I said. "We can't translate it 'hallowed.' Almost nobody today know what 'hallowed' means."

But the argument was, "This is such a well-known verse that we can't change it." They may be right.

It is interesting to see what verses even the NLT would leave alone. (I'm picking here on the NLT because they usually show no hesitancy to change anything.) A great example is, "Love your neighbor as yourself" (Matt 19:19). While the Greek word can mean "neighbor," it also means a "fellow human being" (BDAG, 830). I argued that by translating "love your neighbor," we mistranslate it because if I say "love your neighbor," most Americans are going to think about the person whose lives one or two doors on either side of their house. It certainly does not mean love the person two blocks down the street!

Actually, that's exactly what it means. You love the *other* person, whoever that other person is, whoever it is within your ability to help. That's what the Golden Rule is all about. That's what the parable of the Good Samaritan is all about. The man wanting to justify himself said, "Who's my neighbor?" He's afraid that he must be nice to everybody. Jesus says, "Wrong question." Just as the Good Samaritan helped this person in need, so also you must help anyone who needs you, anyone who is within your ability to help. I still think "love your neighbor" is a mistranslation (I lost that vote), but the verse is just too well known to change.

What Bible Should I Use?

Given these considerations, what Bible would I recommend? Here are my suggestions. (1) Adopt one as your main Bible. For study purposes, I believe formal is better than dynamic. (2) When you are studying a passage, always check at least one other translation. If your main Bible is dynamic, check with a formal translation, and vice versa. (3) I enjoy checking a passage in several dynamic translations, telling myself that I am reading the translators' opinions of what the text means.

Conclusion

There are other issues I could go into detail on, but these are the main issues in my experience that illustrate why translations are different. Translations are different because translators have different translation philosophies. And that's not necessarily bad, but it does make it even more important for you to learn a little Greek, so you can know why they are different. In chapter 30, I will talk about the differences among the different Greek and Hebrew manuscripts, and about how these differences make translations different.

While it perhaps does not need to be stated, I want to stress that ultimately we do not know why the translators chose the specific wording they did unless you can ask one of them. We are only guessing.

Introduction to the Exercises

Most of the exercises show at least two translations of each verse, and the key word or phrase is in bold type in the first verse. (Italicized words are italicized in the biblical text.) Your task is to find the Greek behind the English and see why the translations are different. In many cases, their different translation philosophies will explain the differences. Remember, the translations are not be viewed as saying different things. In most cases, one translation will be vague and the other more specific (i.e., interpretive). Sometimes interpretations will be contradictory.

I will list at least two translations of each verse. It is often helpful for you to look at a few other translations as well as looking at the verse in its fuller context. The computer programs are helpful in doing this.

Matt 2:2 NIV. We saw his star **in the east** and have come to worship him. TNIV. We saw his star when it rose and have come to worship him.

Matt 6:32 ESV. For the **Gentiles** seek after all these things. NIV. For the pagans run after all these things. NET. For the unconverted pursue these things.

Matt 7:3 NASB. Why do you look at the speck that is in your **brother's** eye, but do not notice the log that is in your own eye? NRSV. Why do you see the speck in your neighbor's eye, but do not notice the log in your own eye? NLT. And why worry about a speck in your friend's eye when you have a log in your own?

Mark 1:17 KJV. Come ye after me, and I will make you to become **fishers of men**. NLT. Come, be my disciples, and I will show you how to fish for people! TNIV. "Come, follow me," Jesus said, "and I will send you out to catch people."

Luke 11:41 ESV. But give as **alms** those things that are within. NASB. But give that which is within as charity. NIV. But give what is inside [the dish] to the poor. TNIV. But now as for what is inside you—be generous to the poor.

Luke 22:70 KJV. Then said they all, Art thou then the Son of God? And he said unto them, **Ye say that I am**. NIV. They all asked, "Are you then the Son of God?" He replied, "You are right in saying I am."

John 1:16 NASB. For of His fullness we have all received, and **grace upon grace**. NIV. From the fullness of his grace we have all received one blessing after another. NLT. We have all benefited from the rich blessings he brought to us — one gracious blessing after another.

John 14:23 NIV. Jesus replied, "If anyone loves me, **he** will obey my teaching. My Father will love him, and we will come to him and make our home with him." NRSV. Jesus answered him, "Those who love me will keep my word, and my Father will love them, and we will come to them and make our home with them."

John 17:17 NIV. **Sanctify** them by the truth; your word is truth. NLT. Make them pure and holy by teaching them your words of truth.

Acts 20:30 NIV. Even from your own number **men** will arise and distort the truth in order to draw away disciples after them. NRSV. Some even from your own group will come distorting the truth in order to entice the disciples to follow them.

Rom 3:19 NLT. **Obviously**, the law applies to those to whom it was given. NIV. Now we know that whatever the law says, it says to those who are under the law.

Phil 2:8 NIV. And being found in appearance **as a man**, he humbled himself and became obedient to death — even death on a cross! NLT. And in human form he obediently humbled himself even further by dying a criminal's death on a cross.

Phil 4:13 NASB. I can do **all things** through Him who strengthens me. NIV. I can do everything through him who gives me strength. TNIV. I can do all this through him who gives me strength.

2 Tim 2:3 NIV. Endure hardship **with us**. ESV. Share in suffering. NASB. Suffer hardship with me.

Titus 1:2 NIV. God … promised **before the beginning of time**. ESV. God … promised before the ages began. NLT. God promised them before the world began.

Heb 12:7 NIV. Endure hardship as discipline; God is treating you as **sons**. For what son is not disciplined by his **father**? TNIV. Endure hardship as discipline; God is treating you as his children. For what children are not disciplined by their parents?

1 John 3:9 NRSV. Those who have been born of God **do not sin**. NIV. No one who is born of God will continue to sin.

See the effect of punctuation in the following.

Matt 27:52-53 NIV. "The tombs broke open and the bodies of many holy people who had died were raised to life. They came out of the tombs, and after Jesus' resurrection they went into the holy city and appeared to many people." Compare this to 1 Cor 15:20 and the changes made in the TNIV. "... and the tombs broke open. The bodies of many holy people who had died were raised to life. They came out of the tombs after Jesus' resurrection and went into the holy city and appeared to many people."

1 Cor 6:12-13 Pay special attention to the quotation marks. You may need to check a modern commentary on this one. The same phenomenon may occur in 2 Cor 5:13. NIV. "Everything is permissible for me"—but not everything is beneficial. "Everything is permissible for me"—but I will not be mastered by anything. "Food for the stomach and the stomach for food"—but God will destroy them both. The body is not meant for sexual immorality, but for the Lord, and the Lord for the body. TNIV. "I have the right to do anything," you say—but not everything is beneficial. "I have the right to do anything"—but I will not be mastered by anything. You say, "Food for the stomach and the stomach for food, and God will destroy them both." The body, however, is not meant for sexual immorality but for the Lord, and the Lord for the body.

Advanced Exercises with a Traditional Interlinear

Rom 3:25 Locate the three prepositional phrases that modify ἱλαστήριον and see how the different translations handle them, especially the final of the three.

2 Cor 4:8 Paraphrase this verse, replicating the pun. (Hint, if you read the sentence out loud in Greek, you will hear the pun, even if you do not know the actual words.)

Translation Chart

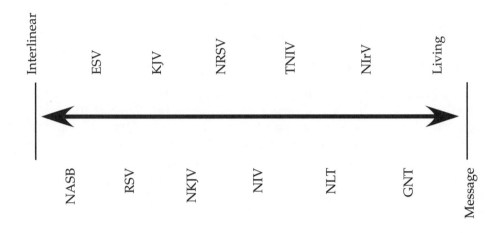

The TNIV and NRSV are difficult to place. If you remove the issue of gender translation, both are a little closer toward the formal equivalent side than the NIV and RSV, but where gender is concerned they move decidedly toward to functional equivalent side.

Please note that there is no midpoint. I do not want to suggest that there is a translation that is necessarily right and all others err to one side or the other. Each is positioned relative to the other translations.

The Building Blocks of Language

Now that you are familiar with the Greek alphabet and have had your first exposure (perhaps) to the nature of translations, it is time to talk about how we understand what God's Word means.

Please don't skip the next three chapters. They are critical if you are to move into serious Bible study. Hopefully you had a good experience learning English grammar in school; but if not, you still need to learn the basics of English grammar. Meaning is conveyed not so much with individual words as it is with groups of words. If you don't understand the basics of English grammar, then you can't make sense of what the Bible is saying with its groups of words.

What if I said the following?

"book red gives friend a a Todd to."

What do I mean? You may be able to piece the words together and hope that you have correctly understood what I mean, but you can't know for sure. Why? Because words need to be conveyed in ways that are in accordance with grammar. If you don't know the grammar, you can't understand what is being communicated.

You have to know the basics of English grammar if you want to be able to study your Bible.

CHAPTER 5

English Grammar: Nouns

Inflection

Sometimes the form of a word changes, such as when it performs different functions in a sentence or when it changes its meaning. This is called "inflection."

For example, the personal pronoun is "he" if it refers to a male and "she" if it refers to a female. It is "she" when it is the subject of the sentence (e.g., "*She* is my wife."), but changes to "her" when it is the direct object (e.g., "The teacher flunked *her*.") If the king and queen have one son, he is the "prince," but if they have two, they are "princes." If their child is a girl, she is called a "princess." All these changes are examples of inflection.

The third-person pronoun is one of the most inflected words in English.

	masculine	*feminine*	*neuter*
subjective singular	he	she	it
possessive singular	his	her	its
objective singular	him	her	it
subjective plural	they	they	they
possessive plural	their	their	their
objective plural	them	them	them

The following grammatical concepts can affect the form of an English word.

Case. Nouns perform different functions in a sentence. These different functions are categorized in "cases." In English there are three cases: subjective, possessive, and objective.

1. If a word is the *subject* of a verb, it is in the **subjective** case.

> *He* is my brother.

The subject is what does the action of an active verb and usually precedes the verb in a sentence.

> *Bill* ran to the store.
> The *ball* broke the window.

Word order shows that both "Bill" and "ball" are the subjects of their verbs. If it is difficult to determine the subject, ask the question "who?" or "what?" For example, Who ran to the store? Bill. What broke the window? The ball.

2. If a word shows *possession*, it is in the **possessive** case.

> *His* Greek Bible is always by *his* bed.

3. If a word is the *direct object*, it is in the **objective** case. The direct object is the person or thing that is directly affected by the action of the verb. This means that whatever the verb does, it does it to the direct object. It usually follows the verb in word order.

> Robin passed her *test*.
> The waiter insulted *Brian*.

Test and *Brian* are the direct objects. You can usually determine the direct object by asking the question "what?" or "whom?" Robin passed what? Her test. The waiter insulted whom? Brian.

case	function	example
Subjective	subject	*He* borrowed my computer.
Possessive	possession	He borrowed *my* computer.
Objective	direct object	He borrowed my *computer*.

Other than pronouns, most English nouns do not change their form as they perform different functions. For example, the word "teacher" stays the same whether it is the subject ("The teacher likes you.") or the direct object ("You like the teacher."). However, to form the possessive, "teacher" adds an "apostrophe s" ("She is the teacher's pet.").

Number. Inflection can also be caused by a word's "number," which refers to whether a word is singular (referring to one thing) or plural (referring to more than one thing). English generally changes a word's number one of two ways. Most words add a "s" to make the word plural.

Students should learn to study like this *student.*

Some words change an internal vowel or some other part of the word.

The *woman* visited the *women.*
The *child* joined in playing with the *children.*

Gender. Some words, mostly pronouns, inflect depending upon whether they are referring to a masculine, feminine, or neuter object. This is called "natural gender."

He gave *it* to *her.*

"He," "it", and "her" are forms of the same pronoun, the third person singular personal pronoun. They are masculine, neuter, and feminine, respectively.

We refer to a man as "he" and a woman as "she." If a word refers to neither a masculine nor feminine thing, then it is neuter. We refer to a rock as an "it" because we do not regard the rock as male or female.

Another example is the word "prince." If the heir to the throne is male, then he is the "prince." If the child is female, she is the "princess."

Most English words do not change to indicate gender. "Teacher" refers to either a woman or a man.

Other Terms

Noun. A noun is a word that stands for someone or something (i.e., a person, place, or thing).

Bill threw his big black *book* at the strange *teacher.*

Adjective. An adjective is a word that modifies a noun or pronoun.

Bill threw his *big black* book at the *strange* teacher.

Declension. In English, there are different ways to form the plural, such as adding an "s" or changing a vowel. You can think of these two ways as different "patterns," or what Greek calls "declensions."

As far as meaning is concerned, it does not matter how a word forms its plural. "Children" and "childs," if the latter were a word, would mean the same thing.

Preposition. A preposition is a word that indicates the relationship between two words. In the sentence, "The book is under the table," the preposition "under" describes the relationship between "book" and "table." The latter word, which follows the preposition, is called the **object of the preposition**. The preposition, its object, and any modifiers, are together called the **prepositional phrase**.

CHAPTER 6

English Grammar: Verbs

Verb. A verb is a word that describes an action or a state of being.

> Tom *hit* the ball.
> Greek *is* the heavenly language.

Person. There are three persons: first, second, and third. *First person* is the person speaking ("I," "we"). *Second person* is the person being spoken to ("you"). *Third person* is everything else ("he," "she," "it," "they," "book").

> *I* am the teacher.
> *You* are the student.
> This *book* is wonderful.

Number. If the subject of a verb is third person singular, English generally inflects the verb by adding a "s."

I kick the ball.	We kick the ball.
You kick the ball.	You kick the ball.
He kicks the ball.	They kick the ball.

Agreement. A verb must "agree" with its subject in person and number. This means that if a subject is singular, the verb must be singular. If the subject is third person, the verb must be third person.

For example, you would not say "Bill *say* to the class that there *is* no tests." Since "Bill" is singular third person, you would say, "Bill *says* to the class." Because "tests" is plural, you would say, "there *are* no tests." The presence or absence of the "s" at the end of the verb, and the difference between "is" and "are," are examples of agreement.

Tense. "Tense" in English refers to the **time** when the action of the verb takes place. If you study your Greek right now, the verb is in the present tense ("study"). If you are planning on doing it tomorrow, the verb is in the future tense ("will study"). If you did it last night, the verb is in the past tense ("studied"). In other words, in English the terms "tense" and "time" refer to the same thing.

English verbs divide into three forms: the present, past, and past participle. These are called the verb's "principal parts." Many verbs do not have three distinct forms.

tense	"to swim"	"to eat"	"to walk"	"to read"
present	swim	eat	walk	read
past	swam	ate	walked	read
past participle	swum	eaten	walked	read

All other tenses are formed from one of these tenses, often with the aid of a helping word (e.g., "will," "have," "being").

Voice. The "voice" of a verb refers to the relationship between a verb and its subject. When a verb is **active**, the subject is doing the action of the verb.

"I *walk* the dog."
"They *called* the preacher."

"I" is the subject of the verb "walk," which means it is doing the action of the verb.

When a verb is **passive**, the subject of the verb is receiving the action. English forms the present passive by adding the helping verb "am/is/are" or "am/are being."

Fido *is walked* by Tyler.
They *are being called* by the preacher.

"Fido" is the subject of the verb "is walked," but "Fido" is not doing the action of the verb "walked." The action of the verb is being performed by "Tyler," and it is being done to the subject, "Fido."

You can often tell if a verb is passive by placing "by" after the verb and seeing if it makes sense. "I was hit." "I was hit by what?" "I was hit by the ball." "Was hit" is a passive verb.

When you use a helping verb to form the passive voice, the time of the verbal construction is determined by the helping verb, not the main verb. For example, the active construction "I remember" shifts to "I am remembered" in the passive. Because "am" is present, the construction "am remembered" is present, even though "remembered" is a past participle.

Aspect. This refers to the "type" of action described by the verb. Some verbs describe an ongoing process ("**continuous**").

> The waves *are lapping* at the side of the boat.
> The ball *was bouncing* down the stairs.
> Peter *used to eat* with the Gentiles.

Other verbs describe a recently completed action that has present consequences ("**perfect**").

> I *have studied* hard and should pass the test.

Other verbs say nothing about the type of action other than the event occurred or occurs ("**undefined**").

> I *enjoy* photography.
> I *studied* all night.

Aspect is not the same thing as time. "I studied," "I was studying," and "I have been studying" are all past time but different aspects.

In English, you form the continuous by adding a helping verb with the present participle ("I am eating; I was eating"), and the perfect by adding the helping words "have" or "has" to the past participle ("I have eaten"; "she has fallen asleep"). The undefined is the simple form of the verb ("I eat; I ate"). Here are the verbal forms we have learned so far.

tense	continuous	perfect	undefined
present active	I am calling	—	I call
present passive	I am being called	—	I am called
past active	I was calling	I have called	I called
past passive	I was being called	I have been called	I was called

Mood. Mood refers to the relationship between the verb and reality. A verb in the indicative describes something that *is*, as opposed to something that *may* or *might* be, or something that is commanded. This includes statements and questions. For example, "I am rich." "Are you rich?" Most of the verbs we will meet for some time are in the indicative mood.

CHAPTER 7

English Grammar: Clauses and Phrases

In a normal English sentence, words don't occur in isolation but in groups. Much of learning to study your Bible has to do with understanding how these groups, or "clauses" and "phrases," work.

Clause and Phrase

A "clause" is a group of related words that includes a subject and verb.

> *After I went home,* the rain stopped.
> I will serve God *because I love him.*

Both "After I went home" and "the rain stopped" are clauses. A "phrase" is a group of words that does not have a subject or an indicative verb.

> *After going home,* the rain stopped.
> *Because of love,* I will serve God.

Dependent (or "Subordinate") and Independent

A **dependent** clause is a clause that cannot grammatically stand on its own. In other words, it doesn't make sense by itself. It isn't a sentence. Do any of the following form a sentence?

> after the rain stops
> because I am tired
> which I read to you

No they don't, and therefore they are "dependent" or "subordinate" clauses. All phrases are dependent.

An **independent** clause is a clause that can stand on its own as a sentence.

> After the rain stops, *I will dry the car.*
> Because I am tired, *I will go to sleep.*
> *Please give me the book,* which I read to you.

The distinction between dependent and independent clauses is crucial for doing Bible study. The author's main thought is usually in an independent clause, and dependent clauses usually modify the main thought. Grammatically, a dependent clause can never contain the main subject/verb of the sentence—the two most important words to locate in a sentence. If you were teaching a Sunday School class, would you rather spend time on the main point, or on qualifications of the main point?

Conjunctions

Conjunctions are (normally) the little words that connect words, phrases, clauses, and sentences (e.g., and, but, for, or, so, yet). They are broken down into two basic categories. **Coordinating** conjunctions connect independent clauses.

> The Word was with God *and* the Word was God.
> Be angry *but* do not sin.
> Jesus has died for us; *therefore,* do not sin.

Subordinate conjunctions begin a dependent clause and often link it to an independent clause (e.g., because, if, since, when, where).

> I studied *because* I want to pass this class. (causal)
> *If* we are faithful to the end, we will be saved. (conditional)

Types of Clauses

There are many types of clauses. As we learn more about exegesis, we will learn to identify the type of clause so we can know how it modifies the meaning of the main statement.

> *Although you know this,* I still need to remind you. (concessive)
> *When he was arguing,* he forgot to mind his manners. (temporal)

Relative clauses are a common type of clause. They always start with a relative pronoun ("who, whose, whom, which, that").

> Write a letter to those *who helped with the fire.*
> Certain people, *whose names I will not mention,* didn't help.

Types of Phrases

There are several types of common phrases. **Prepositional** phrases begin with a preposition and contain the preposition's object and other modifiers. I will discuss prepositions in more detail in chapter 10.

> The flashlight is *under the bed.*
> She went *through the woods* to Grandma's house.

Participial phrases begin with a participle and can include its direct object and other modifiers.

> *After eating the cake,* I started *doing the dishes.*
> The ice cream *eaten by the children* is delicious.
> The dog *sitting in the road* is in real trouble.

Phrases and Clauses Can Act as Parts of Speech

Phrases can act as parts of speech. For example, they can function as a noun.

> *Whoever is with me* is not against me. (subject)
> Give the Bible to *whoever needs it.* (object of preposition)

They can be adjectival.

> He *who is not for us* is against us.
> Good Friday is a day *of joy.* (i.e., "Good Friday is a *joyful* day.")

Phrases can also function adverbially (i.e., as an adverb).

> Drive *with care.* (i.e., "Drive *carefully.*")

Subject and Predicate

A sentence can be broken into two basic parts, the subject and the predicate. (I am sorry we don't have a different word than "subject" since it gets confused with the "subject" of the verb, but nobody checked with me when these grammatical terms were created!)

The **subject** is the subject of the main verb and anything that modifies it. In the sentence,

> The great big dog lying under the table is licking my toes,

"dog" is the subject of the verb "is licking," and "The great big dog lying under the table" is considered the "subject" of the entire sentence as opposed to the "predicate."

The **predicate** is everything else, including the main verb. In the sentence above, "is licking my toes" is the predicate. It contains the verb "is licking," the direct object "toes," and an adjectival modifier "my."

Types of Sentences

There are different types of sentences, grammatically. A **simple** sentence has one subject and one verb.

> I love Greek!

The subject and/or the verb can be compound.

> Mark and I love Greek and Hebrew.

A **compound** sentence has two or more independent clauses connected with a coordinating conjunction or punctuation.

> Kiersten loves Greek and Tyler loves Hebrew.
> Kiersten loves Greek; Tyler loves Hebrew.

A **complex** sentence has one independent clauses and one (or more) dependent clauses.

> Whenever I think back to Hebrew class, I start to sweat.

A **compound-complex** sentence has two (or more) independent clauses and one (or more) dependent clauses.

> I went to class and he went home because he was tired.

In Conclusion

These are not just grammatical niceties. As we get into learning how to study our Bible, we will be analyzing the author's flow of thought and how he constructs his sentences. Grammatical distinctions are a crucial key to analyze meaning.

Advanced Information

Greek is a **hypotactic** language. This means that it tends toward having a main clause with a series of dependent clauses modifying it. This is opposed to a language like English and to a greater degree Hebrew, which are **paratactic**. These languages are more linear, tending to link one independent clause to the next with coordinating conjunctions such as "and" and "but."

This is why understanding clauses and phrases and how they relate to each other is so important; it is a reflection of the way the language is written.

CHAPTER 8

Phrasing

An Introduction to Our Bible Study Method

When I started studying the Bible, I remember looking at a paragraph and having difficulty locating the main idea(s). I am a visual person, and sometimes the words started to blend together.

So I started working on a new way to study my Bible. I would xerox a paragraph of the Bible, cut each verse into its phrases, and lay the pieces out in a way that made sense to me. I would put the main thought all the way to the left, and ideas that were related to that main point were placed under or over it. For example (Mark 8:34):

> If anyone wishes to come after Me,
> he must
> > deny himself, and
> > take up his cross and
> > follow Me.

> In other words, those who want to be a disciple of Jesus must do three things: "deny," "take up," "follow."

When I was done, I would xerox my reconstructed text and have something that visually helped me see the flow of the author's discussion.

As the years passed, I became more sophisticated. I used color pencils! Eventually I used a Bible search program on the computer to get the actual text; I would copy it into my word processor and lay out the passage.

This process helped me more than almost anything else to study my Bible. It forced me to identify the main point (or points) and to see the flow of the author's thought—how he moved from one main point to the next, and how he clarified the main point(s) by adding modifiers.

I eventually named this process "phrasing" because I found that it wasn't normally helpful to break a sentence into every word (which is done in grammatical diagramming). I would break the sentence into its phrases (or clauses) and found that I rarely needed to divide the phrases further. So when you see the examples of phrasing on the following pages, and if you have "baggage" from high school grammar classes, don't freak out. This isn't grammatical diagramming, although it uses grammar.

When I then started teaching phrasing to college and graduate students, I found that they too enjoyed the process because it helped them learn, for themselves, what the Bible was saying.

I also discovered that other people were doing the same type of procedure. They called it by different names—"sentence flow," "discourse analysis"—but they too had learned how laying a passage out visually helped them see what the author meant.

Let me show you how it works.

> On the following pages, the text that is boxed is illustration. Text that is not boxed is my discussion.

By the way, why am I talking about phrasing in a text designed to teach you the basics of Greek grammar? My assumption is that you want to learn to use the language tools *in order to study* your Bible. After trying many other methods, I discovered that the tools are best learned while you are actually doing Bible study, or what is called "exegesis."

Do you have to do phrasing in order to learn a little Greek? No. There are different methods of doing Bible study that are effective. But phrasing works best for me and for my students, and so it becomes the context within which I will teach you how to use the language tools.

Also, one of the goals for this textbook is to help you read good commentaries. While some good commentaries may not actually phrase the text, the essence of the commentary will be to discover the flow of the author's thought and his main points. The better you become at phrasing, the more familiar a good commentary will feel.

Imagine that you have been asked to teach a Bible study on 1 Peter 1:2. How are you going to do it? How will you start?

Phrasing starts with two steps: (1) finding the begining and the end of the passage, (2) and then breaking the passage into manageable sections. Let's walk through the process.

Step 1: Find the Beginning and the End of the Passage

The biblical writers don't intend you to read a single verse in isolation from the verses around it. If you want to understand what one verse means, you have to see how it fits into its context. But which verses provide this context?

The key is to find the beginning and the end of the passage in which your verse occurs. If you are starting with the beginning of a book, the process is a little easier. You start with 1:1 and look for the end of the first passage. But if you are studying a verse somewhere in the middle of a book, it means you must find both the begining and ending of the passage in which that verse occurs.

What is a "passage"? This is my word for the basic "story" that the author wants to tell us. For example, John 3:3 is part of the story of Jesus and Nicodemus, which is John 3:1-21. Romans 3:23 is part of the passage that summarizes justification by faith, which is Romans 3:21-26. In other words, a "passage" is all the verses that make up a complete idea. If your Bible has headings, a passage is the verses under one heading (as far as the editors are concerned).

1:1   Peter, an apostle of Jesus Christ, To God's elect, strangers in the world, scattered throughout Pontus, Galatia, Cappadocia, Asia and Bithynia,

1:2   who have been chosen according to the foreknowledge of God the Father, through the sanctifying work of the Spirit, for obedience to Jesus Christ and sprinkling by his blood: Grace and peace be yours in abundance.

1:3   Praise be to the God and Father of our Lord Jesus Christ! In his great mercy he has given us new birth into a living hope through the resurrection of Jesus Christ from the dead,

1:4   and into an inheritance that can never perish, spoil or fade—kept in heaven for you,

1:5   who through faith are shielded by God's power until the coming of the salvation that is ready to be revealed in the last time.

1:6   In this you greatly rejoice, though now for a little while you may have had to suffer grief in all kinds of trials.

1:7   These have come so that your faith—of greater worth than gold, which perishes even though refined by fire—may be proved genuine and may result in praise, glory and honor when Jesus Christ is revealed.

1:8   Though you have not seen him, you love him; and even though you do not see him now, you believe in him and are filled with an inexpressible and glorious joy,

1:9   for you are receiving the goal of your faith, the salvation of your souls.

1:10   Concerning this salvation, the prophets, who spoke of the grace that was to come to you, searched intently and with the greatest care,

1:11   trying to find out the time and circumstances to which the Spirit of Christ in them was pointing when he predicted the sufferings of Christ and the glories that would follow.

1:12   It was revealed to them that they were not serving themselves but you, when they spoke of the things that have now been told you by those who have preached the gospel to you by the Holy Spirit sent from heaven. Even angels long to look into these things.

1:13   Therefore, prepare your minds for action; be self-controlled; set your hope fully on the grace to be given you when Jesus ...

You find the limits of the passage by reading and rereading the surrounding verses until the limits become apparent. You are looking for the natural breaks in the passage, where the author changes topics, even slightly. To put it another way, you are looking for a unifying theme that ties the verses together. Let the Bible tell you when the author shifts topics. Here are a few of the indicators that the topic has changed.

- Major shifts in the topic of discussion (e.g., Paul has stopped making one point and has gone on to another).
- Shifts in audience (e.g., Jesus stops talking to the Pharisees and starts talking to the disciples).
- Shifts of other types, such as moving from describing what Jesus did to relating what he is teaching.
- Changes in key words and repeated themes.
- Transitional phrases (e.g., "the next day," "after this").

This can be trickier than you think, and the temptation is to trust the chapter, paragraph, and verse divisions of your Bible. But none of these were part of the original Bible, and while usually helpful they can often get in the way. They can also rob you of the joy of exploring and deciding for yourself, and sometimes they are wrong.

Read the first part of 1 Peter (to the left) starting at 1:1 over and over. Where is the break, the end of the first passage? Go ahead and discover it for yourself. (I am working from the NIV translation.)

You probably saw rather quickly that v 2 is part of the letter's salutation that runs from vv 1-2. Once you have found the beginning and the end, write out your heading for 1:1-2. If you are not sure what to call it, make a guess; you can always change it later.

Writing out the heading is crucial: your goal is to get the main point out of each section and then to state that main point in the heading. I call this the "passage heading" as opposed to another type of heading we will meet in a few pages.

Salutation

1:1   Peter, an apostle of Jesus Christ, To God's elect, strangers in the world, scattered throughout Pontus, Galatia, Cappadocia, Asia and Bithynia,

1:2   who have been chosen according to the foreknowledge of God the Father, through the sanctifying work of the Spirit, for obedience to Jesus Christ and sprinkling by his blood: Grace and peace be yours in abundance.

Step 2: Identify the Sections

The next step is to break the passage into sections. You do this by reading and rereading the passage you identified in Step 1 until the natural sections of the passage suggest themselves to you. You then label each section with the main point being made in that section. Writing out the section heading is crucial, just like writing out the passage heading, since the initial goal of phrasing (and exegesis) is to identify the main point. If you are not sure what to write, write it in pencil so you can change it later if necessary.

Don't be in a hurry to get into the details of the passage but take the time to get the *big* picture. So many times when studying the Bible we want to jump right in and see what this word or that phrase "means to me." That's where we are headed, but don't be in a rush. Take your time. God's Word is worth it. Be content to sit back and let the overall picture develop.

During this part of the process you may notice words and phrases that seem important, but you don't know what they mean. Don't stop now to look them up; we are concentrating on the big picture and the day's own trouble is sufficient. Let's concentrate on getting the big picture.

Don't be so concerned with the *meaning* of the verses. Concentrate on seeing the *structure* of the passage, the flow of the author's thought. Ask yourself how the different parts are related to each other. As you read and reread the passage, thinking primarily about structure, you will be surprised at how the passage starts to show you its structure.

Try this now with 1 Peter 1:1-2, before turning the page and seeing what I have done with it.

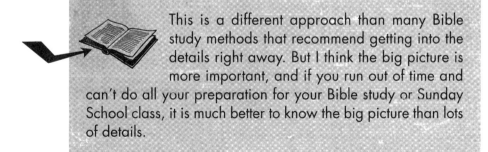

This is a different approach than many Bible study methods that recommend getting into the details right away. But I think the big picture is more important, and if you run out of time and can't do all your preparation for your Bible study or Sunday School class, it is much better to know the big picture than lots of details.

Salutation

Writer

1:1   Peter, an apostle of Jesus Christ,

Recipients

> To God's elect, strangers in the world, scattered throughout Pontus, Galatia, Cappadocia, Asia and Bithynia,

1:2   who have been chosen according to the foreknowledge of God the Father, through the sanctifying work of the Spirit, for obedience to Jesus Christ and sprinkling by his blood:

Greeting

> Grace and peace be yours in abundance

What did you find? You can see my suggestions to the left. I decided that there are three main sections that identify the writer ("Peter"), the recipients ("To God's elect"), and the greeting ("Grace and peace be yours in abundance").

Let me say it again: what you are doing is learning to start your Bible study by breaking up the passage into manageable sections. Of course, you can always cheat yourself out of the joy of discovering the Bible's meaning for yourself and look at a study Bible, or check out a commentary, or ask a friend. But along with losing the joy of discovery, what makes you think that the next time you need help there will be a friend nearby or a study Bible within reach?

One of the nice aspects of phrasing is that if you run out of time after Step 2 and can't continue, you at least have learned something that will help you teach the passage. You know the verses that make up the passage, the main point of the passage, the passage's sections, and the main thought of each section. This provides a great context within which to discuss the verse in question.

Step 3: Identify the Phrases

Now that you have identified the passage (Step 1) and its sections (Step 2), it is time to look at each individual section and divide it into its phrases.

What's a phrase? A phrase is an assertion, a proposition, something that means something. I am using the word "phrase" in a broader way than its grammatical usage. However, many phrases are grammatical phrases such as prepositional phrases, or adverbial phrases, or dependent and independent clauses. As you will see on the next page, many of the phrases I have identified are in fact grammatical phrases and clauses.

For example, if I said, "My father Bob likes to eat chocolate ice cream and drink iced tea," how many assertions did I make? How many phrases are there? In one sense, I only made one assertion. But can you break it down into smaller assertions that have meaning?

Is "Bob" by itself a phrase? Not really. While it may name my father, it says nothing more. How about "to eat chocolate ice cream" and "drink iced tea"? Sure, these are two phrases that have meaning. They may not make complete sense all by themselves (they are dependent constructions), but they do mean something. What does my dad like? He likes (at least) two things: ice cream; iced tea.

Here is where phrasing and grammatical diagramming are different. In grammatical diagramming, every word is shown in its grammatical relationship, and you get something like what you see below. (I hope this doesn't brings back too many bad memories.) This is not what phrasing is, and if you subdivide your phrases too far, they lose their effectiveness.

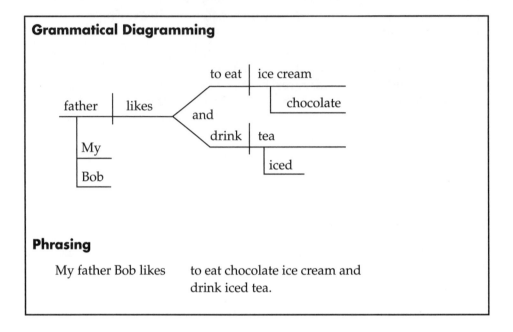

Grammatical Diagramming

Phrasing

My father Bob likes   to eat chocolate ice cream and
                           drink iced tea.

Let me explain it another way. In the sentence, "I want to go to the park but I must study first," how many words does it take until you have a phrase that has real meaning?

1.   I
2.   I want
3.   I want to
4.   I want to go
5.   I want to go to
6.   I want to go to the
7.   I want to go to the park
8   I want to go to the park but
9.   I want to go to the park but I
10. I want to go to the park but I must
11. I want to go to the park but I must study
12. I want to go to the park but I must study first.

While individual words have meaning, you don't really have a phrase that makes any sense until line 7. When you get to line 12, you realize that you have two phrases joined with the conjunction "but": "I want ..." and "I must ...."

Okay, back to 1 Peter. You have identified 1 Peter 1:1-2 as a passage and have seen that it has three sections. Now, break the two verses into its phrases. When done, check my work on the next page.

HΡΩΔΗΣ ΜΟΝΙ-

ΜΟΥ ΚΑΙ ΙΟΥΣΤΟΣ

ΥΙΟΣ ΑΜΑ ΤΟΙΣ

ΤΕΚΝΟΙΣ ΕΚΤΙ-

ΣΑΝ

ΤΟΝ ΚΙΟΝΑ

This inscription is on a column in the synagogue in Capernaum. The synagogue was built on top of a first-century synagogue. The inscription reads, Ἡρώδης Μονιμοῦ καὶ Ἰοῦστος υἱὸς ἅμα τοῖς τέκνοις ἔκτισαν τὸν κίονα, of course without the accents. It means: "Herod (the son) of Monimos and Justos (his) son together with their children erected this column."

Salutation

Writer

1:1   Peter,

         an apostle of Jesus Christ,

Recipients

         To God's elect,

         strangers in the world,

         scattered throughout Pontus, Galatia, Cappadocia, Asia and
         Bithynia,

1:2   who have been chosen

         according to the foreknowledge of God the Father,

         through the sanctifying work of the Spirit,

         for obedience to Jesus Christ and

         sprinkling by his blood:

Greeting

         Grace and peace be yours in abundance.

In "Section 1" ("writer") Peter identifies himself by name and by office. In "Section 2" ("recipients") Peter addresses them as "God's elect" and follows with a series of descriptions. "Section 3" ("greeting") contains the letter's greeting.

Step 4: Identify the Main Phrase(s) and Modifying Phrases

Now comes the real fun. You have established the limits of the passage and its sections and have broken it down into its phrases. As you have been reading and rereading the passage, you have started to identify the main points and the secondary points, and have seen how those secondary points relate to the main. Now it is time to make a commitment as to what is the main point (or points).

Identify the main point(s) in each section and place its phrase furthest to the left. These "main" phrases will be stating the main points the author is making. Most likely a main phrase will have a subject and a verb, and in many cases the verb will be in the indicative mood (and not a subjunctive or a participle).

Indent the other phrases under or over the word they modify. Use extra spacing to separate subsections of thought. If you find it helpful, underline or highlight words or themes that run throughout the discussion. When done, recheck your passage and section headings to be sure they are right. You can see my work on the next page.

Many signs in modern Greece are written in both Greek and English. See if you can pronounce the Greek words on this sign in Corinth.

Salutation

Writer

1:1   Peter,

              an apostle of Jesus Christ,

Recipients

              To God's elect,

                        strangers in the world,

                                      scattered throughout Pontus, Galatia,
                                      Cappadocia, Asia and Bithynia,

1:2   who have been chosen

                        according to the foreknowledge of God the Father,

                        through the sanctifying work of the Spirit,

                        for   obedience to Jesus Christ and

                                sprinkling by his blood:

Greeting

              Grace and peace be yours in abundance.

              To God's elect,

                        strangers in the world,

                                      scattered throughout Pontus,
                                      Galatia, Cappadocia, Asia and
                                      Bithynia,

1:2   who have been chosen

                        according to the foreknowledge of God the Father,

                        through the sanctifying work of the Spirit,

                        for

                          obedience to Jesus Christ and

                          sprinkling by his blood:

Here is how I phrase 1 Peter 1:1-2. Are there other ways this passage could have been laid out? Sure. Since "elect" and "chosen" are the same thing, it would have been nice to align the phrase "strangers …," "according …," "through …," and "for …" in a straight column so you could see that Peter is giving us four descriptions of who the elect are, as in the bottom example to the left. (Actually, there is no Greek behind the phrase "who have been chosen." The NIV inserted it because they wanted the reader to understand that the following prepositional phrases modify the idea of "elect.")

The two phrases "obedience to Jesus Christ" and "sprinkling by his blood" could have been placed under the preposition "for" (see bottom example to the left), but when a word has multiple objects, I like to add the extra space to the right of the word (e.g., "for") so you can see that the following phrases are parallel (see top example to the left).

I also could have listed the five place names ("Pontus, Galatia …") in a column, and often I will do this for a series. It didn't seem to make that much difference here.

Walk through 1 Peter 1:1-2

Now that we have 1 Peter 1:1-2 laid out, let's walk through the passage to see what Peter has to tell us. Here is your Bible study lesson.

Peter begins his letter with a three-part salutation. He first identifies himself by name and adds the qualifier that he is Jesus' apostle.

Peter then identifies to whom he is writing. His primary description is that they are the elect, Christians. He continues by explaining that this means they are strangers, scattered throughout five different areas in modern-day Turkey. (Although they still live on the earth, they are strangers to this land because they are elect.) But what is perhaps more significant is the following theological description of the elect. Their election was "according to the foreknowledge of God," an election accomplished "through the sanctifying work of the Spirit," and an election that has as its goal the "obedience to Jesus Christ" and made possible by the "sprinkling by his blood," Christ's death on the cross.

Peter then concludes with the actual greeting.

Can you see how much help phrasing can be? It helps you get started, rewards you with some understanding of the passage if you are short of time (after Steps 1 and 2), and helps you dig deeper into the passage and discover its primary and secondary points.

Let's try the process again with another passage. Try to do the work on your own before seeing how I do it. We might as well check out the verses following Peter's salutation. (1 Peter 1:3-21 is on the next page.)

1:3	Praise be to the God and Father of our Lord Jesus Christ! In his great mercy he has given us new birth into a living hope through the resurrection of Jesus Christ from the dead,
1:4	and into an inheritance that can never perish, spoil or fade—kept in heaven for you,
1:5	who through faith are shielded by God's power until the coming of the salvation that is ready to be revealed in the last time.
1:6	In this you greatly rejoice, though now for a little while you may have had to suffer grief in all kinds of trials.
1:7	These have come so that your faith—of greater worth than gold, which perishes even though refined by fire—may be proved genuine and may result in praise, glory and honor when Jesus Christ is revealed.
1:8	Though you have not seen him, you love him; and even though you do not see him now, you believe in him and are filled with an inexpressible and glorious joy,
1:9	for you are receiving the goal of your faith, the salvation of your souls.
1:10	Concerning this salvation, the prophets, who spoke of the grace that was to come to you, searched intently and with the greatest care,
1:11	trying to find out the time and circumstances to which the Spirit of Christ in them was pointing when he predicted the sufferings of Christ and the glories that would follow.
1:12	It was revealed to them that they were not serving themselves but you, when they spoke of the things that have now been told you by those who have preached the gospel to you by the Holy Spirit sent from heaven. Even angels long to look into these things.
1:13	Therefore, prepare your minds for action; be self-controlled; set your hope fully on the grace to be given you when Jesus Christ is revealed.
1:14	As obedient children, do not conform to the evil desires you had when you lived in ignorance.
1:15	But just as he who called you is holy, so be holy in all you do;
1:16	for it is written: "Be holy, because I am holy."
1:17	Since you call on a Father who judges each man's work impartially, live your lives as strangers here in reverent fear.
1:18	For you know that it was not with perishable things such as silver or gold that you were redeemed from the empty way of life handed down to you from your forefathers,
1:19	but with the precious blood of Christ, a lamb without blemish or defect.
1:20	He was chosen before the creation of the world, but was revealed in these last times for your sake.
1:21	Through him you believe in God, who raised him from the dead …

Step 1: Find the Beginning and the End of the Passage

Read through these verses to the left until you decide where Peter stops his discussion.

It is a little difficult isn't it? Peter changes his topic several times, and yet each time the new subject is explicitly connected to the previous. Peter starts by describing our salvation, our new birth. Then he moves from rejoicing in that salvation to suffering because of that salvation (vv 6-9), to how the prophets wanted to see the salvation (vv 10-12), and on into how we should live in light of all this (vv 13-17).

The "therefore" that starts v 13 shows Peter is not starting a totally new topic, and yet Peter changes from discussing salvation (vv 3-12) to specifics on how that salvation is to show itself, so perhaps v 13 is a good place to mark the end of the passage.

Step 2: Identify the Sections

While you were working on Step 1, you were also getting ready for Step 2. How many basic sections do you find in vv 3-12? Break the passage into its sections and put a heading with each.

See if you can figure out what
this poster is advertising.

Salvation

1:3   Praise be to the God and Father of our Lord Jesus Christ! In his
        great mercy he has given us new birth into a living hope through
        the resurrection of Jesus Christ from the dead,

1:4   and into an inheritance that can never perish, spoil or fade—kept in
        heaven for you,

1:5   who through faith are shielded by God's power until the coming of
        the salvation that is ready to be revealed in the last time.

Salvation and Suffering

1:6   In this you greatly rejoice, though now for a little while you may
        have had to suffer grief in all kinds of trials.

1:7   These have come so that your faith—of greater worth than gold,
        which perishes even though refined by fire—may be proved gen-
        uine and may result in praise, glory and honor when Jesus Christ is
        revealed.

1:8   Though you have not seen him, you love him; and even though you
        do not see him now, you believe in him and are filled with an inex-
        pressible and glorious joy,

1:9   for you are receiving the goal of your faith, the salvation of your
        souls.

Salvation and the Prophets

1:10   Concerning this salvation, the prophets, who spoke of the grace that
        was to come to you, searched intently and with the greatest care,

1:11   trying to find out the time and circumstances to which the Spirit of
        Christ in them was pointing when he predicted the sufferings of
        Christ and the glories that would follow.

1:12   It was revealed to them that they were not serving themselves but
        you, when they spoke of the things that have now been told you by
        those who have preached the gospel to you by the Holy Spirit sent
        from heaven. Even angels long to look into these things.

Step 3: Identify the Phrases

There is still too much in vv 3-12 for one Bible study (but just the right amount for a three-part series). Let's work with just the first section, vv 3-5. Go through the passage and break it down into its phrases.

_____

It looks as if v 3 begins with the theme statement, and then Peter follows with a series of prepositional phrases and a few relative clauses. As you are dividing these three verses into phrases, you will be starting to get a feel for the main assertions of the section.

1:3   Praise be to the God and Father of our Lord Jesus Christ!

In his great mercy he has given us new birth

into a living hope

through the resurrection of Jesus Christ from the dead,

1:4   and into an inheritance

that can never perish, spoil or fade—

kept in heaven for you,

1:5   who through faith are shielded by God's power

until the coming of the salvation

that is ready to be revealed in the last time.

Step 4: Identify the Main Phrase(s) and Modifying Phrases

Now it is time to identify the main point (or points). Move those phrases to the left, and the modifying phrases under the word they modify. Keep parallel phrases equally indented from the left margin.

_____

1:3   <u>Praise</u> be to the God and Father of our Lord Jesus Christ!

          In his great mercy
        <u>he has given us new birth</u>
                          {1} into a living hope
                through the resurrection of Jesus Christ from the dead,
1:4   {2} and into an inheritance

                            that can never perish, spoil or fade—
                            kept in heaven for you,

1:5   who through faith are shielded by God's power
                              until the coming of the salvation

          that is ready to be revealed in the last time.

By the way, this is great biblical theology. Saying "Praise God" is not praising him. That is not the biblical pattern. To praise God is to give him glory, to describe his character and proclaim his deeds.

The main affirmation of the passage is that we are to praise God. The reason for praising God is that he has given us new birth, and he did this because he is merciful.

Peter then specifies that this new birth has two results. The first is that we now have a living hope. But how was that hope made available? The answer is Jesus' resurrection. Notice from my placement that the prepositional phrase ("through …") modifies the verb "given," telling us how it was given. But I wanted to show that "into a living hope" and "and into an inheritance" are parallel, both telling us something about our new birth. But they are separated by the prepositional phrase "through …." This illustrates one of the problems with phrasing—words can get in the way. One solution is to number them as I have. (I always use curly brackets when I insert something into the phrasing that is not in the text. I don't want to confuse my words with God's!)

The second result of our new birth is that we have an inheritance. But it is not just any inheritance. It is an inheritance that can never perish. Why? Because it is kept in heaven for you. This illustrates another problem of phrasing, but one easily remedied. Due to the nature of how we construct discussions, the visual representation of the flow of thought keeps moving to the right. But eventually you will run out of paper, so I use a line to pull the discussion back to the left. The line should connect a word with what it is modifying. It is especially good to connect pronouns to their antecedents.

"Kept in heaven for you" isn't parallel with "that can never perish, spoil, or fade." It is telling you why our inheritance can never "perish, spoil, or fade." If I wanted to indicate this, I could have placed "kept …" under "never," or I could have drawn a line under the phrase "perish, spoil, or fade" and drawn a second line from it to "kept." In other words, you can make your phrasing more or less specific, depending upon what you need to do in order to understand the passage.

Peter adds one last note to his description of "you." While we look forward to our inheritance in heaven, we live out our lives here and now shielded by God's power. How long will this shielding last? Until our salvation comes in its fullness. When will that be? "In the last time." It is ready right now and waits for the end of time.

Can you see how this simple process of working through the text, seeing its sections, and identifying the main affirmations can make such a significant difference in your Bible study? I hope so.

Another Method

If you do not like working on a computer, you can always write out the phrasing by hand. This has the advantage of slowing you down, which is always a good idea in Bible study.

But what if you want to mark your Bible? Well, we can still follow the basics of phrasing, although you lose the advantage of visually seeing the passage. Here is a suggested procedure.

1. Divide the passage into sections (if necessary) by writing letters (for major sections) and numbers (for subsections) in the margin.

2. Underline or highlight the main clause(s).

3. Draw double slashes to separate the main phrases, and single slashes to separate secondary phrases.

4. Underline (in different colors) the repeated themes and words. Circle the major conjunctions.

---

1 Peter 1:3-5

[3] Praise be to the God and Father of our Lord Jesus Christ! In his great mercy he has given us new birth into a living hope through the resurrection of Jesus Christ from the dead, [4] and into an inheritance that can never perish, spoil or fade—kept in heaven for you, [5] who through faith are shielded by God's power until the coming of the salvation that is ready to be revealed in the last time.

---

[3] <u>Praise be to the God</u> and Father of our Lord Jesus Christ! // In his great mercy he has given us <u>new birth</u> / into a living hope through the resurrection of Jesus Christ from the dead, / [4] and into an inheritance that can never perish, spoil or fade—kept in heaven for you, // [5] who through faith are shielded by God's power / until the coming of the salvation // that is ready to be revealed in the last time

---

Hopefully this gives you a brief look at how phrasing can help you take a portion of Scripture and begin to understand what it says.

Phrasing has a minimum number of rules because it is a personal exercise. What helps one person see the structure of a passage may not help another. What is important is that you adopt the basic approach and then modify it to suit your own tastes and needs.

One of the neat things about phrasing is that you can stop almost anywhere along the process and still have learned your Bible a little better. For example, if all you do is break a larger passage down into its sections, you are well along to learning the passage better even if you don't do the actual phrasing. If all you do is find the main point, it will keep you from emphasizing the details of the passage, which in itself is a significant step forward.

Exercises

Write out the phrasing for the following passages. Please copy the unmarked texts on the next page and use them, not your Bible, for the second and third exercises.

1. 1 Peter 1:6-9 and 1:10-12.
2. Do Steps 1 and 2 on Mark 2:1ff.
3. Phrase the rest of Colossians 1:9 through the end of the passage.
4. 1 Thessalonians 5:16-22 is a good passage to phrase.

Mark 2:1ff.

2:1 A few days later, when Jesus again entered Capernaum, the people heard that he had come home.

2:2 So many gathered that there was no room left, not even outside the door, and he preached the word to them.

2:3 Some men came, bringing to him a paralytic, carried by four of them.

2:4 Since they could not get him to Jesus because of the crowd, they made an opening in the roof above Jesus and, after digging through it, lowered the mat the paralyzed man was lying on.

2:5 When Jesus saw their faith, he said to the paralytic, "Son, your sins are forgiven."

2:6 Now some teachers of the law were sitting there, thinking to themselves,

2:7 "Why does this fellow talk like that? He's blaspheming! Who can forgive sins but God alone?"

2:8 Immediately Jesus knew in his spirit that this was what they were thinking in their hearts, and he said to them, "Why are you thinking these things?

2:9 Which is easier: to say to the paralytic, 'Your sins are forgiven,' or to say, 'Get up, take your mat and walk'?

2:10 But that you may know that the Son of Man has authority on earth to forgive sins. . . ." He said to the paralytic,

2:11 "I tell you, get up, take your mat and go home."

2:12 He got up, took his mat and walked out in full view of them all. This amazed everyone and they praised God, saying, "We have never seen anything like this!"

2:13 Once again Jesus went out beside the lake. A large crowd came to him, and he began to teach them.

2:14 As he walked along, he saw Levi son of Alphaeus sitting at the tax collector's booth. "Follow me," Jesus told him, and Levi got up and followed him.

2:15 While Jesus was having dinner at Levi's house, many tax collectors and "sinners" were eating with him and his disciples, for there were many who followed him....

Colossians 1:9ff.

1:9   For this reason, since the day we heard about you, we have not stopped praying for you and asking God to fill you with the knowledge of his will through all spiritual wisdom and understanding.

1:10   And we pray this in order that you may live a life worthy of the Lord and may please him in every way: bearing fruit in every good work, growing in the knowledge of God,

1:11   being strengthened with all power according to his glorious might so that you may have great endurance and patience, and joyfully

1:12   giving thanks to the Father, who has qualified you to share in the inheritance of the saints in the kingdom of light.

1:13   For he has rescued us from the dominion of darkness and brought us into the kingdom of the Son he loves,

1:14   in whom we have redemption, the forgiveness of sins.

1:15   He is the image of the invisible God, the firstborn over all creation.

1:16   For by him all things were created: things in heaven and on earth, visible and invisible, whether thrones or powers or rulers or authorities; all things were created by him and for him.

1:17   He is before all things, and in him all things hold together.

1:18   And he is the head of the body, the church; he is the beginning and the firstborn from among the dead, so that in everything he might have the supremacy.

1:19   For God was pleased to have all his fullness dwell in him,

1:20   and through him to reconcile to himself all things, whether things on earth or things in heaven, by making peace through his blood, shed on the cross.

1:21   Once you were alienated from God and were enemies in your minds because of your evil behavior.

1:22   But now he has reconciled you by Christ's physical body through death to present you holy in his sight, without blemish and free from accusation—

1:23   if you continue in your faith, established and firm, not moved from the hope held out in the gospel. This is the gospel that you heard and that has been proclaimed to every creature ...

How Do We Modify Ideas?

We are well on our way. Now that we have a feel for how phrasing is done, we are going to start learning how a knowledge of the Greek tools can make our phrasing better as well as continue to help us understand why translations are different.

In the next several chapters we will learn more about the "connecting tissue" of a language, how the parts are held together (conjunctions), and how thoughts are modified and clarified (adjectives, phrases, and clauses).

Let me first ask a question. How do you modify a thought, or even a word? Let's say you start with the word "Paul." What can you do to it?

- You could modify it with another noun: "Paul, an apostle."
- You could use an adjective: "tired Paul"; "Paul is tired."
- You could also use a phrase: "Paul, an apostle to the Gentiles"; "Paul of Antioch"; "Paul, while going to Damascus."
- And you could use clauses: "Paul, whom we love."
- You can also use conjunctions to append ideas: "Paul and Barnabas."

My point is that the main thought is "Paul," and we recognize that the modifiers are telling us something about "Paul." In a sense, this is what exegesis is all about, locating the main thought and seeing how the other thoughts modify that main thought. Remember our mission: to see how the biblical writers have put their ideas together, to identify the main and the secondary thoughts, and in so doing come to a deeper understanding of what the author means.

CHAPTER 9

Conjunctions

In chapter 7, I gave you a short introduction to conjunctions. I need to fill out that discussion and then dig a little deeper into Greek to look for more ways Greek conjunctions can help us understand the Bible.

Significance

Conjunctions are linking words that connect thoughts. In exegesis, they are important because they tell us the specific relationship between different units of thought. By seeing this, we can better understand the author's flow of thought and therefore his meaning.

However, Greek can use conjunctions differently than we do in English. For example, almost every sentence in Greek narrative begins with a conjunction. One-third of all the sentences in John begin with καί, which generally means "and." It is "poor English" to start so many sentences with conjunctions, so they are often dropped in translation. But they are there, and they might give us a clue as to the relationship between ideas.

Greek conjunctions, like all words, have a range of meanings. δέ can mean "but" or "and." How do translators decide which meaning to use in a specific instance? Right! Context. In other words, they will use the meaning that makes the best sense in that sentence and paragraph. Sometimes it is obvious what a Greek conjunction means. Other times it is an issue of interpretation; when this is the case, translations differ.

In this chapter we will learn to identify these conjunctions and then use them to specify the relationship between the different phrases. Conjunctions break into two basic divisions, *coordinate* and *subordinate*. Some conjunctions are also *correlatives*.

In what follows, I usually list two translations for most examples. The first illustrates the point I am making. The second often shows another translation that treats the conjunction differently.

Coordinate Conjunctions

Coordinate conjunctions connect grammatically equal units. They can connect two independent clauses (i.e., two sentences), two direct objects, two subjects, etc. They can even link paragraphs. Following are the main coordinate conjunctions in Greek.

1. **καί** is the most common of all Greek conjunctions (occurring 9,161 times). It can mean "and."

> Phil 4:9. The things you have learned *and* (καί) received *and* (καί) heard *and* (καί) seen in me, practice these things, *and* (καί) the God of peace will be with you. (NASB)

> Whatever you have learned *or* (καί) received *or* (καί) heard from me, *or* (καί) seen in me—put it into practice. *And* (καί) the God of peace will be with you. (NIV)

καί can also add emphasis to another word, as in the English "even" or "also." This use is sometimes left untranslated.

> Matt 5:46. For if you love those who love you, what reward have you? Do not *even* (καί) the tax collectors do the same? (RSV)

> Rom 8:29. For those God foreknew he *also* (καί) predestined to be conformed to the likeness of his Son, that he might be the firstborn among many brothers. (NIV)

καί can also be used in a context in which the two clauses contrast each other, and καί is translated "but" by some translations while others use "and."

> Matt 12:43. When an evil spirit leaves a person, it goes into the desert, seeking rest *but* (καί) finding none. (NLT)

> When an evil spirit comes out of a man, it goes through arid places seeking rest *and* (καί) does not find it. (NIV)

When καί occurs at the beginning of a sentence, it is often marking the simple fact that the clause is a continuation of the previous discussion. Because we do not tend to do this in English, this type of καί is often left untranslated.

> Heb 9:15. (καί) For this reason Christ is the mediator of a new covenant, that those who are called may receive the promised eternal inheritance. (NIV)

> *And* (καί) for this cause he is the mediator of the new testament ... they which are called might receive the promise of eternal inheritance. (KJV)

2. **δέ** (2,792t) is a "weaker" connective, which means all it necessarily says is that there is a connection between the preceding and following.

Often, when a sentence starts with δέ, it is not translated. The NET Bible has literally hundreds of footnotes that indicate every place they did not translate δέ.

> Matt 1:2. Abraham was the father of Isaac, (δέ) Isaac the father of Jacob, (δέ) Jacob the father of Judah and his brothers. (NIV)
>
> Abraham was the father of Isaac, *and* (δέ) Isaac the father of Jacob, *and* (δέ) Jacob the father of Judah and his brothers. (ESV)
>
> Rom 7:25. (δέ) I thank God—through Jesus Christ our Lord! So then, with the mind I myself serve the law of God, *but* (δέ) with the flesh the law of sin. (NKJV)

Sometimes the force of the δέ is a little stronger and is translated as "and."

> John 3:19. *And* (δέ) this is the judgment, that the light has come into the world, and (καί) men loved darkness rather than light, because their deeds were evil. (RSV)
>
> (δέ) This is the verdict: Light has come into the world, but (καί) men loved darkness instead of light because their deeds were evil. (NIV)

Sometimes the δέ is helping the story to continue, and "now" or "then" among other words is used.

> Acts 2:5. *Now* (δέ) there were staying in Jerusalem God-fearing Jews from every nation under heaven. (NIV)
>
> (δέ) Godly Jews from many nations were living in Jerusalem at that time. (NLT)
>
> Luke 24:31. *Then* (δέ) their eyes were opened and (καί) they recognized him, and (καί) he disappeared from their sight. (NIV)
>
> *And* (δέ) their eyes were opened, and (καί) they recognized him. And (καί) he vanished from their sight. (ESV)
>
> *Suddenly* (δέ), their eyes were opened, and (καί) they recognized him. And (καί) at that moment he disappeared! (NLT)

δέ can also introduce a contrasting idea and is translated "but." This is called an "adversative" conjunction because it contrasts the following with the preceding. However, δέ is a "weak" adversative, which means it usually indicates a slight adversative relationship.

> Mark 15:23. (καί) They tried to give Him wine mixed with myrrh; *but* (δέ) He did not take it. (NASB).
>
> Luke 16:17. *But* (δέ) it is easier for heaven and (καί) earth to pass away than for one dot of the Law to become void. (ESV)
>
> (δέ) It is easier for heaven and (καί) earth to disappear than for the least stroke of a pen to drop out of the Law. (NIV)

> *But* (δέ) that doesn't mean that the law has lost its force in even the smallest point. It is stronger and more permanent than heaven and (καί) earth. (NLT)

> Acts 2:13. Some, *however,* (δέ) made fun of them and said, "They have had too much wine." (NIV)

> *But* (δέ) others in the crowd were mocking. "They're drunk, that's all!" they said. (NLT)

> John 1:12. *Yet* (δέ) to all who received him, to those who believed in his name, he gave the right to become children of God. (NIV)

> *But* (δέ) to all who did receive him, who believed in his name, he gave the right to become children of God. (ESV)

If you want to get even more sophisticated, you can see that the English paragraph marker can perform the same function as the δέ, since it indicates a change of some sort. Luke 24:36-43 contains one of Jesus' post-resurrection appearances. V 44 starts a new paragraph introduced with δέ.

> (δέ) He said to them, "This is what I told you while I was still with you: Everything must be fulfilled that is written about me in the Law of Moses, the Prophets and the Psalms." (NIV)

> *Now* (δέ) He said to them, "These are My words which I spoke to you while I was still with you, that all things which are written about Me in the Law of Moses and the Prophets and the Psalms must be fulfilled." (NASB)

> *Then* (δέ) he said to them, "These are my words that I spoke to you while I was still with you, that everything written about me in the Law of Moses and the Prophets and the Psalms must be fulfilled." (ESV)

In Matthew 28:11-15 we read about the Jewish leaders formulating the lie to explain away the empty tomb. V 16 then, in essence, starts a new paragraph by telling us what the disciples did.

> *But* (δέ) the eleven disciples proceeded to Galilee, to the mountain which Jesus had designated. (NASB)

> *Now* (δέ) the eleven disciples went to Galilee, to the mountain to which Jesus had directed them. (RSV)

> *Then* (δέ) the eleven disciples went to Galilee, to the mountain where Jesus had told them to go. (NIV)

How does the translator know when to translate δέ and when to drop it? Context! Are you seeing why translations can be so different? The translators' sense of English style and how they want to express these relationships can vary significantly.

3. **γάρ** (1,041t) gives the reason or explanation for something. It is usually translated "for."

> John 4:7-8. There came a woman of Samaria to draw water. Jesus said to her, "Give Me a drink." *For* (γάρ) His disciples had gone away into the city to buy food. (NASB)

> Soon a Samaritan woman came to draw water, and Jesus said to her, "Please give me a drink." (γάρ) He was alone at the time because his disciples had gone into the village to buy some food." (NLT)

> Rom 12:4. *For* (γάρ) as in one body we have many members, and the members do not all have the same function.... (ESV)

> (γάρ) Just as each of us has one body with many members, and these members do not all have the same function.... (NIV)

But γάρ can also indicate that the author is simply continuing his discussion, and these occurrences are usually not translated, as illustrated by the second occurrence of γάρ in Romans 1:20.

> Rom 1:19-20. For (διότι) what can be known about God is plain to them, *because* (γάρ) God has shown it to them. (γάρ) Ever since the creation of the world his invisible nature, namely, his eternal power and (καί) deity, has been clearly perceived in the things that have been made. So they are without excuse. (RSV)

> since (διότι) what may be known about God is plain to them, *because* (γάρ) God has made it plain to them. *For* (γάρ) since the creation of the world God's invisible qualities—his eternal power and (καί) divine nature—have been clearly seen, being understood from what has been made, so that men are without excuse. (NIV)

4. **ἀλλά** (638t) is a "strong" *adversative* conjunction, indicating that the following clause stands in contrast to the preceding. It is usually translated "but," but it can be translated many other ways that indicate a contrast.

> Matt 5:17. Do not think that I have come to abolish the Law or the Prophets; I have not come to abolish them *but* (ἀλλά) to fulfill them. (NIV)

> Matt 5:15. Neither do people light a lamp and (καί) put it under a bowl. *Instead* (ἀλλά) they put it on its stand, and (καί) it gives light to everyone in the house. (NIV)

> Nor do people light a lamp and (καί) put it under a basket, *but* (ἀλλά) on a stand, and (καί) it gives light to all in the house. (ESV)

Matt 9:17. Neither do men pour new wine into old wineskins. (δέ) If they do, the skins will burst, (καί) the wine will run out and (καί) the wineskins will be ruined. *No* (ἀλλά), they pour new wine into new wineskins, and (καί) both are preserved. (NIV)

Nor do people put new wine into old wineskins; otherwise (δέ) the wineskins burst, and (καί) the wine pours out and (καί) the wineskins are ruined; *but* (ἀλλά) they put new wine into fresh wineskins, and (καί) both are preserved. (NASB)

Matt 11:8. *If not* (ἀλλά), what did you go out to see? A man dressed in fine clothes? No, those who wear fine clothes are in kings' palaces. (NIV)

What *then* (ἀλλά) did you go out to see? A man dressed in soft clothing? Behold, those who wear soft clothing are in kings' houses. (ESV)

Mark 4:22 . For (γάρ) there is nothing hid, except to be made manifest; nor is anything secret, *except* (ἀλλά) to come to light. (RSV)

For (γάρ) whatever is hidden is meant to be disclosed, and whatever is concealed is meant (ἀλλά) to be brought out into the open. (NIV)

Rom 6:5. If we have been united with him like this in his death, we will *certainly* (ἀλλά) also be united with him in his resurrection. (NIV)

Since we have been united with him in his death, we will (ἀλλά) also be raised as he was. (NLT)

5. **οὖν** (499t) is the main *inferential* conjunction and is often translated "therefore."

Rom 12:1. *Therefore* (οὖν) I urge you, brethren, by the mercies of God, to present your bodies a living and (*no Greek conjunction*) holy sacrifice, acceptable to God, which is your spiritual service of worship. (NASB)

And so (οὖν), dear brothers and sisters, I plead with you to give your bodies to God. Let them be a living and (*no Greek conjunction*) holy sacrifice—the kind he will accept. When you think of what he has done for you, is this too much to ask? (NLT)

Its force can weaken to indicate a transition or continuation of the narrative.

John 9:18. The Jews *then* (οὖν) did not believe it of him, that he had been blind and (καί) had received sight. (NASB)

The Jews (οὖν) did not believe that he had been blind and (καί) had received his sight. (ESV)

The Jews *still* (οὖν) did not believe that he had been blind and (καί) had received his sight. (NIV)

6. ἤ (343t) is the main conjunction for saying "or."

> Matt 5:18. For (γάρ) truly I say to you, until heaven and (καί) earth pass
> away, not the smallest letter *or* (ἤ) stroke shall pass from the Law until all
> is accomplished. (NIV)

> For (γάρ) truly, I say to you, until heaven and (καί) earth pass away, not
> an iota, (ἤ) not a dot, will pass from the Law until all is accomplished.
> (ESV)

Did you notice how the comma performs the function of ἤ in the ESV
example above?

Subordinate Conjunctions

Subordinate conjunctions introduce dependent clauses, which means
these clauses will modify a main phrase. This is significant for phrasing as
you attempt to differentiate primary and secondary thoughts.

1. ὅτι (1,296t) can indicate the basis for an action and is usually translated "because."

> Rom 5:5. And (δέ) hope does not disappoint us, *because* (ὅτι) God's love
> has been poured into our hearts through the Holy Spirit which has been
> given to us. (RSV)

ὅτι can also be the equivalent of "that" after certain types of verbs.

> John 15:18. If the world hates you, know *that* (ὅτι) it has hated me before
> it hated you. (RSV)

2. ἵνα (663t) generally indicates *purpose* and can be translated "in order
that," "so that."

> John 3:16. For (γάρ) God so loved the world that he gave his only Son, *so
> that* (ἵνα) everyone who believes in him will not perish but (ἀλλ᾽) have
> eternal life. (NLT)

> Matt 7:1. Do not judge *so that* (ἵνα) you will not be judged. (NASB)
> Judge not, *that* (ἵνα) you be not judged. (ESV)
> Do not judge, *or* (ἵνα) you too will be judged. (NIV)
> Stop judging others, *and* (ἵνα) you will not be judged. (NLT)

It can also indicate the *result*, translated with "that."

> Matt 26:56. But (δέ) this has all taken place that (ἵνα) the writings of the
> prophets might be fulfilled. (NIV)

The difference between purpose and result is subtle. If there was intention,
it is purpose. If the action simply occurred, it is result. Some commentaries
will try to split this hair.

ἵνα can also lose all of its purpose/result nuance and simply introduce the content of what is expressed by the verb.

> Mark 9:30. He did not want (ἵνα) anyone to know it. (NRSV)

3. εἰ (502t) is the main *conditional* conjunction meaning "if."

> Luke 22:67. *If* (εἰ) you are the Christ, tell us. (RSV)

4. ἐάν (334t) is another form of εἰ, also meaning "if."

> Matt 5:13. You are the salt of the earth; but (δέ) *if* (ἐάν) the salt has become tasteless, how can it be made salty again? It is no longer good for anything, except (εἰ μή) to be thrown out and (*no Greek conjunction*) trampled under foot by men. (NASB)

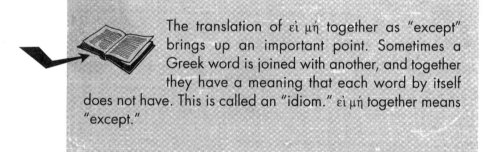

The translation of εἰ μή together as "except" brings up an important point. Sometimes a Greek word is joined with another, and together they have a meaning that each word by itself does not have. This is called an "idiom." εἰ μή together means "except."

5. ὅτε (103) is the main temporal conjunction meaning "when."

> Gal 4:4. But (δέ) *when* (ὅτε) the right time came, God sent his Son, born of a woman, subject to the law. (NLT)

Correlative Conjunctions

Correlative conjunctions are pairs of conjunctions that work together. The most common are:

μέν ... δέ	on the one hand ... but on the other
καί ... καί	both ... and
ἤ ... ἤ	either ... or
μήτε ... μήτε	neither ... nor
οὔτε ... οὔτε	neither ... nor
οὐκ ... ἀλλά (or δέ)	not ... but
τε ... καί	both ... and

Rev 3:15. I know your works: you are *neither* (οὔτε) cold *nor* (οὔτε) hot. Would that you were cold or (ἤ) hot! (RSV).

Often the first of the pair is not translated because of English style.

Matt 9:37. Then he said to his disciples, "(μέν) The harvest is plentiful, *but* (δέ) the laborers are few." (RSV)

The translation of conjunctions can become quite nuanced. For example, in the NASB of 1 Corinthians 7:7 the μέν … δέ is represented by the change from "one" to "another."

1 Cor 7:7. *one* (μέν) in this manner, and *another* (δέ) in that.

In *EGNT*, I have tried to keep these correlatives at the beginning of their phrases. In Greek word order, 1 Peter 2:4 reads,

ὑπο	ἀνθρώπων	μὲν	ἀποδεδοκιμασμένον	παρὰ	δὲ	θεῷ	ἐκλεκτόν
by	men		rejected	before	but	God	chosen

Notice how μέν comes after ὑπὸ ἀνθρώπων and δέ after παρά. In *EGNT* I listed μέν and δέ as the first word in each phrase.

	rejected	by	men	but	chosen	by	God
μὲν	ἀποδεδοκιμασμένον	ὑπὸ	ἀνθρώπων	δὲ	ἐκλεκτὸν	παρὰ	θεῷ
pl	pt.rp.asm	p.g	n.gpm	cj	a.asm	p.d	n.dsm
3525	627	5679	476	1254	1723	4123	2536

This is the first time I have shown you my "reverse interlinear." The first line is the NIV. I called it a "reverse" interlinear because I kept the order of the English words, not the Greek as other interlinears do. The second line is the Greek word(s) beneath the English. The third line is the Greek word's parsing; the parsing codes are explained in *EGNT*. For example, the English word "men" is a translation of ἀνθρώπων, which is a noun, genitive plural masculine. The fourth row is the GK number; the GK number for ἀνθρώπων is *476*, which is the number you use for word studies.

How to Identify the Greek word

All of this discussion on Greek conjunctions is a mute point, of course, unless you can discover the Greek word behind the English. And you are not going to be able to do the homework for this chapter until you can find the Greek.

I am going to discuss this issue in detail next week in chapter 19. For right now, the easiest way is to use my *English-Greek New Testament*. Here is Colossians 1:6b-7a.

God's		grace		in	all	its	truth.	7		You	learned it
⌞τοῦ	θεοῦ⌟	⌞τὴν	χάριν⌟	ἐν			ἀληθείᾳ		καθὼς	→	ἐμάθετε
d.gsm	n.gsm	d.asf	n.asf	p.d			n.dsf		cj		v.aai.2p
3836	2536	3836	5921	1877			237		2777		3443

With which conjunction does Colossians 1:7 begin that is not translated by the NIV? καθὼς, word #2777. What is the Greek preposition translated "in"? ἐν, word #1877. You get the idea.

If you do not have access to this book, you may want to look ahead to chapter 19 and skim over it.

Vocabulary

Conjunctions occur 18,180 times in the New Testament. If you would memorize four conjunctions, καί, δέ, γάρ, and ὅτι, you would know 13,474 of these occurrences.

Exercises

In Weeks 3-6 there are not exercises for every chapter. The last chapter in each Week has its own exercises, and the remaining chapters in the Week share one set of exercises, given after the next to last chapter in each Week.

CHAPTER 10

Adjectives

English

An adjective is a word that modifies a noun (or another adjective). In the sentence, "The big dog attacked the strange person," the words "big" and "strange" are adjectives that modify nouns. In the sentence, "The dark brown Bible costs too much," "dark" is an adjective modifying another adjective, "brown."

Adjectives can function **adjectivally** (i.e., like a regular adjective, also called an **attributive** adjective).

> He is a *good* student.

An adjective can also function **substantivally** (i.e., as if it were a noun). In this case the adjective does not modify anything but performs a function in the sentence, such as the subject, direct object, etc.

> The *Good*, the *Bad*, and the *Ugly* are all welcome here.
> Out with the *old* and in with the *new*.

Adjectives can appear in the predicate, which means they occur after the verb.

> The Bible is *black*.

Other parts of speech can also function adjectivally. For example, a prepositional or participial phrase can modify a noun.

> The man *on the street* is walking this way.
> The woman *sitting on the chair* is looking at me.

A phrase can also function substantivally.

> *Sitting on the dock* is great relaxation.

Greek

If you were studying full Greek, there would be much to learn about how to tell when an adjective is modifying a noun, and even to tell which noun it modifies. Unlike English, adjectives are not always right before the noun. Because *EGNT* follows English order, this is generally not an issue for you; but you do need to understand the basics of what is going on in Greek, especially if you are using a regular interlinear.

Greek can use adjectives in the order article–adjective–noun.

Phil 1:15	ἀπὸ	τῆς	πρώτης	ἡμέρας	ἄχρι	τοῦ	νῦν
	from	the	first	day	until	the	now

from the *first* day until now

This is the first time I have used this layout for a verse, so let me explain what I am doing, using Mark 2:5.

τέκνον,	ἀφίενταί	σου	αἱ ἁμαρτίαι.
child	*they are forgiven*	your	the sins

NLT: My son, your sins *are forgiven.*

- The first line is the Greek. To save space, I have usually kept the definite article ("the") with the following word (e.g., αἱ is with ἁμαρτίαι). You can tell αἱ is the article because the word "the" is underneath it.

- The second line is a word-for-word translation of the Greek. I have italicized the translation of the Greek word that I am using for the illustration. For example, because I am using Mark 2:5 as an illustration of the present tense, the italicized *they are forgiven* shows that ἀφίενταί is a present tense verb.

- The third and following lines (if present) are normal translations of the verse. The first translation has been chosen to illustrate the point I am making. If there is no indication of which translation I am using, I translated it myself to clearly illustrate the point. If there is a fourth line, it generally shows another way to translate the verse. Usually the difference will be one of clarity; one translation will bring out the nuance of the tense and the other will leave it vague. Rarely do translations clearly contradict each other.

It is easy to see that τῆς πρώτης ἡμέρας means "the first day," with τῆς meaning "the" (the article), πρώτης being the adjective, and ἡμέρας the noun. It is "easy" because that is how English does it.

However, often Greek lists the adjective in the order article–noun–article–adjective, as below.

Eph 4:30 τὸ πνεῦμα τὸ ἅγιον
      the spirit the holy
      The *Holy* Spirit

In fact, Greek could write "the Holy Spirit" or "the Spirit the Holy" with no significant difference in meaning. In *EGNT* these two phrases are listed like this.

from	the	first	day	until	now	
ἀπὸ	τῆς	πρώτης	ἡμέρας	ἄχρι	⌞τοῦ	νῦν⌟
p.g		a.gsf	n.gsf	p.g		adv
608		4755	2465	948		3814

the	Holy	Spirit
τὸ	⌞τὸ ἅγιον⌟	πνεῦμα
	a.asn	n.asn
	41	4460

As you can see in the second example, I keep the second article with its adjective. Notice the parsing code for adjectives; under ἅγιον the code starts with "a" (meaning "adjective").

You may also have noticed that the adjective is in the same case, number, and gender of the word it modifies ("Holy" and "Spirit" are both "asn"). This is called "agreement," which means that the adjective is the same case, number, and gender as the word it modifies. (We will discuss "case, number, gender" in more detail in Week 6.)

Substantival

Greek adjectives can also function substantivally. It is often necessary to add a word to the translation to make sense of this usage, and it is usually clear from context what word needs to be added. In Matthew 1:19, δίκαιος is an adjective meaning "righteous." If the translator's sense of English wants to treat the adjective substantivally, you need to add a word like "man."

Matt 1:19 Ἰωσὴφ δὲ ὁ ἀνὴρ αὐτῆς, δίκαιος ὢν
     Joseph but the husband of her righteous being
     NIV: Because Joseph her husband was a righteous *man*

The most famous example of a possible substantival adjective is from the Lord's Prayer. The question is, are we to pray that we be delivered from evil, or the evil one, i.e., Satan? (πονηροῦ is an adjective meaning "evil.")

Matt 6:13	ῥῦσαι	ἡμᾶς	ἀπὸ	τοῦ	πονηροῦ
	deliver	us	from	the	evil

NASB: deliver us from evil
NIV: deliver us from the evil *one*

In adding "one," the NIV is not "adding to" Scripture. This is simply how language functions, and these words are often necessary if you are going to say in one language what was said in another.

Predicate

As in English, the Greek adjective can be in the predicate, and there does not have to be an actual verb in the Greek sentence. The translator will have added the verb, normally a form of the verb "to be." (ἀναγκαιότερον is a comparative adjective meaning "more necessary.")

Phil 1:24	τὸ	ἐπιμένειν	[ἐν]	τῇ	σαρκὶ	ἀναγκαιότερον	δι᾽	ὑμᾶς.
	the	to remain	in	the	flesh	more necessary	for	you

NASB: yet to remain on in the flesh *is more necessary* for your sake.

In *EGNT*, the verb will not have any Greek under it.

it	*is*	more	necessary	for	you	that	I	remain
	→		ἀναγκαιότερον	δι᾽	ὑμᾶς		⌊τὸ	ἐπιμένειν⌋
			a.nsn.c					f.pa
			338					2152

Definite Article

In English the word "the" is the definite article, as opposed to "a," which is the indefinite article. Greek has a word, ὁ, which we usually call the Greek "definite article," but it is much more than that. It actually has one of the widest ranges of meaning of all Greek words.

Its function is *not* to make something definite that would otherwise be indefinite. This is a common mistake in exegesis, even by students who have learned Greek. The use of the article is actually quite complicated and is best left alone at the "baby Greek" stage, except to notice its flexibility. (You may notice in the examples below how the Greek article changes its form. I will discuss this in Week 6.)

It can function as the definite article.

Luke 5:33	οἱ	μαθηταὶ	Ἰωάννου	νηστεύουσιν	πυκνὰ
	the	disciples	of John	they fast	often

NASB: *The* disciples of John often fast.

It can function as a grammatical marker, for example showing that the following word modifies the previous.

Mark 8:38	μετὰ	τῶν	ἀγγέλων	τῶν	ἀγίων.
	with	the	angels	*the*	holy

NIV: with the holy angels

Greek uses the article when English does not, such as with proper names.

Matt 3:15	ἀποκριθεὶς	δὲ	ὁ	Ἰησοῦς	εἶπεν	πρὸς	αὐτόν
	answering	but	*the*	Jesus	said	to	him

NASB. But Jesus answering said to him

Sometimes it functions with a participle (e.g., ἔχοντι) or an adjective to make it into a noun, even with words between them (τὴν ξηρὰν χεῖρα).

Mark 3:3	λέγει	τῷ	ἀνθρώπῳ	τῷ	τὴν ξηρὰν	χεῖρα	ἔχοντι·
	he says	to the	man	*the*	the withered	hand	*having*

He says to *the one who has* the withered hand
ESV: he said to the man *with* the withered hand

Other times Greek doesn't use the article when English requires it.

John 1:1	Ἐν	ἀρχῇ	ἦν	ὁ	λόγος
	in	beginning	was	the	Word

NIV: In *the* beginning was the Word.

ὁ can function as a personal, possessive, or relative pronoun.

Luke 5:33	Οἱ	δὲ	εἶπαν	πρὸς	αὐτόν
	the	and	said	to	him

NASB: And *they* said to Him

Eph 5:25	Οἱ	ἄνδρες,	ἀγαπᾶτε	τὰς	γυναῖκας
	the	men	love!	*the*	wives

NASB: Husbands, love *your* wives.

Luke 7:32	ὅμοιοί	εἰσιν	παιδίοις τοῖς	ἐν	ἀγορᾷ	καθημένοις
	like	they are	children *who*	in	marketplace	sitting

NASB: They are like children *who* sit in the market place.
NIV: They are like children sitting in the marketplace.

CHAPTER 11

Phrases

In chapter 7, I gave you a short introduction to phrases, and now it is time to dig a little deeper into the grammar of prepositional and participial phrases. Again, the purpose is not simply to learn grammar but to gain a better understanding of how the biblical writers communicate their thoughts.

A phrase is often categorized by the type of word with which it begins (e.g., preposition, participle). Sometimes a phrase is categorized by its function (e.g., "adverbial," "temporal").

Because a "phrase" by definition does not have a subject or verb, all phrases are dependent constructions. Normally, the author's main thought is in the independent clause, and the dependent clause modifies that main thought.

Please do not confuse my terminology. I am talking here about a *grammatical* phrase, which is different from my more generic use of *phrase* when I am discussing *phrasing*. In the case of the latter, a "phrase" is any group of words with meaning.

Review of the Cases

I introduced English grammar relating to cases in chapter 5, but let me give you a quick review. In English we have three cases: subjective, possessive, objective. In Greek there are basically four cases that roughly line up as follows.

English	Greek	usage
Subjective	Nominative	subject
Possessive	Genitive	possession
—	Dative	indirect object
Objective	Accusative	direct object

Each Greek noun or adjective will be in one case. (I will discusses Greek cases in detail in Week 6.)

Prepositional Phrases

Prepositional phrases are common in Greek, and you must have a good understanding of them if you are going to do exegesis properly.

A **preposition** is a word that indicates the relationship between two words. In the sentence, "The book is under the table," the preposition "under" describes the relationship between "book" and "table," which in this case is a spatial relationship. What are some other prepositions in English? The relationship can be spatial, temporal, or many others.

> The Greek text is *by* the bed.
> The student always studies *after* the ball game.

The word that follows the preposition is called the **object of the preposition**. In the example above, the object of the preposition "by" is "bed." The preposition together with its object and modifiers is called a **prepositional phrase**.

A Preposition and Its Object

Regarding the Greek language, we say that a preposition "governs" the case of its object, controls it. Some prepositions always require their objects to be in one case: ἐν will always have an object in the dative, ἐκ in the genitive, and εἰς in the accusative.

However, other prepositions are followed by an object that can be in one of two or even three cases. διά can have an object in the genitive or accusative; ἐπί can take an object in all three. (The object of a preposition will never be in the nominative except under unusual circumstances).

This is different from English, where the object of the preposition is always in the objective case. You would not say, "The book is under he." You would say, "The book is under him." "He" is subjective and "him" is objective.

The Meaning of a Preposition

There are two important points to remember about prepositions. They can have a wide range of meanings. The preposition ἐν can mean "in," "among," "into," "with," "because," "while," etc. In many instances the meaning will be obvious, but in others the decision will be necessarily interpretive. Translations are different.

Second, prepositions that take an object in only one case have one set of meanings (although that one set can contain a wide variety of possibilities). But if a prepostion takes an object in more than one case, the preposition has a different set of meanings for each case. This is why a Greek dictionary divides its discussion of prepositions based on the case of its object. The translator will identify the case of the object before translating the preposition.

For example, the preposition διά means "through" if its object is in the genitive case, but it means "on account of" if its object is in the accusative.

Matt 2:5	οὕτως	γὰρ	γέγραπται	διά		τοῦ	προφήτου
	in this way	for	it is written	*through*		the	prophet

NASB: for this is what has been written *by* the prophet
NIV: for this is what the prophet has written

Matt 10:22	ἔσεσθε	μισούμενοι	ὑπὸ	πάντων	διά		τὸ	ὄνομά	μου
	you will be	hated	by	all	*on account of*		the	name	my

NIV: All men will hate you *because of* me
RSV: you will be hated by all *for* my name's *sake*

More on Prepositions

Greek regularly drops the definite article in a prepositional phrase. "In the world" could be written in Greek as ἐν τῷ κόσμῳ. "In the world" can also be written without the article (in this case τῷ) as ἐν κόσμῳ. In this situation, and if it fits the context, the translator may put the article back in.

Rom 5:13	ἁμαρτία	ἦν	ἐν	κόσμῳ
	sin	was	in	world

NIV: sin was in *the* world
NLT: people sinned

In the last chapter I showed you that adjectives can occur in the "article—noun—article—adjective" position. Actually, that last word should be "modifier": article–noun–article–modifier. Even a prepositional phrase can act as a modifier. Take the following for example. (τό is the article.)

Phil 2:9	τὸ	ὄνομα	τὸ	ὑπὲρ	πᾶν	ὄνομα
	the	name	the	above	every	name

RSV: the name which is above every name

The second τό shows that the following prepositional phrase (ὑπὲρ πᾶν ὄνομα) modifies the preceding noun (ὄνομα). Because we do not have the same construction in English, translations handle this situation in different ways. Usually the "article + prepositional phrase" is turned into a relative clause, which means a verb must be added ("which *is* above every name"). Other times the article will not be translated, which is fine since all it is doing is showing that the following phrase is modifying the previous word.

Phil 3:11   τὴν ἐξανάστασιν τὴν ἐκ   νεκρῶν
             the resurrection   the from dead
             RSV: the resurrection from the dead

Participial Phrases

Another common type of phrase is a participial phrase. A **participle** is an "-ing" word like "eating," "sleeping," "studying." A participle can have an object ("seeing the big *man*") with modifiers ("seeing *the big* man"), all of which form a **participial phrase**. Because it is a phrase, it is always dependent.

Participles are flexible in how they can be translated; you will often find words that appear to be inserted before the participle. For example, in Matthew 1:24 "woke" is actually a participle, and "when" has been inserted to make the meaning of the participle clear.

> *When* Joseph *woke* from sleep, he did as the angel of the Lord commanded him; he took his wife. (RSV)

Participles will be the topic of discussion in Week 5; we are dealing here more with participial phrases.

It is common for translators to change a dependent construction into an independent one, especially a participial phrase. Mark 10:23 in the NIV reads,

> Jesus looked around and said to his disciples, "How hard it is for the rich to enter the kingdom of God!"

"Looked around" is a participle, and "said" is the main verb. The translators change dependent into independent constructions for at least two reasons, both of which have to do with English style.

(1) Because Greek is inflected, it can handle long sentences built with a lengthy series of phrases and clauses. English tends to avoid this type of complicated construction, so what can the translators do?

They often break a long Greek sentence into two or more English sentences. For example, Ephesians 1:3-14 can be viewed as one Greek sentence.* The NIV breaks it into eight sentences and two paragraphs. In order to do this, translators often turn participial phrases into independent clauses, and the participle into a regular verb. When this happens,

---

* The repeated "in whom" (ἐν ᾧ) can be viewed as starting a new sentence, at vv 7, 11, 13.

words need to be added to the beginning of the second sentence, normally supplying the subject.

The NIV of Ephesians 1:4b-5a reads,

sight.	In	love		⁵ he	predestined	us	to be	adopted
κατενώπιον	ἐν	ἀγάπῃ	→		προορίσας	ἡμᾶς	εἰς ←	υἱοθεσίαν
p.g	p.d	n.dsf			pt.aa.nsm	r.ap.1	p.a	n.asf
2979	1877	27			4633	7005	1650	5625

The "pt" below "predestined" (third row) shows that προορίσας is a participle, translated here as the finite "he predestined." The same is true of "he made known" (γνωρίσας) in v 9.

(2) Greek is fond of using a participle followed by a regular verb. For the sake of English style, this participle is often turned into a regular verb, such as "called" in Matthew 2:7.

> Then Herod *called* the Magi secretly and *found out* from them the exact time the star had appeared. (NIV)

This verse actually has only one indicative verb, "found out."

This is not necessarily bad translation practice. After all, the point of translation is to make something understandable. However, because it blurs the grammatical distinction between independent and dependent constructions, and because the author's main thought tends to be in the independent clauses, this practice can obscure the relationship between phrases and makes exegesis more difficult. This is one reason why formal equivalent translations tend to be better for serious Bible study.

The opposite can also happen; an independent clause can be translated as dependent. Consider Romans 4:19.

> He *did not weaken* in faith when he *considered* his own body, which was as good as dead because he was about a hundred years old. (RSV)

"Did not weaken" is a participle in a subordinate clause. "When he considered" is the main verb in Greek, but in the RSV it is a temporal subordinate clause. Paul's point is how Abraham looked at his aging body ("considered"), and adds that in doing so he "did not weaken" in his faith, a fact obscured by the RSV. The NIV does a better job in this regard.

> *Without weakening* in his faith, he *faced the fact* that his body was as good as dead—since he was about a hundred years old.

Another good example is the "Great Commission" (Matt 28:19-20). The NIV reads,

> Therefore *go* and *make disciples* of all nations, *baptizing* them in the name of the Father and of the Son and of the Holy Spirit, and *teaching* them to obey everything I have commanded you.

What is the main point? It appears that the apostles are told to do *two* things: "go!" and "make disciples!" However, if you look at the Greek, you will find that there is only one imperative: "make disciples!" "Go" is a participle, like "baptizing" and "teaching." Jesus is telling his disciples (and us): "Therefore, *as* you go, make disciples by baptizing and by teaching." Wherever you are, wherever you go (whether, I would add, you are in full-time ministry as a missionary or as a stay-at-home Christian), you are to make disciples.

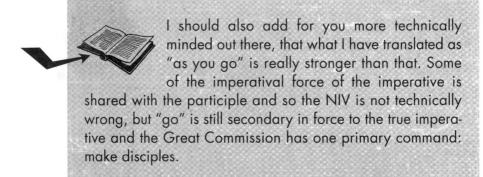

I should also add for you more technically minded out there, that what I have translated as "as you go" is really stronger than that. Some of the imperatival force of the imperative is shared with the participle and so the NIV is not technically wrong, but "go" is still secondary in force to the true imperative and the Great Commission has one primary command: make disciples.

Advanced Information

Prepositions that end in a vowel might change their form when the following word begins with a vowel. The final vowel of the preposition may be dropped and marked with an apostrophe. This is called **elision**.

μετὰ αὐτόν ‣ μετ᾽ αὐτόν

When a preposition ends in a vowel and the following word begins with a vowel and a rough breathing, the consonant before the final vowel in the preposition often changes as well. These changes were necessary in order to pronounce the combination of sounds more easily.

μετὰ ἡμῶν ‣ μετ᾽ ἡμῶν ‣ μεθ᾽ ἡμῶν

CHAPTER 12

Clauses

Clauses are like phrases except that they have a finite verb and therefore a subject of that verb. Clauses can modify a word or perform a function in the sentence.

> *After I study Greek,* I drift off into a beautiful sleep.
> *Whoever is not for me* is against me.

Relative clauses

A relative pronoun is a noun substitute: who(m); whose; that; which; what(ever). The first word in a relative clause is the relative pronoun.

> The man *who is sitting at the table* is my pastor.
> *Whoever is for me* is not against us.

When Greek relative clauses perform a function, it is often necessary for the translator to add a pronoun to the clause to make better sounding English. For example, in the sentence "Who will be first will be last," the relative clause "Who will be first" is the subject of the verb "will be." To make the translation smoother you could add a word such as a person pronoun, "*He* who will be first will be last."

Pronouns and Antecedents

The **antecedent** is the word the pronoun represents. In your phrasing, try to connect a relative pronoun to its antecedent. How do you identify a pronoun's antecedent? The relative pronoun must agree with its antecedent in number and gender. So, for example, if the pronoun is masculine plural, look for an antecedent that is masculine plural.

There are several situations in which a translator might substitute the antecedent for the pronoun. (1) Because Greek is an inflected language, Greek writers are comfortable separating pronouns from their antecedents

104   *Greek for the Rest of Us*

by quite some distance. The grammar would allow the Greek reader to see the pronoun's antecedent. However, English requires pronouns to be much closer to their antecedent. Because of this difference, translators often substitute the antecedent for the pronoun if they think that the English reader might not be able to identify the pronoun's antecedent. Consider Romans 6:10.

Rom 6:10	ὃ	γὰρ	ἀπέθανεν,	τῇ	ἁμαρτίᾳ	ἀπέθανεν	ἐφάπαξ
	which	for	he died,	to the	sin	he die	once for all

KJV: For in *that* he died, he died unto sin once.
ESV: The *death* he died, he died to sin once for all.
NLT: *He* died once to defeat sin.

For the pronoun ὃ the ESV substitutes "death" from v 9. The NLT ignores the relative pronoun altogether.

(2) Sometimes a Greek sentence is too long and must be broken into smaller units for the sake of English style. When this is done, relative clauses are often used to start a new sentence, and in this case the antecedent is normally supplied for the pronoun. A word-for-word translation of Romans 2:5b-6 reads something like this:

ἀποκαλύψεως	δικαιοκρισίας	τοῦ θεοῦ	ὃς	ἀποδώσει
revelation	of righteous judgment	of God	who	he will give

ἑκάστῳ	κατὰ	τὰ ἔργα	αὐτοῦ
to each	according to	the works	of him

There is no question of the identity of the "who" (ὃς), especially since it immediately follows "God" (θεοῦ). However, if the translators feel that the sentence is too long and they decide to start a new sentence at ὃς, the "who" becomes spearated from its antecedent.

The NASB does not start a new sentence,

> *who* will render to each person according to his deeds.

The ESV starts a new paragraph at v 6 and so can't write "who." It says,

> *He* will render to each one according to his works

The NIV supplies the antecedent of the relative pronoun.

> *God* "will give to each person according to what he has done."

Sometimes the pronoun refers back to an idea in general, or to a group of words. In Colossians 2:23, the antecedents of the pronoun translated "such regulations" are those specifically mentioned in v 21. "Do not handle! Do not taste! Do not touch!" The NIV translates,

> *Such regulations* indeed have an appearance of wisdom, with their self-imposed worship, their false humility and their harsh treatment of the body, but they lack any value in restraining sensual indulgence.

The translators are not "adding to" Scripture. The Greek makes the connection between pronoun and its antecedent(s) clear, and they don't want you to misunderstand.

While I am on this topic, I should add that this is true of other pronouns, not just relative pronouns. Personal pronouns ("he, she, it, they") are sometimes replaced by their antecedent, as in Matthew 8:24.

> Without warning, a furious storm came up on the lake, so that the waves swept over the boat. But *Jesus* was sleeping. (NIV)

The Greek only has "he was sleeping." On Matthew 9:10 the ESV writes,

> And as Jesus reclined at table in the house, behold, many tax collectors and sinners came and were reclining with Jesus and his disciples.

The footnote on "Jesus" reads, "Greek *he*."

Adverbial Clauses

There are many other types of clauses, and I will go into them in more detail in the Advanced Information section in the next chapter. As far as phrasing is concerned, just work to keep your adverbial clauses together. Be sure you can identify the beginning and end of the phrase.

Also be aware that if a translator wants to break a Greek sentence into multiple sentences, the break will almost always come between clauses, and this will often necessitate adding some words to the clause to make it into a sentence. For example, the NIV adds "I pray" to the beginning of Ephesians 3:16 since in Greek it is a content clause (ἵνα) and not a complete sentence.

> *I pray* that (ἵνα) out of his glorious riches he may strengthen you with power through his Spirit in your inner being.

Conditional Clauses

A "conditional sentence" is an "if... then... " type sentence. The "if" clause is called the **protasis**, and the "then" clause the **apodosis**. There are four basic types of conditional sentences in Greek based on their form, and each one has its own nuance of meaning.

1. **First class**. Also call a "condition of fact." The protasis begins with εἰ ("if") and the verb is in the indicative. These sentences are saying that if something is true, and let's assume for the sake of the argument that it is true, then such and such will occur.

Matt 5:29. If your right eye causes you to sin, tear it out and throw it away. For it is better that you lose one of your members than that your whole body be thrown into hell. (ESV)

Sometimes the apodosis is clearly true, and translators might use "since" instead of "if." But it seems to me that there is something to be gained by saying "if …" even when you know it is true. It causes you to affirm the truthfulness of the apodosis.

Daniel Wallace tells the rather "crude" (his word) illustration of a young man who knew only enough Greek to be dangerous. The young man understood the first class condition to be a "statement of fact" and thought εἰ should be translated "since." So in obedience to Matthew 5:29 cited above, he "proceeded to gouge his eye with a screwdriver" (GGBB, p. 681). Let's not make that same mistake.

Please note that just because a sentence is a first class condition, this does not mean that the apodosis actually is true. It is assumed true for the sake of the argument, but that does not make it really true.

1 Cor 15:13. But *if there is no resurrection of the dead,* then not even Christ has been raised. (ESV)

2. **Second class**. Also called "contrary to fact." The protasis begins with εἰ ("if") and the verb is in the indicative. These sentences are saying that if something is true, even though it is not, then such and such would occur. The falseness of the protasis is assumed in the argument.

1 Cor 2:8. None of the rulers of this age understood it, for *if they had,* they would not have crucified the Lord of glory. (NIV)

3. **Third class**. Also called a "more probable future" condition. The protasis begins with ἐάν ("if") and the verb is in the subjunctive mood (chapter 21). There are two subcategories of a third class condition, although they are identical in their form.

(a) Sometimes this type of condition is used to say that if some specific event in the future happens, as it is likely (in the mind of the author) to happen, then something else will happen.

> Matt 4:9. Satan says to Jesus, "All these I will give you, *if you will fall down and worship me.*"

I am a little nervous telling you that this type of condition "probably" will occur. This is the way it is discussed in many Greek grammars and commentaries, but there is ample evidence that often, if not usually, this assumption is wrong. It seems doubtful Satan really thought Jesus would worship him. Be very careful with this nuance.

(b) This same form (ἐάν with the subjunctive) is also used to state a general truth, an axiomatic truth. The subjunctive mood is appropriate because the truth of the statement is timeless.

> John 11:9. *If anyone walks in the day,* he does not stumble, because he sees the light of this world.

Obviously, this distinction between specific and general is important for exegesis.

4. **Fourth class**. Also called a "less probable future" condition. The writer is saying that if something happens, as it is *not* likely (in the mind of the author) to happen, then something else will happen. There is no complete illustration of this form in the New Testament. You should also know that the forms of conditional sentences can be mixed; people don't always follow grammar.

Exercises for Chapters 9-12

Matt 1:16 Explain the shift from the NIV to the TNIV in this verse. (Hint: it has to do with the relative pronoun.) NIV. Joseph, the husband of Mary, of whom was born Jesus. TNIV. Joseph, the husband of Mary, and Mary was the mother of Jesus.

Matt 1:18 ESV. ¶ **Now** the birth of Jesus Christ took place in this way. NIV. ¶ This is how the birth of Jesus Christ came about.

Mark 4:31 NIV. It is like a mustard seed, which is the smallest seed you plant in the ground. TNIV. It is like a mustard seed, which is the smallest of all seeds on earth. You may want to check the commentaries to see why the TNIV changed the translation.

Luke 17:21 KJV. Neither shall they say, Lo here! or, lo there! for, behold, the kingdom of God is **within** you. NIV. Nor will people say, 'Here it is,' or 'There it is,' because the kingdom of God is within you." TNIV. Nor will people say, 'Here it is,' or 'There it is,' because the kingdom of God is in your midst."

Luke 18:11 NIV. The Pharisee stood up and prayed **about himself**. NASB. The Pharisee stood and was praying this to himself. KJV. The Pharisee stood and prayed thus with himself.

1 Cor 2:10 NASB. **For** to us God revealed them through the Spirit. NIV. But God has revealed it to us by his Spirit.

1 Tim 4:7 KJV. **But** refuse profane and old wives' fables. NIV. Have nothing to do with godless myths and old wives' tales.

1 John 1:5 What represents the καί in this verse? NIV. ¶ This is the message we have heard from him and declare to you: God is light; in him there is no darkness at all.

We did not study οὕτως or ἔτι, but read its entry in a lexicon and explain the following differences.

John 3:16 KJV. For God **so** loved the world, that he gave his only begotten Son, that whosoever believeth in him should not perish, but have everlasting life. NET. For this is the way God loved the world: he gave his one and only Son that everyone who believes in him should not perish but have eternal life.

Rom 11:26 ESV. And **in this way** all Israel will be saved. NIV. And so all Israel will be saved.

Luke 1:15 NIV. He will be filled with the Holy Spirit **even from** birth. NRSV. Even before his birth he will be filled with the Holy Spirit. ESV. He will be filled with the Holy Spirit, even from his mother's womb. NASB. He will be filled with the Holy Spirit while yet in his mother's womb.

Advanced

Relative pronouns can be changed to indefinite relative pronouns (e.g., to "whoever, whichever, whatever") when they are followed by ἄν or occur as an alternate form such as ἐάν.

> Matt 5:19. "*Anyone* (ὃς ἐὰν) who breaks one of the least of these commandments and teaches others to do the same will be called least in the kingdom of heaven, but *whoever* (ὃς ἐὰν) practices and teaches these commands will be called great in the kingdom of heaven " (NIV)

There are certain forms of the relative pronoun that are both masculine and neuter. Every once in a while this can make exegesis a bit tricky.

CHAPTER 13

Fine-Tuning Phrasing

In Week 2 we learned the basics of phrasing. Let's review! The purpose of phrasing is to identify the beginning and end of the passage, divide it into manageable sections if necessary, find the main point(s) of each section, and then see how the remaining phrases relate to that main point.

I found in class that one week is not enough time to become comfortable with phrasing, so we are going to do some more phrasing, this time with the letter of Jude. This is a harder book to phrase, but if you can get through Jude, you can deal with most of the New Testament.

I also want to help you get a little more specific in seeing how the phrases actually are related to each other. In other words, what we will do is discover the specific nature of that relationship. For example, "Jesus came in order to save sinners." "Jesus came" is the main clause and "in order to save sinners" tells us what? It tells us the *purpose* of Jesus' coming.

Here is another example that is less obvious. Paul writes to the Romans, in 12:3-5,

> [3]For by the grace given to me I say to everyone among you not to think of himself more highly than he ought to think, but to think with sober judgment, each according to the measure of faith that God has assigned. [4] *For* as in one body we have many members, and the members do not all have the same function, [5] so we, though many, are one body in Christ, and individually members one of another. (ESV)

What is the relationship between v 3 and vv 4-5? Some translations don't start v 4 with the word "for," but the ESV has correctly translated the initial γάρ. "For" tells you that vv 4-6 are not a new topic but are giving you the *reason* for v 3. We should not be prideful *because*, despite the diversity of gifts in the church, we are one body in Christ and members one of another.

This is a lectionary from the thirteenth to fourteenth century (see pg. 254), containing parts of Matthew and John. Photo provided by the Center for the Study of the New Testament Manuscripts (Dan Wallace, director) and used by permission of Institut für neutestamentliche Textforschung.

What we are going to do this week is help you slow down, look at the phrases, and make the decisions as to the actual relationships of the phrases.

By the way, remember that one of our goals in this text is for you to be able to read good commentaries. Specifying the precise relationship between ideas is at the heart of an exegetical commentary. We will conclude our discussion of how to read commentaries in chapter 29.

Jude

I have listed the NIV text of Jude on the next two pages without paragraphs and headings. Make a copy of the pages and work from it, not your Bible.

Step 1: Find the Beginning and the End

Because we want to phrase all of Jude, this step is done for us. We are going to work with all its 25 verses.

Step 2: Identify the Sections

Work through Jude and discover how many basics sections it has. Place headings with each. My work is on page 114, so don't look ahead until you are done.

It would seem obvious what these signs are giving directions to.

Jude

1:1   Jude, a servant of Jesus Christ and a brother of James,

       To those who have been called, who are loved by God the Father and
       kept by Jesus Christ:

1:2   Mercy, peace and love be yours in abundance.

1:3   Dear friends, although I was very eager to write to you about the
       salvation we share, I felt I had to write and urge you to contend for
       the faith that was once for all entrusted to the saints.

1:4   For certain men whose condemnation was written about long ago
       have secretly slipped in among you. They are godless men, who
       change the grace of our God into a license for immorality and deny
       Jesus Christ our only Sovereign and Lord.

1:5   Though you already know all this, I want to remind you that the
       Lord delivered his people out of Egypt, but later destroyed those
       who did not believe.

1:6   And the angels who did not keep their positions of authority but
       abandoned their own home—these he has kept in darkness, bound
       with everlasting chains for judgment on the great Day.

1:7   In a similar way, Sodom and Gomorrah and the surrounding towns
       gave themselves up to sexual immorality and perversion. They serve
       as an example of those who suffer the punishment of eternal fire.

1:8   In the very same way, these dreamers pollute their own bodies, reject
       authority and slander celestial beings.

1:9   But even the archangel Michael, when he was disputing with the
       devil about the body of Moses, did not dare to bring a slanderous
       accusation against him, but said, "The Lord rebuke you!"

1:10   Yet these men speak abusively against whatever they do not under-
       stand; and what things they do understand by instinct, like unrea-
       soning animals—these are the very things that destroy them.

1:11   Woe to them! They have taken the way of Cain; they have rushed for
       profit into Balaam's error; they have been destroyed in Korah's
       rebellion.

1:12   These men are blemishes at your love feasts, eating with you without the slightest qualm—shepherds who feed only themselves. They are clouds without rain, blown along by the wind; autumn trees, without fruit and uprooted—twice dead.

1:13   They are wild waves of the sea, foaming up their shame; wandering stars, for whom blackest darkness has been reserved forever.

1:14   Enoch, the seventh from Adam, prophesied about these men: "See, the Lord is coming with thousands upon thousands of his holy ones

1:15   to judge everyone, and to convict all the ungodly of all the ungodly acts they have done in the ungodly way, and of all the harsh words ungodly sinners have spoken against him."

1:16   These men are grumblers and faultfinders; they follow their own evil desires; they boast about themselves and flatter others for their own advantage.

1:17   But, dear friends, remember what the apostles of our Lord Jesus Christ foretold.

1:18   They said to you, "In the last times there will be scoffers who will follow their own ungodly desires."

1:19   These are the men who divide you, who follow mere natural instincts and do not have the Spirit.

1:20   But you, dear friends, build yourselves up in your most holy faith and pray in the Holy Spirit.

1:21   Keep yourselves in God's love as you wait for the mercy of our Lord Jesus Christ to bring you to eternal life.

1:22   Be merciful to those who doubt;

1:23   snatch others from the fire and save them; to others show mercy, mixed with fear—hating even the clothing stained by corrupted flesh.

1:24   To him who is able to keep you from falling and to present you before his glorious presence without fault and with great joy—

1:25   to the only God our Savior be glory, majesty, power and authority, through Jesus Christ our Lord, before all ages, now and forevermore! Amen.

Salutation

1:1   Jude, a servant of Jesus Christ and a brother of James,

To those who have been called, who are loved by God the Father and kept by Jesus Christ:

1:2   Mercy, peace and love be yours in abundance.

Occasion for Writing

1:3   Dear friends, although I was very eager to write to you about the salvation we share, I felt I had to write and urge you to contend for the faith that was once for all entrusted to the saints.

1:4   For certain men whose condemnation was written about long ago have secretly slipped in among you. They are godless men, who change the grace of our God into a license for immorality and deny Jesus Christ our only Sovereign and Lord.

Description and Condemnation of the Troublemakers

1:5   Though you already know all this, I want to remind you that the Lord delivered his people out of Egypt, but later destroyed those who did not believe.
. . . . .

1:19   These are the men who divide you, who follow mere natural instincts and do not have the Spirit.

Call to Perseverance

1:20   But you, dear friends, build yourselves up in your most holy faith and pray in the Holy Spirit.

1:21   Keep yourselves in God's love as you wait for the mercy of our Lord Jesus Christ to bring you to eternal life.

1:22   Be merciful to those who doubt;

1:23   snatch others from the fire and save them; to others show mercy, mixed with fear—hating even the clothing stained by corrupted flesh.

Doxology

1:24   To him who is able to keep you from falling and to present you before his glorious presence without fault and with great joy—

1:25   to the only God our Savior be glory, majesty, power and authority, through Jesus Christ our Lord, before all ages, now and forever-more! Amen.

So how did we do? I see five basic sections. The salutation and doxology are pretty evident, I think. Vv 3-4 tell us why Jude wrote and introduces us to the troublemakers.

The heart of the letter is vv 5-23, but there is a shift between v 19 and v 20 as Jude moves from describing the troublemakers to encouraging the church to persevere. In other words, there is a shift of audience and a shift in his basic message.

Some people don't split it this way. Some see a shift at 1:17, especially because of the beginning "Dear friends." That's okay. I may not be right. But when I break a passage into its sections, what I am looking for is a unifying theme, something that holds the verses together. In vv 5-23 I see Jude doing the same thing: whether he is describing people or explicitly judging them, all of it functions as a condemnation of sin, asserting that God always punishes evil.

Steps 3-4

Go ahead and phase the salutation. It has similarities to 1 Peter 1:1-2 and shouldn't give you a problem. Also phrase vv 3-4. Pay special attention to why Jude says they are godless.

When you are done, check my work on the next page.

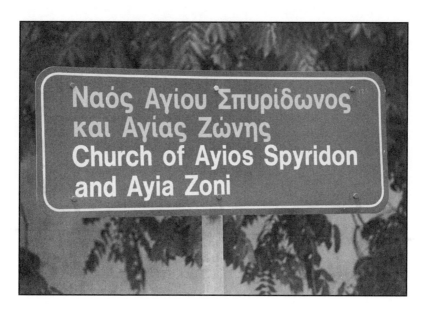

A sign of a church. Can you spot any variances from the transliteration scheme you were instructed in this book?

Salutation

1:1   Jude,

      a servant of Jesus Christ and

      a brother of James,

   To those

      who have been called,

      who are   loved by God the Father and

          kept by Jesus Christ:

1:2   Mercy, peace and love be yours in abundance.

Occasion for Writing

1:3   Dear friends,

      although I was very eager to write to you about the salvation we share,

   I felt I had to write and urge you to contend for the faith

         that was once for all entrusted to the saints.

1:4   For

  certain men ... have secretly slipped in among you.

      whose condemnation was written about long ago

      They are godless men,

           who change the grace of our God into a license for immorality and

           deny Jesus Christ our only Sovereign and Lord.

We have the usual threefold salutation, with Jude emphasizing that those who have been called are loved and kept both by God the Father and Jesus Christ.

Jude then moves into the occasion for writing. He had wanted to write a different type of letter, one about the salvation he shares with the church; but instead, because of the troublemakers, he felt the need to write them to contend, to fight, for the faith. Why? Because certain godless men had snuck into the church, and their heresy was twofold. They taught that holiness didn't matter, that God's grace gave them license to live immoral lives. Second, they denied that Jesus was the believer's only Sovereign and Lord.

I connected the "for" in v 4 back to "felt," precisely identifying v 4 as the *reason* for why Jude felt this way. Without the line, it may not have been visually clear that "For" is indented under "felt."

Notice the use of ellipsis in v 4: "certain men ... have secretly slipped in." While I prefer to keep the word order of the translation, sometimes it is not possible. The phrase, "whose condemnation was written about long ago," separates the subject "men" from its verb "slipped in" and is parallel with the following, "they are godless men." So I pulled the phrase out, marked its place with an ellipsis, and placed it under "men."

Notice also what I did with the last two statements. They were too long to fit on one line, so I put extra space between the two. Without that space, you might think there were four phrases modifying "men."

A picture of the ruins of Acropolis, towering over the city of Athens.

Description and Condemnation of the Troublemakers

1:5　Though you already know all this, I want to remind you that the Lord delivered his people out of Egypt, but later destroyed those who did not believe.

1:6　And the angels who did not keep their positions of authority but abandoned their own home—these he has kept in darkness, bound with everlasting chains for judgment on the great Day.

1:7　In a similar way, Sodom and Gomorrah and the surrounding towns gave themselves up to sexual immorality and perversion. They serve as an example of those who suffer the punishment of eternal fire.

1:8　In the very same way, these dreamers pollute their own bodies, reject authority and slander celestial beings.

1:9　But even the archangel Michael, when he was disputing with the devil about the body of Moses, did not dare to bring a slanderous accusation against him, but said, "The Lord rebuke you!"

1:10　Yet these men speak abusively against whatever they do not understand; and what things they do understand by instinct, like unreasoning animals—these are the very things that destroy them.

1:11　Woe to them! They have taken the way of Cain; they have rushed for profit into Balaam's error; they have been destroyed in Korah's rebellion.

1:12　These men are blemishes at your love feasts, eating with you without the slightest qualm—shepherds who feed only themselves. They are clouds without rain, blown along by the wind; autumn trees, without fruit and uprooted—twice dead.

1:13　They are wild waves of the sea, foaming up their shame; wandering stars, for whom blackest darkness has been reserved forever.

1:14　Enoch, the seventh from Adam, prophesied about these men: "See, the Lord is coming with thousands upon thousands of his holy ones

1:15　to judge everyone, and to convict all the ungodly of all the ungodly acts they have done in the ungodly way, and of all the harsh words ungodly sinners have spoken against him."

1:16　These men are grumblers and faultfinders; they follow their own evil desires; they boast about themselves and flatter others for their own advantage.

1:17　But, dear friends, remember what the apostles of our Lord Jesus Christ foretold.

1:18　They said to you, "In the last times there will be scoffers who will follow their own ungodly desires."

1:19　These are the men who divide you, who follow mere natural instincts and do not have the Spirit.

Repeat of Steps 1 and 2

But now what are we going to go with vv 5-19? We have seen that Jude is describing the troublemakers and condemning them, and he is also talking about other people who got in trouble. But vv 5-19 are probably too many verses to handle at one time, so what is a "phraser" to do?

Basically, we treat the section (vv 5-19) as a new passage, and repeat Step 2 by dividing the section into its subsections. Read and reread vv 5-19 until the Bible tells you where the natural breaks are. Go ahead and do it now, and be sure to write a heading for each subsection. (Write the subsection headings in some form that differentiates them from the main section headings.) Then do Steps 3 and 4 for each subsection. My work is on the next few pages.

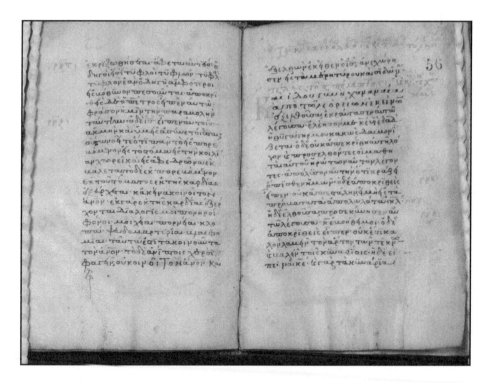

This photo is of a cursive (see pg. 258) New Testament manuscript, copied in the twelfth century. It contains Matthew 15:13-27a. Photo provided by the Center for the Study of the New Testament Manuscripts (Dan Wallace, director) and used by permission of Institut für neutestamentliche Textforschung.

Three Parallels

1:5   Though you already know all this, I want to remind you that

          {1} the Lord delivered <u>his people</u> out of Egypt,

               but later destroyed those who did not believe.

1:6   And

          {2} the <u>angels</u> who did not keep their positions of authority but
          abandoned their own home

               —these he has kept in darkness, bound with everlasting chains
               for judgment on the great Day.

1:7   In a similar way,

          {3} <u>Sodom and Gomorrah</u> and the surrounding towns gave them-
          selves up to sexual immorality and perversion.

               They serve as an example of those who suffer the punishment
               of eternal fire.

I see six subsections. I could be wrong, but that is how the passage divides to my way of thinking.

(1) Vv 5-7 spell out *three situations* that parallel the situation Jude is addressing: people delivered from Egypt; angels; Sodom and Gomorrah. The parallelism is that these three groups represent that fact that God always punishes sin. The first two groups are especially privileged people, and even they were punished. The implication is that these "certain men" in Jude's time will likewise be punished for their sins.

Notice that I numbered the three points. As I said last week, whenever I want to add something in my phrasing to the biblical text, I use curly brackets so I never confuse my scribblings with God's Word.

I could have broken v 6b into two parts, showing that the angels {1} have been kept in darkness and {2} are bound with everlasting chains. But I divided it up the way I did because I like to see the symmetry of three groups of beings who each experienced punishment: the Israelites were destroyed; the angels are bound in darkness; the people of Sodom and Gomorrah were punished with fire.

For large Greek cities, roadsigns have Greek and English. If you want to go to smaller localities, you will need to know how to read Greek.

Description of the Troublemakers

1:8   In the very same way,

           these dreamers

                    {1} pollute their own bodies,

                    {2} reject authority and

                    {3} slander celestial beings.

1:9   But even the archangel Michael, –>

                         when he was disputing with the devil about the
                         body of Moses,

                -> did not dare to bring a slanderous accusation against
                   him,

                   but said, "The Lord rebuke you!"

1:10   Yet these men

                    {4} speak abusively against whatever they do not under-
                    stand; and

                    {5} what things they do understand by instinct, like
                    unreasoning animals—these are the very things that
                    destroy them.

(2) In vv 8-10 we see Jude doing two things. First, he is describing the troublemakers, the "dreamers," and emphasizing how bad they are. In v 8 he gives three characteristics, and two more in v 10. But what is v 9 about?

As you worked on your phrasing, hopefully you saw that v 9 goes with the third description of the dreamers. They "slander celestial beings" (v 8), but even the archangel Michael wouldn't slander Satan but simply said, "The Lord rebuke you!" (Don't go looking for this story in your Bible.)

Notice my use of space (e.g., between v 8 and v 9) to group different ideas. Notice also how underlining the most essential elements of the discussion help you focus on the basics of the passage and not become lost in the details.

In v 9 the subject ("Michael") and the main verb ("did not dare") are separated by the temporal clause ("when ..."). The arrows ("->") are my way of hooking "Michael did not dare" together.

It is probably a good thing both Greek and English are written here. The Greek phrase literally reads, "Do not come near."

Statement of Judgment

1:11   Woe to them!

{1} They have taken the way of Cain;

{2} they have rushed for profit into Balaam's error;

{3} they have been destroyed in Korah's rebellion.

1:12   {4} These men are blemishes at your love feasts,

eating with you without the slightest qualm

—shepherds who feed only themselves.

{5} They are clouds without rain, blown along by the wind;

{6} autumn trees, without fruit and uprooted—twice dead.

1:13   {7} They are wild waves of the sea, foaming up their shame;

{8} wandering stars, for whom blackest darkness has been reserved forever.

Prophecies

1:14   Enoch, the seventh from Adam, prophesied about these men:

"See, the Lord is coming with thousands upon thousands of his holy ones

1:15   to judge everyone, and

to convict all the ungodly

of all the ungodly acts they have done in the ungodly way, and

of all the harsh words ungodly sinners have spoken against him."

Continued Descriptions

1:16   {1} These men are grumblers and faultfinders;

{2} they follow their own evil desires;

{3} they boast about themselves and flatter others for their own advantage.

(3) The third subsection moves into Jude's statements of woe, his statement of judgment on these dreamers. Again, notice the numbering of the series.

(4) Jude continues by pointing out that Enoch prophesied about these men. Enoch didn't prophesy that these specific men would come, but that the Lord would judge all the ungodly for what they said and did.

(5) In v 16 Jude resumes his description of the dreamers. If you wanted to connect them back to vv 11-13, you could continue the numbering with {9}, {10}, and {11}. However, you may have noticed that Jude likes series of three, so I left them {1}, {2}, and {3}.

The entrance to an archaeological site of ancient Corinth.

Prophecies

1:17   But, dear friends,

        remember what the apostles of our Lord Jesus Christ foretold.

1:18   They said to you,

          "In the last times there will be scoffers

                                  who will follow their own
                                  ungodly desires."

1:19   These are the men   who divide you,

                       who follow mere natural instincts and

                       do not have the Spirit.

(6) In the sixth subsection, Jude refers to the prophecies of the apostles, that evil people will come in the last days; the dreamers are the fulfillment of those prophecies. What is important to note, in all these descriptions, is that Jude is also condemning them, and that note of judgment is what ties vv 5-19 together.

Some people see a major break at v 17, which starts with what appears to be a transitional phrase ("But, dear friends") and which addresses the church directly. It is good to have a sensitivity to this type of change. However, because the overall thrust of this subsection is once again to describe the dreamers as evil people and so continue the judgment theme, I prefer to keep vv 17-19 with the preceeding and not start a new subsection.

How do my subsections compare to yours? How about our headings? If you found a different structure, you may want to go back and reread the passage. But again let me stress that the point here is for *you* to study *your* own Bible and to let the Bible and the Holy Spirit talk to you about what it is saying.

Okay, we are almost done. Phrase vv 20-25 (below) and then turn the page.

Call to Perseverance

1:20   But you, dear friends, build yourselves up in your most holy faith and pray in the Holy Spirit.

1:21   Keep yourselves in God's love as you wait for the mercy of our Lord Jesus Christ to bring you to eternal life.

1:22   Be merciful to those who doubt;

1:23   snatch others from the fire and save them; to others show mercy, mixed with fear—hating even the clothing stained by corrupted flesh.

Doxology

1:24   To him who is able to keep you from falling and to present you before his glorious presence without fault and with great joy—

1:25   to the only God our Savior be glory, majesty, power and authority, through Jesus Christ our Lord, before all ages, now and forevermore!

Call to Perseverance

1:20   But you, dear friends,

      {1} build yourselves up in your most holy faith and

      {2} pray in the Holy Spirit.

1:21   {3} Keep yourselves in God's love

           as you wait for the mercy of our Lord Jesus Christ to bring you to eternal life.

1:22   {4} Be merciful to those who doubt;

1:23   {5} snatch others from the fire and save them;

      {6} to others show mercy, mixed with fear

      {7}—hating even the clothing stained by corrupted flesh.

Doxology

1:24   To him

        who is able   to keep you from falling and

                to present you before his glorious presence

                    without fault and with great joy—

1:25   to the only God our Savior

   be glory, majesty, power and authority,

     through Jesus Christ our Lord,

     before all ages, now and forevermore!

   Amen.

Vv 20-23 are a call to perseverance in face of the opposition from the dreamers. This is the point to which Jude has been heading. He is not describing them just to condemn them; he wants his "dear friends" to see that the dreamers are evil people and to stand firm in the face of their opposition.

Vv 24-25 end with a glorious doxology. Did you notice the themes in the doxology that were introduced in the first two verses? These themes of God's protection and the person of Jesus Christ serve as theological bookends to Jude's call for perseverance.

Let me again stress that while phrasing is not grammatical diagramming, noticing conjunctions and dependent clauses goes a long way in helping us see the author's flow of thought.

Do you see what just happened? You took twenty-five verses that perhaps were not the easiest to understand, you discovered their main points, you identified several other assertions, and you can see how they all relate to the main points. Welcome to the heart of Bible study!

You figure out what works for you. That's the point. There isn't always a right and wrong way to do this process. You can take this basic process and mold and shape it until it works for you, until you find a way that helps you see most clearly what the Bible is saying. And what works for me may not work for you. But take the time, experiment, and let the Bible teach you what it says and means.

One last point. One of the purposes of this text is to help you be able to read the better commentaries. The kind of work we have been doing here is also the kind of work you will see being done in the better commentaries. Perhaps the authors will not be as deliberate and obvious as I have been, but this is precisely the type of work that underlies a good commentary. When we conclude our discussion of how to understand commentaries in chapter 24, this phrasing will prove itself invaluable.

Colossians 1:1-18

1:1   Paul, an apostle of Christ Jesus by the will of God, and Timothy our brother,

1:2   To the saints and faithful brothers in Christ at Colossae: Grace to you and peace from God our Father.

1:3   We always thank God, the Father of our Lord Jesus Christ, when we pray for you,

1:4   since we heard of your faith in Christ Jesus and of the love that you have for all the saints,

1:5   because of the hope laid up for you in heaven. Of this you have heard before in the word of the truth, the gospel,

1:6   which has come to you, as indeed in the whole world it is bearing fruit and growing—as it also does among you, since the day you heard it and understood the grace of God in truth,

1:7   just as you learned it from Epaphras our beloved fellow servant. He is a faithful minister of Christ on your behalf

1:8   and has made known to us your love in the Spirit.

1:9   And so, from the day we heard, we have not ceased to pray for you, asking that you may be filled with the knowledge of his will in all spiritual wisdom and understanding,

1:10   so as to walk in a manner worthy of the Lord, fully pleasing to him, bearing fruit in every good work and increasing in the knowledge of God.

1:11   May you be strengthened with all power, according to his glorious might, for all endurance and patience with joy,

1:12   giving thanks to the Father, who has qualified you to share in the inheritance of the saints in light.

1:13   He has delivered us from the domain of darkness and transferred us to the kingdom of his beloved Son,

1:14   in whom we have redemption, the forgiveness of sins.

1:15   He is the image of the invisible God, the firstborn of all creation.

1:16   For by him all things were created, in heaven and on earth, visible and invisible, whether thrones or dominions or rulers or authorities—all things were created through him and for him.

1:17   And he is before all things, and in him all things hold together.

1:18   And he is the head of the body, the church. He is the beginning ...

Advanced Phrasing: Terminology for the Relationships

It is time to take the final step in phrasing, and that is to specify the precise relationship between phrases. This is a little advanced, so it may not be for everyone. One of my favorite passages in the New Testament is Paul's prayer for the Colossians, especially verse 9. Go ahead and completely phrase the prayer. Please use the ESV to the left. I am sure you know the steps by now:

1. Find the beginning and end of the passage, in this case, the prayer.

2. Divide it into sections and include headings.

3. Break it into phrases.

4. Indicate the main phrases and the subordinate phrases.

My work is on page 132.

Colossians 1:9-14

1:9　And so, from the day we heard, we have not ceased to pray for you, asking that you may be filled with the knowledge of his will in all spiritual wisdom and understanding,

1:10　so as to walk in a manner worthy of the Lord, fully pleasing to him, bearing fruit in every good work and increasing in the knowledge of God.

1:11　May you be strengthened with all power, according to his glorious might, for all endurance and patience with joy,

1:12　giving thanks to the Father, who has qualified you to share in the inheritance of the saints in light.

1:13　He has delivered us from the domain of darkness and transferred us to the kingdom of his beloved Son,

1:14　in whom we have redemption, the forgiveness of sins.

Paul's Prayer for the Colossians

Content

1:9   And so,

                        from the day we heard,
           we have not ceased to pray for you,

                asking that you may be filled with the knowledge of his will

                in all spiritual wisdom and understanding,

Purpose

1:10   so as to walk in a manner worthy of the Lord,

                                fully pleasing to him,
                                bearing fruit in every good work and
                                increasing in the knowledge of God.

1:11   May you be strengthened with all power,

                        according to his glorious might,
                   for   all endurance and
                        patience with joy,

1:12   giving thanks to the Father,

                        who has qualified you to share in the inheri-
                        tance of the saints in light.

Father

1:13   He has   delivered us from the domain of darkness and
                transferred us to the kingdom of his beloved Son,

Son

1:14   in whom we have redemption,

                        the forgiveness of sins.

It looks as if the prayer goes from v 9 through v 14. Paul begins by telling the Colossian church that he has not ceased praying for them, specifying the content of that prayer and adding something more about God's knowledge. He then moves on to the purpose of being filled with the knowledge of God's will. He wants them to walk in a manner worthy of the Lord, and he wants them to be strengthened by God's might for their own endurance and patience. I moved "giving thanks" (v 12) back to the left because it looks like the phrase is telling us another major point about Paul's prayer.

In typical fashion (for Paul), his mention of the Father leads him to praise him for two things he has done, and mention of the Son leads Paul to tell us one final point about Jesus, namely, that in him we have redemption, and redemption is the forgiveness of our sins.

There is much more that we could talk about and is reflected in the phrasing, but I want to move on to the next and final stage. Let's start with an easy question. What is the relationship between "pray" (v 9) and the phrase "asking that you may be filled with the knowledge of his will"? Right! The latter tells us the *content* of the prayer. What is the relationship between "filling" and the following "in all spiritual wisdom and understanding"? The latter tells us the *manner* in which they are to be filled.

What word does the opening phrase in v 10 refer back to, and what is its precise relationship to that word? It goes back to "pray" (we could have drawn a line if that had been helpful), and it tells us the *purpose* of the prayer. Paul did not want the Colossians simply to know about God and not have that knowledge affect their lives (as if a true knowledge of God doesn't always motivate one toward godly living—but I digress).

These terms that I am using—*content, manner, purpose*—specify the precise relationship between phrases.

The question then becomes, how do we use our phrasing to specify this precise relationship? A common recommendation is to draw brackets to the left of the verses and label them. Something like this:

```
┌─   we have not ceased to pray for you,
│
Content
│
└────────────────        asking that you may be filled with the
                         knowledge of his will
```

The *content* of Paul's prayer was that the Colossians be filled with knowledge.

9a		And so,
b	duration	from the day we heard,
c	**assertion**	**we have not ceased to pray for you,**
d	content	asking that you may be filled
e	content	with the knowledge of his will
f	manner	in all spiritual wisdom and understanding,
10a	purpose	so as to walk
b	manner	in a manner worthy of the Lord,
c	manner	fully pleasing to him,
d	result	bearing fruit in every good work and
e	result	increasing in the knowledge of God.
11a	result	May you be strengthened
b	instrument	with all power,
c	accordance	according to his glorious might,
d	purpose	for all endurance and patience with joy,
12a	result	giving thanks to the Father,
b	description	who has qualified you to share in the inheritance of the saints in light.
13a	description	He has delivered us from the domain of darkness and
b		transferred us to the kingdom of his beloved Son,
14	description	in whom we have redemption,
		the forgiveness of sins.

What about the opening phrase in v 10?

```
┌──  we have not ceased to pray for you,
Purpose
└──────────────────────  so as to walk in a manner worthy of the Lord
```

The *purpose* of prayer is to walk worthily. You get the idea.

Another method is to run a column down the left side of the page showing these connections, as I have done on page 134. You could also specify the relationships by using curly brackets like this:

```
                {concession} although I was very eager ...
    {main} I felt I had to write ... faith
                        {explanation} that was once for all ...
```

This process can go on and on, to any degree of detail that you wish. At some point the process becomes exhausting, but I would encourage you to always be deliberate as to the precise relationships among the main phrases.

Just imagine a Bible study in which the leader says something like this. From the first day that Paul heard the gospel had spread to Colossae, he has not stopped praying for them. Specifically, Paul has been praying that they be filled with the knowledge of God's will. Paul wants them to know God, and know God's will for their lives; but this knowledge specifically includes both spiritual wisdom and understanding; it is more than head knowledge. But it is not enough just to know God. Paul insists that their knowledge of him leads on to right behavior, that their daily walk be worthy of the Lord. What does a worthy walk look like? It is one that is pleasing to God, bears fruit in good works, and comes full circle to help them understand more of God. But Paul also wants them to be strengthened, a strengthing by God's glorious might (and not their own), a strengthening necessary for their lives to be characterized by endurance and joyful patience (in the face of suffering), all the while thanking the Father who has made it possible for the Colossians to share in their inheritance. Paul concludes with two sets of theological affirmations. He is giving thanks to the Father because of what God has done; specifically, he has saved them from darkness and into the kingdom of his Son. And Jesus, his Son, is the source of their redemption; specifically, he is the source of forgiveness.

This is the type of specificity and cohesiveness with which you can understand and present the Bible, if you can learn to see the author's flow of thought and main points.

Exercise

Go through Jude and identify at least ten different relationships between phrases. For example, in Jude 1:1 you have the main thought ("I felt I had to write …") with two modifying thoughts ("Although I was…"; "that was once …"). The first is a statement of "concession" and the second is an "explanation." Write these words down the left column.

Types of Phrases

The following is only for students who want to go even further into phrasing. Much of the discussion in commentaries is concerned with the precise nature of the relationships between phrases, and the writer will use a label to describe the relationship such as "manner" or "temporal."

If you come up with your own labels for the connections between the major phrases, you will be doing well. But sometimes it is difficult to come up with the right terminology, so here are some suggestions. They have been taken (with permission) from a textbook written by some good friends of mine, George Guthrie and Scott Duvall. If you want to know more about the use of brackets, see their book *Biblical Greek Exegesis* (Zondervan, 1998). The following verses are from the ESV unless otherwise noted. Many of the terms listed below are the technical terms used in the better commentaries

Foundational Expressions

Many of the main phrases you come across can be categorized in one of these "foundational" categories.

1. **Assertion**. Making a statement.

    John 15:1. I am the true vine.

2. **Event/Action**. Something that happened.

    1 John 1:2. The life was made manifest.

3. **Rhetorical question**. A question used to make a declaration.

    Heb 1:5. For to which of the angels did God ever say,"You are my Son?"

4. **Desire** (wish/hope). Expression of a wish or hope.

    3 John 1:14. I hope to see you soon.

5. **Exclamation**.

    Rom 7:24. Wretched man that I am!

6. **Exhortation** (command/encouragement).

> Mark 8:33. "Get behind me, Satan!"

7. **Warning**.

> Heb 10:26. For if we go on sinning deliberately after receiving the knowledge of the truth, there no longer remains a sacrifice for sins.

8. **Promise**.

> Heb 13:5. I will never leave you nor forsake you.

9. **Problem/Resolution**. The stating of a problem followed by its resolution.

> Eph 2:1-5. And you were dead in the trespasses and sins.… But God … made us alive together with Christ.

10. **Entreaty**. A polite request made to a superior.

> Matt 6:11. Give us this day our daily bread.

Modifications

These are different ways to modify the main assertion.

Temporal

1. **Time**. A simple statement of the time an event, action, or state occurred. It answers the question, "When did this occur?"

> Acts 13:3. Then *after fasting and praying* they laid their hands on them and sent them off.

2. **Simultaneous**. Two or more events or states expressed as happening at the same time.

> Rom 8:10. But if Christ is in you, although your *bodies are dead* because of sin, your *spirits are alive* because of righteousness.

3. **Sequence**. Two or more events expressed as happening one after the other.

> 1 Cor 15:5. He appeared to Cephas, *then* to the twelve.

4. **Progression**. Same as "sequence," but the emphasis is placed on the developmental nature of the actions.

> John 15:6. If a man does not abide in me, he *is cast forth* as a branch and withers; and the branches are *gathered, thrown* into the fire and *burned*.

Location

5. **Place**. Where the event, action, or state occurred. Answers the question, "Where?"

> Acts 17:1. Now when they had passed *through Amphipolis and Apollonia,* they came *to Thessalonica,* where there was a synagogue of the Jews.

6. **Sphere**. The domain or realm of existence.

> Rom 8:9. But you are not in the flesh, you are *in the Spirit,* if in fact the Spirit of God dwells in you.

7. **Source**. The point of origin. Answers the question, "From where?"

> 2 Cor 4:7. But we have this treasure in earthen vessels, to show that the transcendent power *belongs to God* and not to us.

8. **Separation**. Creating distance between two parties.

> Matt 6:13. And lead us not into temptation, but deliver us *from evil.*

Adverbial

9. **Measure**. Answers the question, "How long?" "How many?" or, "How far?"

> Matt 20:6. Why do you stand here idle *all day?*

10. **Circumstance**. Situations surrounding events or actions.

> 1 Thess 5:18. Give thanks *in all circumstances.*

11. **Cause**. An event or state that produces some result. Answers the question, "What brought this about?"

> Rom 5:1a. *Since we have been justified by faith,* we have peace with God.

12. **Result**. An outcome of some action or attitude.

> Rom 5:1b. Since we have been justified by faith, *we have peace with God.*

13. **Purpose**. An outcome that one intends to take place. Answers the question, "What did he wish to occur?"

> John 3:16. For God so loved the world, that he gave his only Son, *that whoever believes in him should not perish but have eternal life.*

14. **Means**. The tool or instrument used in carrying out an action. Answers the question, "How did he do that?"

> 1 Cor. 15:10. But *by the grace of God* I am what I am.

15. **Manner**. How the instrument is used. Answers the question, "In what way did he do this?"

> Phil 1:18. Only that *in every way,* whether *in pretense* or *in truth,* Christ is proclaimed, and in that I rejoice.

16. **Agency**. The personal agent who performs the action. Answers the question, "By whom?" or, "Through whom?"

> Rom 5:1. We have peace with God *through our Lord Jesus Christ.*

17. **Reference**. An expression of relation. Answers the question, "With reference to whom or what?"

> Eph 4:22. You were taught, *with regard to your former way of life,* to put off your old self.

18. **Advantage or Disadvantage**. For whom or against whom an action takes place.

> Rom 5:7. For one will scarcely die *for a righteous person.*
> Matt 23:31. Thus you witness *against yourselves* that you are sons of those who murdered the prophets.

19. **Association**. Expresses the idea of accompaniment.

> Matt 5:41. And if anyone forces you to go one mile, go *with him* two miles.

20. **Relationship**. Expresses some form of personal relationship.

> Col 1:3. We always thank God, the Father *of our Lord* Jesus Christ.

21. **Possession**. Expresses ownership.

> Matt 5:40. And if anyone would sue you and take *your* tunic, let him have *your* cloak as well.

Logic

22. **Basis**. The grounds upon which a statement or command is made.

> Matt 5:3. *Blessed are the poor in spirit,* for theirs is the kingdom of heaven.

23. **Condition**. A requirement that must be fulfilled.

> Jam 3:2. *If anyone does not stumble in what he says,* he is a perfect man.

24. **Inference**. The logical conclusion drawn from an idea.

> Jam 3:2. If anyone does not stumble in what he says, *he is a perfect man.*

25. **Concession**. A reservation or qualification.

> Heb 5:8. *Although he was a son,* he learned obedience through what he suffered.

26. **Contrast**. Two conditions, ideas, or actions put together in order to point out differences.

> Eph 5:17. Therefore *do not be foolish, but understand* what the will of the Lord is.

27. **Comparison**. Two conditions, ideas, or actions put together in order to point out similarities.

> John 20:21. *As the Father has sent* me, *even so I am sending* you.

28. **General/Specific**. When a general and a specific statement are put side-by-side to show the relationship between a broader and a particular concept, truth, or action.

> Heb 5:4-5. *No one takes this honor for himself,* but only when called by God, just as Aaron was. So also *Christ did not exalt himself to be made a high priest,* but was appointed.

Clarification

29. **Restatement**. The same idea is expressed in a different way.

> Heb 8:12. For I will be merciful toward their iniquities, and *I will remember their sins no more.*

30. **Description**. Functions to provide vivid detail of a person, event, state, or object.

> Rev 12:3. A *great red dragon,* with *seven heads and ten horns,* and on his heads *seven diadems.*

31. **Identification**. Information used to specify a person or thing. Answers the question, "Which one?"

> John 3:1. Now there was a man of the Pharisees *named Nicodemus,* a ruler of the Jews.

32. **Illustration**. To elucidate by use of examples.

> Heb 6:12-15. So that you may not be sluggish, but imitators of those who through faith and patience inherit the promises. *For when God made a promise to Abraham ... he swore by himself.... And thus Abraham, having patiently waited, obtained the promise.*

33. **Apposition**. A noun or participle that follows immediately another noun or participle with which it shares a common referent.

> Eph 3:1. For this reason I, Paul, *a prisoner* for Christ Jesus.

34. **Explanation**. The addition of clarifying statements to a main proposition.

> Matt 6:7. And when you pray, do not heap up empty phrases as the Gentiles do, *for they think that they will be heard for their many words.*

35. **Alternative** (either . . . or). When one condition, action, or place is expressed as a possible substitute for another.

> Matt 6:24. Either he will hate the one and love the other, *or he will be devoted to the one and despise the other.*

36. **Question and answer**. I'll let you figure this one out.

> Mark 8:29. And he asked them, *"But who do you say that I am?"* Peter answered him, *"You are the Christ."*

Form

37. **Introduction**. A passage that presents the opening of a discussion or narrative, such as Hebrews 1:1-4.

38. **Conclusion**. To bring to an end by way of summary or final decisive statement, such as Acts 4:32-37.

39. **List**. A number of things, normally of the same kind, mentioned one after the other.

> 1 Pet 1:1. To God's elect, strangers in the world, scattered throughout *Pontus, Galatia, Cappadocia, Asia and Bithynia.*

40. **Series**. The joining of equally prominent assertions or commands in a loose association.

> 1 Thess 5:16-18. *Rejoice always, pray without ceasing, give thanks in all circumstances.*

41. **Parallel**. Two or more elements correspond verbally or conceptually.

> Matt 5:13-14. You are the salt of the earth.... *You are the light of the world.*

Exercises

Go back through your phrasing of 1 Peter 1:6-12 and Colossians 1:9ff. and enter labels for each major phrase.

How Do We Describe Action?

This week you are going to start learning about the Greek verbal system in the indicative mood. You will learn the basics of Greek verbal grammar and then the different indicative tenses. I will conclude with showing you how to use different paper and electronic tools like concordances and Bible search software.

As you work through the next two weeks, you are going to see new reasons why translations are different. Any form of any Greek verb generally carries several nuances, nuances related to the meaning of the verb as well as the verb's tense, voice, and mood. Remember: languages are not codes. We generally cannot say in English exactly what the Greek is saying. Translations will either over- or under-translate. And remember what I said in Chapter 4: "Translators are traitors!"

CHAPTER 14

Greek Grammar: Verbs

In chapter 6 I introduced you to the basics of English verbal grammar. Now I need to talk about the basics of Greek verbal grammar.

Person and number. Like English, Greek verbs have person (1st, 2nd, and 3rd) and number (singular and plural). Greek verbs indicate their person and number by adding different suffixes to the end of the word. These endings are called *personal endings.* This is somewhat like adding a "s" to an English verb when its subject is third person singular.

> I love.
> She loves.

Agreement. A Greek verb must agree with its subject in person and number. This means that if the subject is singular, the verb must be singular. If the subject is first, second, or third person, then so must the verb.

The verb does this by using different personal endings. For example, if the subject is "you," the verb would use a second person singular personal ending such as εις. λέγεις means "You say." If the subject is "we," the verb could end in ομεν. λέγομεν means "We say."

Here is a Greek paradigm of the verb ἀκούω, which means "I hear." Notice how the endings change depending on the subject's person and

There is no such thing as case or gender in verbs. Case and gender belong to the noun system.

number. (You do not have to memorize these endings; just be aware of how they function.)

person and number	Greek	Translation
first person singular	ἀκούω	I hear
second person singular	ἀκούεις	You hear
·third person singular	ἀκούει	He/she/it hears
first person plural	ἀκούομεν	We hear
second person plural	ἀκούετε	You hear
third person plural	ἀκούουσι	They hear

Aspect is perhaps the most difficult concept to grasp in Greek verbs, and yet it is the most important and most misunderstood. The basic genius of the Greek verb is not its ability to indicate *when* the action of the verb occurs (time), but what *type of action* it describes, or what we call "aspect."

For example, what is the difference between saying "I studied last night" and "I was studying last night"? The first merely says that an event occurred last night; it describes a simple event. It does not give you a clue as to the precise nature of your study time. The second pictures the action of studying as an ongoing action, a process, something that took place over a period of time. This difference between a simple event ("studied") and a process ("was studying") is what we mean by "aspect."

In Galatians 2:12 the RSV reads,

> For before certain men came from James, he *ate* with the Gentiles; but when they came he drew back and separated himself, fearing the circumcision party.

What does Paul mean by "ate"? Did Peter eat one meal or did he eat often with the Gentiles? Is Paul confronting Peter for doing just one thing wrong? I always thought so, until I learned that this particular Greek verb indicates an ongoing action. Peter *ate often* with the Gentiles before he pulled back under pressure from some of the Jewish Christians. This is why the NIV uses "used to" in their translation.

> Before certain men came from James, he *used to eat* with the Gentiles. But when they arrived, he began to draw back and separate himself from the Gentiles because he was afraid of those who belonged to the circumcision group.

Another example is Jesus' words to his disciples in Mark 8:34:

> If anyone wishes to come after me, let him *deny* himself and *take*
> *up* his cross and *follow* me.

"Deny" and "take up" in the Greek are described as simple events while
the aspect of the verb "follow" is a process. The aspect of "deny" and
"take up" does not tell us anything about the nature of those actions. They
do not tell us whether the "deny and take up" occur only once in your life,
or if you are to do this every day. But the aspect of "follow" emphasizes
that the commitment to discipleship involves a day-to-day following, as
you might assume from the meaning of the word.

In Greek there are three aspects. The *continuous* aspect means that the
action of the verb is thought of as an ongoing process.

> In pointing out these things to the brethren, you will be a good servant
> of Christ Jesus, *constantly nourished* on the words of the faith and of the
> sound doctrine which you have been following. (1 Tim 4:6; NASB)

The *undefined* aspect means that the action of the verb is thought of as a
simple event, without commenting on whether or not it is a process.

> For God so *loved* the world that he *gave* his only Son, that whoever
> believes in him should not perish but have eternal life. (John 3:16; RSV)

The *perfect* aspect describes an action that was brought to completion and
has effects carrying into the present. Of course, the time of the verb is from
the viewpoint of the writer/speaker, not the reader; the effects are present
to the writer, not necessarily to the reader.

> Jesus *has died* for our sins.
> For *it is written* that Abraham had two sons. (Gal 4:22)
> That which *is born* of the flesh is flesh, and that which *is born* of the Spirit
> is spirit. (John 3:6; RSV)

Tense. In Greek, a tense carries two connotations: aspect and time. For
example, the aorist tense (chapter 17) describes an undefined action
(aspect) that normally occurs in the past (time). In this text, I use the term
"tense" to refer only to the *form* of the verb (e.g., present tense, future
tense, aorist tense), and I do not use the term to designate *when* the action
of a verb occurs. I always use the term "time" to describe *when* the action
of that verb occurs. Please do not confuse "tense" and "time."

Lexical form. The lexical form of a verb is the first person singular, present indicative. In the full language approach, you would have to be able to
figure out the lexical form from an inflected form. But in our approach, the
tools will tell us the lexical form.

Some of the older grammars and some modern commentaries list the infinitive form (λέγειν, "to say") as the lexical form, but lexicons are consistent now in listing verbs in the first person singular, present indicative (λέγω, "I say").

GK Numbers. For many years we have had access to what are called "Strong's numbers." Each Greek and Hebrew word was tagged with a unique number by Dr. James Strong. This way, no matter what inflected form a word took, it could always be identified by the same number. ἀκούεις and ἀκούομεν are both #191.

Because Strong's numbers originally omitted many Greek and Hebrew words, Zondervan introduced a new set of numbers (done by Ed Goodrick and John Kohlenberger; hence, "GK"), and it is these numbers that I am using in this text and in *EGNT*. In the back of *EGNT* you will find a conversion chart to move between the two numbering systems. ἀκούω in the GK system is #201.

Voice and Deponent Verbs

Greek verbs have active and passive voice, just like English. Greek uses different personal endings to differentiate active from passive. You don't need to memorize the following paradigm, but it illustrates how this works.

	active		*passive*	
1 sg	λύω	I loose	λύομαι	I am loosed
2 sg	λύεις	You loose	λύῃ	You are loosed
3 sg	λύει	He/she/it looses	λύεται	He/she/it are loosed
1 pl	λύομεν	We loose	λυόμεθα	We are loosed
2 pl	λύετε	You loose	λύεσθε	You are loosed
3 pl	λύουσι(ν)	They loose	λύονται	They are loosed

However, Greek does have a category of verbs called "deponent" verbs. A deponent verb is one that is passive in its *form* but active in its *meaning*. Its form is always passive but its meaning is always active. It can never have a passive meaning.

Most tools will list these forms as "passive" and not "deponent," including *EGNT* and my *Analytical Lexicon to the Greek New Testament.* How then will you know how they are to be translated? Well, the translators know which verbs are deponent, and they have translated these words with active meanings. How do they know? Actually it is quite easy. Nondeponent verbs have lexical forms ending in ω or μι (λύω, δίδωμι). But if the lexical form of the word ends in ομαι, it is deponent in the present tense.

Deponent verbs become a little more complicated than this, though. Just because a word is
deponent in the present does not mean it is
deponent in other tenses. Likewise, a verb can
be nondeponent in the present but deponent in other tenses.
For the "baby Greek" approach, you only need to know that
deponent forms exist, and in doing your word studies you will
treat them as actives.

Middle Voice

Greek also has a third voice, the "middle." There are three points you
need to know.

(1) In some tenses the middle and passive forms are identical. The
present tense ἀκούομαι could be middle or passive. In other tenses, the
middle will be distinctly different from the passive. For the seasoned
translator, this rarely is confusing. Some tools such as *EGNT* distinguish
between middle and passive (which is an interpretive decision and may
be wrong). Others, however, simply say it is "middle/passive."

(2) Most middles are deponent and therefore have active meanings.
About 75 percent, in fact, of all middles in the New Testament are deponents. (In other words, deponents properly defined are verbs that are *middle or passive* in form but active in meaning.)

(3) What about the other 25 percent? The proper definition of the middle voice is that the *subject does the action of verb in some way that concerns
itself.* The subject still does the action of the verb and the direct object still
receives the action (as opposed to the passive), but in the middle the subject is acting on its own behalf. The words in brackets below draw out the
significance of the middle verb.

> Matt 27:12. Jesus *answered* nothing [in his defense].
> Luke 10:42. Mary *has chosen* [for herself] the good part.
> Acts 5:2. He (Ananias) *kept back* [for himself] some of the price.

Be cautious about placing too much weight on the middle. Even students of full Greek struggle with being able to feel the nuanced difference
between the active and middle. Beware of preachers basing their sermon
or Bible study on the middle voice; most of the sermons I have heard that
bring up the middle voice have done so incorrectly.

In classical Greek, the middle voice could even be used to express the
reflexive idea.

> Matt 27:5. Judas *hung himself.*
> Matt 14:54. Peter *warmed himself* by the fire.

However, by biblical times, this would normally be expressed with an active verb and a reflexive pronoun. (Language is always changing.)

Greek Passives and Translators

Sometimes context shows that when a verb is passive, God is doing the action of the verb. This is called a "divine passive."

> Matt 5:4. Blessed are those who mourn, for *they shall be comforted.*

Comforted by whom? God. English style, however, prefers active verbs, and so many Greek passives are changed to actives.

> *Matt 27:63*   μετὰ   τρεῖς   ἡμέρας   ἐγείρομαι
> after   three   days   *I will be raised*
> ESV: After three days *I will arise.*
> NIV: After three days *I will be raised* from the dead.

Subjects and Objects

A Greek sentence does not require an expressed subject. A verb by itself can be a complete sentence. Both ἐγὼ λέγω and λέγω mean "I say." (ἐγώ is the first person personal pronoun, "I.")

It is also common for Greek to drop a verb's direct object, and English translators must add them back in (since English doesn't allow this for the most part).

> *1 Pet 1:8*   ὃν   οὐκ   ἰδόντες   ἀγαπᾶτε
> whom   not   seeing   you love
> NIV: Though you have not seen him, you love *him.*
> KJV: Whom having not seen, ye love.

Translations rarely (if ever) indicate in the footnotes when they add in the direct object. It is just too common.

Remember back in chapter 12 I pointed out how sometimes a translator will replace a relative pronoun with its antecedent if the English is confusing. The same type of thing can happen with a verb. Take, for example, Hebrews 4:7-9.

> He again fixes a certain day, "Today," saying through David after so long a time just as has been said before, "Today if you hear His voice, Do not harden your hearts." For if Joshua had given them rest, *He* would not have spoken of another day after that. So there remains a Sabbath rest for the people of God. (NASB)

Who is the "He" who "would not have spoken"? It may appear, initially, to be Joshua; that is what the normal rules of English grammar would require. However, the subject of the verb is God, who is spoken of in v 8. That is why the NASB capitalizes "He," and why the NIV replaces "He" with "God."

> For if Joshua had given them rest, *God* would not have spoken of another day later on.

The ESV supplies the antecedent "God" and adds a footnote, "Greek *he*" as is its custom in this situation. Likewise, the ESV adds "Jews" to Romans 3:9 and marks it with a footnote, "Greek *Are we*."

> What then? Are we *Jews* any better off? No, not at all. For we have already charged that all, both Jews and Greeks, are munder sin.

A subject that is neuter plural will have a singular verb when the subject is being viewed as a collective whole. For example, "Therefore, if anyone is in Christ, he is a new creation. The old *has passed away*; behold, the new *has come*" (2 Cor 5:17). The "old" are the "old things" that all have passed away.

CHAPTER 15

Present Indicative

English

The present indicative describes an action that generally occurs in the present. The active voice is used when the subject is performing the action of the verb, and the passive when the action of the verb is directed toward the subject. The indicative mood describes a fact or asks a question.

"*I see the tall man.*" "See" describes an action that is being performed by the subject of the sentence "I" at the present time. "*I am seen by a tall woman.*" "Am seen" is passive and so the subject "I" does not do the action but receives the action of the verb.

Greek

The present indicative verb in Greek is basically the same as in English. It describes an action that usually occurs in the present time.

Person, number. We have already seen that Greek uses different personal endings to distinguish person and number. The tools will simply "parse" this information for you, i.e., tell you the verb's person and number (along with other information about the verb).

Aspect. The present tense indicates either a continuous or undefined action. The translator can choose either "I am studying" or "I study," based on which fits the context best.

Time. The present tense verb generally—but not always—indicates an action occurring in the present time. And while the following may seem obvious, it is amazing how many times it is forgotten: *the time frame of the verb is from the time frame of the speaker/writer, not the hearer/reader.* Of course, what was presently true for Paul may still be presently true for you, but this is a function of theology and not grammar.

Voice. In the present tense, the middle and passive forms of the verb are identical. λύομαι could be either middle or passive.

Uses of the Present Tense

You are now going to start seeing what we talked about several weeks back when we discussed the nature of languages. Languages are not nice and neat. They do not fit into square boxes. While a tense may have a general use, it is only a general use and there may be many other options and variations.

What follows are some of the more common ways in which the present tense is used in Greek. The primary function of these examples is to give you a feel for the variety of usages and to see why so much of translation is interpretive and therefore why translations are often different. Does this mean you can look at a present tense verb and decide for yourself what its nuance is? Probably not. Does this mean you can argue with a commentary or translation based on your knowledge of Greek. Absolutely not. You just don't know enough Greek. Will you be able to see why translations are different and be able to follow the discussion in commentaries? Yes.

I am not showing you all the usages, nor will I in the following chapters. There are too many. But I have picked the common usages to give you a feel for the tense. This means you may come across passages in the Bible that illustrate one of those omitted uses. There are Greek grammars that do list all the uses (such as Daniel Wallace's *Greek Grammar Beyond the Basics*), but they may be beyond the reach of the "baby Greek" approach.

The terms in parentheses at the end of each category are its technical names. As you will see, Greek grammarians have not settled on one name per category. These are the terms the commentators will use.

1. Sometimes a Greek present describes an action that happens immediately. In other words, it has no real continuous nature (*instantaneous, aoristic, punctiliar*).

> *Mark 2:5*　　τέκνον,　ἀφίενταί　　　σου　αἱ ἁμαρτίαι.
> 　　　　　　　child　　*they are forgiven*　your　the sins
> 　　　　　　　NLT: My son, your sins *are forgiven.*

2. The Greek present can describe an ongoing action, even though in real time the action does not last very long (*progressive, descriptive*).

> *1 Cor 14:14*　ἐὰν　προσεύχωμαι　γλώσσῃ,　τὸ πνεῦμά　μου　προσεύχεται
> 　　　　　　　　if　　I am praying　　tongue,　the spirit　　my　*it is praying*
> 　　　　　　　　For if I am praying in a tongue, my spirit *is praying.*
> 　　　　　　　　ESV: For if I pray in a tongue, my spirit *prays.*

3. Some actions occur repeatedly (*iterative*).

Matt 17:15 πολλάκις γὰρ πίπτει εἰς τὸ πῦρ
often   for he falls into the fire
ESV: For often he falls into the fire.

4. Actions occur regularly but not necessarily at the same time (*customary, habitual, general*).

Luke 18:12 νηστεύω δὶς   τοῦ σαββάτου
I fast   twice the week
I *customarily fast* twice a week.
NIV: I *fast* twice a week.

5. Sometimes the Greek present tense will be used to express a timeless fact (*gnomic*).

2 Cor 9:7 ἱλαρὸν δότην ἀγαπᾷ ὁ θεός
cheerful giver he loves the God
ESV: God *loves* a cheerful giver.

6. Finally, because the Greek verb system views time as secondary to aspect, it is possible for the Greek present tense to refer to an action that occurs in the past. The idea is to make the telling of the past event more vivid by using the present tense (*historical, dramatic*). We have the same construction in English, but the Greeks used it much more than we do, so this usage is often translated with the past tense.

John 1:29 βλέπει τὸν Ἰησοῦν ἐρχόμενον πρὸς αὐτὸν
he sees the Jesus coming to him
NRSV: The next day *he saw* Jesus coming toward him.

The event could also be in the future (*futuristic*).

Rev 22:20 ναί, ἔρχομαι   ταχύ.
yes I am coming soon
NASB: Yes, I *am coming* quickly.
KJV: Surely I *come* quickly.

How do translators decide which of these usages is correct in any one instance? It is easier than you may think, but it does involve some linguistic sensitivity. They look at the context and especially the meaning of the word, and make their decision. But learning a language is both a science (i.e., there are rules to follow) and an art. It is the art side that takes years to develop, and it is the art side that enables the translator to make these types of decisions.

Advanced Information

Often Greek adds a *connecting vowel* between the stem of a verb and its personal ending. This is to aid in pronunciation. For example, λέγετε means "You say." The stem is *λεγ. The connecting vowel is the second ε, and τε is the second person plural personal ending.

For the Curious

Although our approach does not require you to be able to identify the parts of the Greek verb, it can be helpful to understand the concepts.

The *stem* of a verb is the part of the verb that carries its basic meaning. The form λύομεν means "we destroy." The stem is *λυ (I put an asterisk in front of a stem). While it is possible for the stem of a verb to undergo some changes, most of the changes are to the beginning and ending of the verb.

Greek often adds a *connecting vowel* between the stem of a verb and its personal ending. This is to aid in pronunciation. For example, λέγετε means "You say." The stem is *λεγ. The connecting vowel is the second ε, and τε is the second person plural personal ending.

CHAPTER 16

Future Indicative

English

The future indicative describes an action that will occur in the future. To form the future you add a helping verb ("will"/"shall") to the present tense stem of the verb.

> I *will work* hard.
> You *shall persevere.*

The basic rule in older English for the future tense is that "shall" is used for the first person and "will" for the second and third.

> I *shall* work hard.
> You *will* work hard.
> He *will* slack off.

That distinction has generally fallen into disuse today.

Greek

The future tense in Greek has the same meaning as in English. Of all the Greek tenses, the future has the strongest emphasis on time, describing an action that will occur in the future, from the time frame of the writer.

As a general rule, the future is translated with the undefined aspect ("I will eat") rather than the continuous ("I will be eating").

Uses of the Future

1. The basic use of the future is to describe something that will happen in the future (*predictive*).

> *Phil 1:6*　ὁ ἐναρξάμενος　ἐν　ὑμῖν　ἔργον　ἀγαθὸν　ἐπιτελέσει
> 　　　　　the beginning　in　you　work　good　*he will complete*
> 　　　　　ESV: He who began a good work in you *will bring it to completion.*

2. As in English, the Greek future can express a command (*imperatival*).

Matt 22:37	ἀγαπήσεις	κύριον	τὸν θεόν	σου
	you will love	Lord	the God	your

ESV: *You shall love* the Lord your God.
NET: *Love* the Lord your God.

3. The future can also state that a generic event will occur. It does not say that a particular occurrence is in mind, but that such events do occur (*gnomic*).

Matt 4:4	οὐκ	ἐπ᾽	ἄρτῳ	μόνῳ	ζήσεται	ὁ ἄνθρωπος
	not	on	bread	alone	*he will live*	the man

NASB: Man *shall* not *live* on bread alone.
NRSV: One *does* not *live* by bread alone.

For the Curious

Here is a paradigm of the future active indicative. The σ is called a *tense formative* because it is used to form the future tense stem, and is placed between the stem and the connecting vowel/personal ending.

		active	*translation*
1 sg		λύσω	I will loose
2 sg		λύσεις	You will loose
3 sg		λύσει	He/she/it will loose
1 pl		λύσομεν	We will loose
2 pl		λύσετε	You will loose
3 pl		λύσουσι(ν)	They will loose

CHAPTER 17

Two Past Tenses (Imperfect and Aorist)

English

English has a simple past that we call the punctiliar: "Bob studied." English also has a continuous past formed with a helping verb: "Bob was studying."

Greek

Greek actually has two tenses that indicate past time. The difference between the two is aspect.

- The *imperfect* describes a *continuous* action that normally occurs in the past. "I *was studying* last night."
- The *aorist* tense describes an *undefined* action that normally occurs in the past. "I *studied* last night."

Aspect

We have already met this distinction in aspect between the continuous and undefined in the present tense. But unlike the present tense—which can be either continuous or undefined—in the past tenses the difference is made explicit. The imperfect is always continuous; the aorist is always undefined.

As is the case with the present, so also in the past tenses this distinction is important for exegesis. The ESV translates John 19:3 as,

> They *came up* to him, saying, "Hail, King of the Jews!" and *struck* him with their hands.

But how often did the soldiers approach Jesus, and how often did they strike him? Only once? The NET and NRSV make the English as clear as the Greek.

They came up to him *again and again* and said, "Hail, King of the Jews!"
And they *struck* him *repeatedly* in the face. (NET)
They *kept coming up* to him, saying, "Hail, King of the Jews!" and *striking*
him on the face. (NRSV)

Time

Notice that I defined these tenses as describing actions that "normally" occur in the past. As in the present tense, so also in the aorist/
imperfect, time is secondary to aspect. The Greek writers are primarily
trying to tell you the "type" of action and only secondarily the "time" of
the action. As you will see below, the aorist and imperfect tenses can
describe actions occurring in the present and in the future, or the time significance is absent.

Uses of the Imperfect

1. Generally, the imperfect describes an ongoing action that happened
in the past (*progressive, durative*).

Mark 9:31	ἐδίδασκεν	τοὺς μαθητὰς	αὐτοῦ
	He was teaching	the disciples	his

NIV: *He was teaching* his disciples.
KJV: *He taught* his disciples.

2. It can also place emphasis on the beginning of the action (*ingressive,
inceptive*). Translators may add the word "began" to bring out this significance.

Matt 4:11	ἄγγελοι	προσῆλθον	καὶ	διηκόνουν	αὐτῷ
	angels	they came	and	*they were ministering*	to him

NASB: Angels came and *began to minister* to Him.
NIV: Angels came and *attended* him.

3. Some continuous actions do not occur constantly but rather repeti-
tively (*iterative*). The translator can add a phrase like "kept on" to bring
this out.

Luke 18:3	ἤρχετο	πρὸς	αὐτὸν
	she was coming	to	him

NIV: The widow *kept coming* to the judge.
KJV: *She came* unto him.

John 19:3	ἤρχοντο	πρὸς	αὐτὸν	καὶ	ἔλεγον·	χαῖρε
	They were coming	to	him	and	*they were saying*	Hail!

NRSV: *They kept coming* up to him, *saying*, "Hail."

NIV: (They) *went up* to him *again and again, saying*, "Hail"

NASB: *They began to come up* to Him and *say*, "Hail."

4. Other actions occur regularly, such as expressed by the English "used to" (*customary*).

Mark 15:6	Κατὰ	δὲ	ἑορτὴν	ἀπέλυεν		αὐτοῖς	ἕνα	δέσμιον
	at	now	feast	*he was releasing*		for them	one	prisoner

NASB: Now at the feast *he used to release* for them any one prisoner.

NET: During the feast *it was customary to release* a prisoner to them.

NIV: Now *it was the custom* at the Feast *to release* a prisoner.

KJV: Now at that feast *he released* unto them one prisoner.

5. The imperfect can also describe what a person wishes to do (*voluntative*), tries to do (*conative*), or almost does (*tendential*). Often it is difficult to tell the difference between these three, and, as always, context is the guide.

Gal 1:13	ἐδίωκον	τὴν ἐκκλησίαν	τοῦ θεοῦ	καὶ	ἐπόρθουν	αὐτήν
	I was persecuting	the church	of God	and	*I was destroying*	it

NASB: I *used to persecute* the church of God ... and *tried to destroy* it.

ESV: I *persecuted* the church of God ... and *tried to destroy* it.

NET: I *was persecuting* the church of God ... and *trying to destroy* it.

Matt 3:14	ὁ	δὲ	Ἰωάννης	διεκώλυεν	αὐτόν
	the	but	John	*he was preventing*	him

NIV: But John *tried to deter* him.

ESV: John *would have prevented* him.

Rom 9:3	ηὐχόμην	γὰρ	ἀνάθεμα	εἶναι	αὐτὸς	ἐγὼ
	I was wishing	for	accursed	to be	myself	I

NASB: For *I could wish* that I myself were accursed.

NLT: *I would be willing* to be forever cursed.

Uses of the Aorist

6. Generally, the aorist looks at an action as a whole and does not tell us anything about the precise nature of the action (*constative*).

Matt 15:39   ἐνέβη εἰς τὸ πλοῖον καὶ ἦλθεν εἰς τὰ ὅρια   Μαγαδάν.
            he got into the boat and *he went* into the region of Magadan.
            ESV: *He got* into the boat and *went* to the region of Magadan.

This does not mean that the action was not a process; the writer simply does not tell us. This fact has been widely misunderstood in popular discussions; a person will say that because the verb is an aorist, then it must describe something that happened immediately, or once for all. This simply is not true.

Rev 20:4   ἐβασίλευσαν μετὰ   τοῦ Χριστοῦ χίλια   ἔτη.
         They reigned with   the Christ   thousand years
         ESV: (They) *reigned* with Christ for a thousand years.

In this example, "reigned" is obviously continuous because of the meaning of the word, but for some reason it was not important for John to make this point grammatically explicit. I imagine John felt the meaning of the word made it sufficiently clear.

7. Other times the aorist places emphasis on the beginning of an action (*ingressive*). The translator may use a word like "became" to bring out the significance.

Matt 22:7 ὁ   δὲ   βασιλεὺς ὠργίσθη
        the   but   king   *he was angry*
        NLT: Then the king *became furious.*
        RSV: The king *was angry.*

8. The aorist can be used to describe a timeless truth (*gnomic*). Here the time significance of the aorist completely falls away and only its aspect is significant. These are often translated into English with the present tense.

1 Pet 1:24 ἐξηράνθη ὁ χόρτος, καὶ τὸ ἄνθος ἐξέπεσεν
         It withered the grass and the flower *it fell off*
         NIV: The grass *withers* and the flowers *falls.*
         NET: The grass *withers* and the flower *falls off.*

9. Because time is secondary to aspect, the Greek speaker can even use the aorist to describe an action that will occur in the future (*proleptic*). This stresses the certainty that the event will occur.

Rom 8:30	οὓς	ἐδικαίωσεν,	τούτους	καὶ	ἐδόξασεν.
	whom	he justified	these	also	*he glorified*

NLT: And he gave them right standing with himself, and *he promised them his glory.*

RSV: And those whom he justified *he* also *glorified.*

For the Curious

Greek generally indicates a past tense verb by adding an *augment* to the beginning of a verb (which is often an ε) and sometimes a *tense formative* (below, the σα) to the end, which is followed by a personal ending. The personal endings used with the imperfect and aorist are different from those used with the present.

- πιστεύω   is present tense and means, "I believe."
- ἐπίστευον   is imperfect and means "I was believing."
- ἐπίστευσα   is aorist and means "I believed."

Advanced Information

One of the primary areas of confusion in Greek exegesis comes when people confuse the Greek aorist with the English punctiliar aspect. The English punctiliar describes an action that occurs in a single point of time. "The tidal wave *hit* the boat." However, the Greek aorist is not necessarily punctiliar. It tells you nothing about the action of the verb other than it happened.

It is interesting that Luke's version of Jesus' statement on discipleship is a little different from Mark's. He says,

> If anyone wishes to come after me, let him deny himself and *take up* his cross *daily,* and follow me. (Luke 9:23)

Luke includes the adverb "daily" to emphasize that the action of "taking up" occurs every day. Does this contradict the Markan account (Mark 8:34) that simply says, "take up"? No. Both Mark and Luke use the same undefined aspect—the aorist—when saying "take up." The verb does not specify the nature of the action; it merely says that it should occur. But Luke includes the adverb "daily" to clarify that this action is a daily action. He could have just as easily used the continuous aspect for "take up" and arrived at the same meaning.

Part of the misconception surrounding the aorist and its aspect is because it can be used to describe a punctiliar action. However, such a verb is punctiliar not because it is an aorist but because of the context and the meaning of the word. You will find this mistake in many commentaries, so be careful.

CHAPTER 18

Perfect Indicative

English

In English, the past tense indicates that something happened in the past. When you use the helping verbs "have" or "has," the action is described as completed in the recent past but as having implications in the present.

> I *ate* last night.
> I *have eaten* and am still full.

The English present tense can also describe a past action with current consequences.

> It *is written.*

These last two examples are close to the Greek perfect.

Greek

The Greek perfect is one of the more interesting tenses and is often used to express great theological truths. The Greek perfect describes an action that was brought to completion and whose effects are felt in the present—the present, of course, from the time frame of the writer. Because it describes a completed action, the action described by the perfect verb normally occurred in the past.

For example, "Jesus died" is a simple statement of an event that happened in the past. In Greek this would be in the aorist. But if we used the Greek perfect to say, "Jesus has died," then we would expect the verse to continue, for example, by spelling out the present significance of that past action. "Jesus has died for my sins."

Another example is the verb "to write." When the Bible says, "It is written," this is usually in the perfect tense. Scripture was written in the past but is applicable in the present. That is why some translations choose the present "It is written," instead of "It has been written." This emphasizes its abiding significance.

Uses of the Perfect

1. Sometimes the emphasis is on the fact that the action was completed (*consummative, extensive*).

2 Tim 4:7	τὸν καλὸν	ἀγῶνα	ἠγώνισμαι,	τὸν δρόμον	τετέλεκα
	the good	fight	*I have fought*	the race	*I have finished*

NIV: I have fought the good fight, I have finished the race.

Rom 5:5	ἡ ἀγάπη	τοῦ θεοῦ	ἐκκέχυται	ἐν	ταῖς καρδίαις	ἡμῶν
	the love	of the God	*has been poured*	in	the hearts	of us

ESV: God's love *has been poured* into our hearts.

KJV: the love of God *is shed abroad* in our hearts.

2. Other times the emphasis is on the resulting state of the action (*intensive*) and is generally translated with the English present.

Luke 5:20	ἄνθρωπε,	ἀφέωνταί	σοι	αἱ ἁμαρτίαι	σου
	man	*they have been forgiven*	to you	the sins	of you

RSV: Man, your sins *are forgiven* you.

Exercises for Chapters 14 - 18

Try to identify the grammatical category of each bolded verb below (e.g., inceptive imperfect) and explain the different translations.

Matt 27:30 ESV. And they spit on him and took the reed and *struck* him on the head. NASB. They spat on Him, and took the reed and began to beat Him on the head. NIV. They spit on him, and took the staff and struck him on the head again and again.

Luke 3:9 ESV. Even now the axe *is laid* to the root of the trees. Every tree therefore that does not bear good fruit *is cut down* and *thrown* into the fire. NIV. The ax is already at the root of the trees, and every tree that does not produce good fruit will be cut down and thrown into the fire.

Acts 9:34 How can the present tense describe a continuous action and yet Jesus heals him instantly? NIV. "Aeneas," Peter said to him, "Jesus Christ *heals* you. Get up and take care of your mat." Immediately Aeneas got up.

Acts 26:11 Where does the "tried" come from? Check the Greek. NIV. Many a time I went from one synagogue to another to have them punished, and I *tried* to force them to blaspheme.

Rom 7:19 NRSV. For I do not do the good I want, but the evil I do not want is what I *do*. ESV. For I do not do the good I want, but the evil I do not want is what I keep on doing.

1 Cor 3:16 How many people does it take to be the temple of God? ESV. Do you not know that *you* are God's temple and that God's Spirit dwells in *you*? NIV. Don't you know that you yourselves are God's temple and that God's Spirit lives in you? NLT. Don't you realize that all of you together are the temple of God and that the Spirit of God lives in you?

1 Cor 16:5 NASB. *I am going through* Macedonia. ESV. I intend to pass through Macedonia. NLT. I am planning to travel through Macedonia.

Gal 5:15 Explain why this is an acceptable translation of an aorist verb. NIV. If you keep on biting and devouring each other, watch out or you *will be destroyed* by each other. ESV. But if you bite and devour one another, watch out that you are not consumed by one another.

Explain the differences in how the perfect tense functions in the following.

Rom 3:10 NIV. As it *is written*: "There is no one righteous, not even one."

Rom 5:5 NIV. God *has poured* out his love into our hearts by the Holy Spirit.

In the last chapter we learned the "ingressive aorist." A.T. Robertson says that John 11:35, "Jesus wept," is actually an ingressive aorist and "more exactly means, 'Jesus burst into tears'" (*The Minister and His Greek New Testament*, Baker, 1977).

CHAPTER 19

How to Use the Paper and Electronic Tools

Now that you have learned quite a bit about Greek, it is time to discuss the tools you can use to get at the Greek behind the English translations. Much of what I have to say here also applies to Hebrew, but I will talk about Hebrew-specific tools in the Appendix. I will also show you other tools you can use for advanced Bible study.

Getting at the Greek behind the English

There are several tools that will show you the Greek behind the English. You will excuse me if I am a little biased, but my favorite is a book I wrote, *Interlinear for the Rest of Us: The Reverse Interlinear for New Testament Word Studies* (Zondervan, 2006). The whole point behind this book is to give people who do not know "full Greek" access to the Greek words behind the English, the Greek word's parsing, and its GK number.

I called it a "reverse" interlinear because it does one thing significantly different from standard interlinears. Most interlinears keep Greek word order and include a word-for-word English translation under each Greek word. Because English word order is often fundamentally different from Greek, the interlinear English translations generally do not make sense. *EGNT* keeps the English word order and alters the Greek to match the English text of the NIV. This way you can read the English and drop down to the Greek whenever you wish.

Man		does	not	live	on	bread	alone,
ͺὁ	ἄνθρωπος⌋ ↦		οὐκ	ζήσεται	ἐπ᾽	ἄρτῳ	μόνῳ
d.nsm	n.nsm		adv	v.fmi.3s	p.d	n.dsm	a.dsm
3836	476	2409	4024	2409	2093	788	3668

For example, the Greek behind "live" is ζήσεται. It is a verb, future middle indicative, third person singular. For word studies, all you need to know is that its GK number is 2409.

Most of the example verses I have given you so far have been in the traditional interlinear format. Sometimes the Greek and English word order is sufficiently close that you can understand the English translation.

Matt 4:4	οὐκ	ἐπ'	ἄρτῳ	μόνῳ	ζήσεται	ὁ ἄνθρωπος
	not	on	bread	alone	*he will live*	the man

At other times it borders on nonsense to the English reader. But it is also the inclusion of the parsing and the GK numbers that makes *IRU* indispensable—of course, I am biased! You can also get some of the same information from *The Complete Word Study New Testament,* by Spiros Zodhiates (AMG Publishers), who based his work on the KJV.

Software

Another easy way to get at the Greek behind the English is to use a good software program. There are several I could use for illustrations, but my favorite is Accordance (Macintosh computers only). In Accordance you simply find a verse and move the cursor over the Greek word. Its definition, GK number, and lexical form (in Greek and transliteration) appears in the amplify window (see next page). If you have purchased the NASB or KJV modules, you can also move the cursor over the English and it will show the Greek in the amplify window.

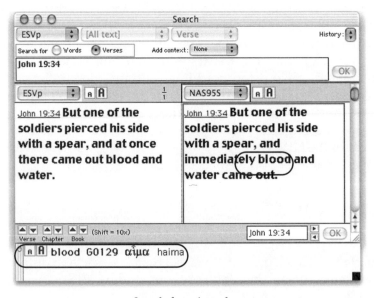

Sample from Accordance

If you use a Microsoft Windows computer, there are several good options. BibleWorks is especially good for showing you the original languages, as long as you use the KJV and/or the NASB with codes. Zondervan's new Pradis also does an excellent job. Further information about all three can be obtained from the respective web sites of the companies that produce these Bible programs.

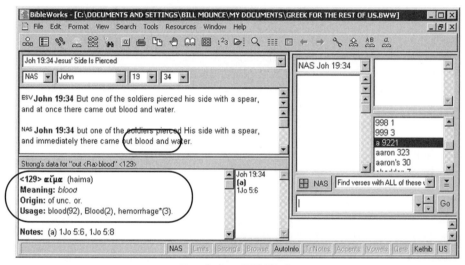

Sample from BibleWorks

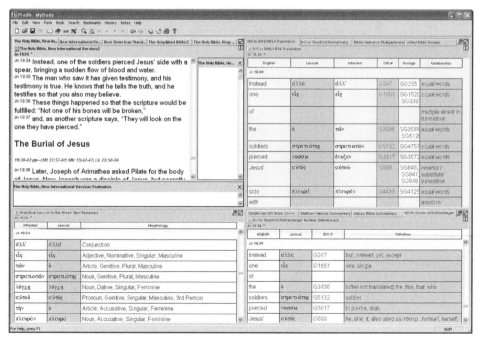

Sample from Pradis

LOVE (551) [BELOVED, LOVED, LOVELY, LOVER, LOVER'S, LOVERS, LOVES, LOVING, LOVING-KINDNESS, LOVINGLY]

Ge	20:13	`This is how you can show your *l* to me:	2876
	22: 2	your only son, Isaac, whom *you l,*	170
	29:18	Jacob *was in l with* Rachel and said,	170
	29:20	a few days to him because of his *l for* her.	173
	29:32	Surely my husband *will l* me now."	170
		. . . . .	
Mt	3: 17	Son, whom I *l;* with him I am well pleased."	28
	5: 43	`L your neighbor and hate your enemy.'	26
	5: 44	*L* your enemies and pray for those who	26
	5: 46	If *you l* those who love you,	26
	5: 46	If you love those who *l* you,	26
	6: 5	for *they l* to pray standing in the	5797
	6: 24	Either he will hate the one and *l* the other,	26
	12:18	the one I *l,* in whom I delight;	28
	17: 5	whom I *l;* with him I am well pleased.	28
	19:19	and `*l* your neighbor as yourself.' "	26
	22:37	" `L the Lord your God with all your heart	26
	22:39	`L your neighbor as yourself.'	26
	23: 6	*they l* the place of honor at banquets and	5797
	23: 7	they *l* to be greeted in the marketplaces	NIG
	24:12	the *l* of most will grow cold,	27
Mk	1: 11	"You are my Son, whom I *l;*	28
	9: 7	"This is my Son, whom I *l.*	28
	12:30	*L* the Lord your God with all your heart	26
	12:31	`L your neighbor as yourself.'	26
	12:33	*To l* him with all your heart,	26
	12:33	and *to l* your neighbor as yourself.'	26
Lk	3: 22	"You are my Son, whom I *l;*	28
	6: 27	*L* your enemies, do good to those who hate	26
	6: 32	"If *you l* those who love you,	26
	6: 32	"If you love those who *l* you,	26
	6: 32	Even `sinners' *l* those who love them.	26
	6: 32	Even `sinners' love those who *l* them.	26
	6: 35	But *l* your enemies, do good to them,	26
	7: 42	Now which of them *will l* him more?"	26
	10:27	" `L the Lord your God with all your heart	26
	10:27	and, `L your neighbor as yourself.' "	NIG
	11:42	but you neglect justice and the *l* of God.	27
	11:43	because *you l* the most important seats in	26
	16:13	Either he will hate the one and *l* the other,	26
	20:13	I will send my son, whom I *l;*	28

The NIV Exhaustive Concordance

Concordances

You could also find the Greek word behind the English the old fashioned way, using an exhaustive concordance. Let's do this using the NIV text and the *NIV Exhaustive Concordance* (sample on the previous page).

What is a concordance? A concordance is a book that lists the words in the Bible, and under each word shows you the verses in which that word occurs. So, for example, if you looked up "love," you would find that the word occurs 551 times in 505 verses. (I didn't count; I let Accordance tell me.)

What is an exhaustive concordance? It is a concordance that lists *every* word in the Bible and lists *every* verse in which each word occurs. There are shorter concordances, published as separate books or in the back of your Bible, but they do not show every word, and sometimes do not show you every verse in which the words occur. The serious student needs a serious concordance. Get an exhaustive.

But exhaustive concordances also give you one more invaluable piece of information. They show you the GK (or Strong's) number of the Greek word used in the sentence. So let's say you want to find the Greek word behind the English word "love" in Matthew 19:19, "You shall love your neighbor as yourself." Look up the word "love" and look through the entries until you find the verse. This concordance lists the entry as, "and 'l your neighbor as yourself.'" The editor made a decision as to which words to the left and the right to include, and also abbreviated "love" to "l" and bolded it. This is standard practice. Now look on the next page and you will see the GK number, "26."

This is the key piece of information especially for word studies. Go to the back of the concordance and look up the number in the Greek lexicon (not the Hebrew, which is the first of the three dictionaries in the back). You will find that the lexical form of the Greek word # 26 is ἀγαπάω, which is transliterated as *agapaō*.

If you use the KJV, there are several exhaustive concordances available. In my opinion, the best is the *Strongest Strongs*, not because Zondervan (my publisher) published it, but because it is the best. They worked from the best English KJV text, and they provide the best helps in the back of the book. (I will talk about those below.) John Kohlenberger outdid himself on this one (along with his editor and team)! The original Strong's concordance is published by several publishers as is Young's. There is an exhaustive concordance for the NASB and the RSV as well. Most use Strong's numbers; the *NIV Exhaustive* and I use the GK numbers (and there are conversion charts in the back so you can move from GK to Strong and back again).

More on Software

There is much you can learn about the Bible from software programs; I will only mention a few. If you are serious about studying your Bible and if you have a computer, these tools are modestly priced and will prove themselves invaluable. I will use Accordance as an example.

The software originally was written so you could look up occurrences of words quickly. Today this is viturally instantaneous. You can do what are called "wild card" searches. Searching for "love*" (with the asterisk) will find verses that have "love, loved, lovely, lover, lover's, lovers, loves, loving, loving-kindness," and "lovingly." You can also limit your search to certain books, such as just the Minor Prophets.

Different software displays the biblical text differently. Accordance can show you versions in parallel or in a more traditional concordance format. The more advanced software should also be able to provide analysis for your search. For example, Accordance will show you the distribution of "hits," i.e., where the words occur in the Bible.

Many software products also let you store your notes along with the text, kind of like writing in the margins of your Bible. But the future of software lies in its ability to include reference books. Some software comes with the reference books; others require you to purchase them. Let's say you are studying James 1:12. "Blessed is the man who perseveres under trial, because when he has stood the test, he will receive the crown of life that God has promised to those who love him" (NIV). If you want help on a word or the verse, you can just click on something (every program does it differently) and a dictionary or commentary will appear, helping you with that word or verse. I predict that the software that provides the best resources will be the best seller in the long run.

But a word to the wise on this topic. Many software products make huge claims. "Buy me and I come with 60 different versions of the Bible." Now really, how many of us really want access to five Spanish versions and three Portugese? If I were Spanish or Portugese, would I really care if the software contained twenty-seven English versions? Probably not. I also have seen some software vendors make huge claims about all the reference materials they provide for free. There generally are reasons the material is free; it is in the public domain and they can distribute it without royalties. So a word to the wise. While the feature-set of the software, price, support, and interface are important issues, the most important is the quality of materials you can access with the software. And bigger is not always better.

You can also get Bible search software on your hand-held computer. Check out MyBible™ and PocketBible® from www.Laridian.com, BibleReader™ from www.OliveTree.com, and the offerings from www.Gramcord.org.

More on Books

Concordances

Let me go back first to concordances. I previously talked about how to get to the Greek behind the English, but let me say a few things about concordance usage in general. Suppose you have been reading your Bible (I will use the ESV for my examples below) and vaguely remember a verse that speaks about Jesus being a "propitiation." You look up the word "propitiation" and quickly see that the ESV uses the word four times.

PROPITIATION (4)
God put forward as a p by his blood,	Rom 3:25
to make p for the sins of the people.	Heb 2:17
He is the p for our sins, and not for ours	1 Jn 2:2
sent his Son to be the p for our sins.	1 Jn 4:10

From this listing you should be able to identify the verse you were reading, and in the process you also find the other three times the word is used. These verses help to provide the context for your verse and the concept of "propitiation."

When you are looking for that elusive verse, pick the more specific or unusual word. Let's say you want to find the verse where Paul says he "delivered" two men "to Satan that they may learn not to blaspheme." If you looked up the word "delivered," you would find 160 verses. Looking up "Satan" would locate 53 verses, and "blaspheme" locates 6 verses. It will be much faster to find "blaspheme" in the concordance and look through those 6 verses. Of course, if you are not sure what specific words occur in the verse, it may be a bit hit and miss until you find the right word.

Do not forget about related words. You may be confident that the verse for which you are looking has the word "believe," but try as you might you cannot find the verse. As it turns out, the verse might actually have the form "believes." A word to the wise.

You also need to respect the limitations of concordances. Let's say you want to find all the verses in the Bible that talk about prayer. You can look up the entries for pray, prayed, prayer, prayers, praying, and prays. These verses will show you many of the verses that discuss prayer, but they will not show you all of them. Why? Because the Bible talks about prayer without using the actual word. For example, none of these listings contain Matthew 7:7. "Ask, and it will be given you; seek, and you will find; knock, and it will be opened to you." This would be a serious omission in your Bible study, and it is one of the limitations of using a concordance.

LOVE [*170, 171, 172, 173, 1856, 2668, 2876, 2883, 3137, 3351, 8163, 8533, *26, 27, 28, 921, 5789, 5797*].

NIV+ BELOVED, LOVED, LOVELY, LOVER, LOVER'S, LOVERS, LOVES, LOV-ING, LOVING-KINDNESS, LOVINGLY

(1Co 13; 14:1; Col 1:8; 2:2; 1Th 1:3; 5:8; 1Ti 6:11; 2Ti 1:7; Phm 5; Heb 10:24; 1Jn 4:7,16-18).

The theme of the Song of Solomon, and often allegorized representing the love of the Messiah for the church and of his church for the Messiah (SS 1-8). *See Church, Loved.*

Love of Person For Person: (Ro 5:7; Jas 1:27).

Defined—

1Co 13:1 If I speak in the tongues of men and of angels, but have not love, I am only a resounding gong or a clanging cymbal. ² If I have the gift of prophecy and can fathom all mysteries and all knowledge, and if I have a faith that can move mountains, but have not love, I am nothing. ³ If I give all I possess to the poor and surrender my body to the flames, but have not love, I gain nothing.

⁴ Love is patient, love is kind. It does not envy, it does not boast, it is not proud. ⁵ It is not rude, it is not self-seeking, it is not easily angered, it keeps no record of wrongs. ⁶ Love does not delight in evil but rejoices with the truth. ⁷ It always protects, always trusts, always hopes, always perseveres.

⁸ Love never fails. But where there are prophecies, they will cease; where there are tongues, they will be stilled; where there is knowledge, it will pass away. ⁹ For we know in part and we prophesy in part, ¹⁰ but when perfection comes, the imperfect disappears. ¹¹ When I was a child, I talked like a child, I thought like a child, I reasoned like a child. When I became a man, I put childish ways behind me. ¹² Now we see but a poor reflection as in a mirror; then we shall see face to face. Now I know in part; then I shall know fully, even as I am fully known.

¹³ And now these three remain: faith, hope and love. But the greatest of these is love.
In the parable of the good Samaritan (Lk 10:25-37).

Is edifying—

1Co 8:1 Now about food sacrificed to idols: We know that we all possess knowledge. Knowledge puffs up, but love builds up.

Is precious—

Pr 15:17 Better a meal of vegetables where there is love than a fattened calf with hatred.

Is unquenchable—

Pr 17:17 A friend loves at all times, and a brother is born for adversity.
SS 8:6 Place me like a seal over your heart, like a seal on your arm; for love is as strong as death, its jealousy unyielding as the grave. It burns like blazing fire, like a mighty flame. ⁷ Many waters cannot quench love, rivers cannot wash it away. If one were to give all the wealth of his house for love, it would be utterly scorned.

Is a fruit of the Spirit—

Gal 5:22 But the fruit of the Spirit is love, joy, peace, patience, kindness, goodness, faithfulness,

Topical Bibles like Nave's will help solve this problem (see sample on p. 172).

There is another limitation to concordances, but one that is easily remedied. You need to use the concordance that is based on the version of the Bible that you read. Let's say you want to find the verse that says, "If I speak in the tongues of men and of angels, but have not love, I am a noisy gong or a clanging cymbal." If you use a concordance that is based on the King James Version of the Bible, you will not find this verse listed under "love" because the KJV uses the word "charity" in 1 Corinthians 13:1. Likewise, if you were looking for the verse with "propitiation" in the concordance for the Revised Standard Version you would not find it, because the RSV uses the word "expiation." There are specific concordances for the KJV, NIV, RSV, NRSV, NASB, NLT, ESV, and perhaps others.

Finally, a more serious limitation is that the concordance only shows a limited context for the word. "Context" is the most important tool in determining the meaning of a verse. The more context you have—in other words, the more words you have—the better job you can do interpreting the verse. So let's say you are studying on the "will of God" and you find this entry: "For this is the will of God" (1 Thess 4:3). There are insufficient words to make the meaning of the verse clear. However, if the entry had a few more words, the verse would be clearer: "For this is the will of God, your sanctification." And if you had even more, it would be even clearer: "For this is the will of God, your sanctification: that you abstain from sexual immorality." So the moral of the story is, once you find the verse in the concordance, you should always look it up in your Bible and read it in its fuller context.

There are three basic types of concordances for the English reader. (1) Many Bibles have an abbreviated concordance in the back. These concordances do not list every word in the Bible, nor do they list every verse that uses each word. For example, the word "love" occurs 888 times in the ESV, but there are only 120 verses under "love" in the Bible's concordance. These 120 are some of the better known verses using the word "love," but the specific verse for which you are looking may not be one of them.

(2) "Complete" concordances list all the words in the Bible except for the most common (like "a," "an," "be," etc.), and then list all the verses that use each of those words. These omitted words are so common that it is doubtful you would use them to look up a verse. These words should be listed somewhere in the book.

(3) An "exhaustive" concordance, as I said previously, adds one more feature. It will tell you what Hebrew, Aramaic, or Greek word lies behind each concorded word. This way you can do word studies based on the

original language without knowing that language. Exhaustive concordances usually do not list all the verses that use the common words. They will often list the word (for example, "a"), and then only the verse references where the word "a" occurs; they do not actually list the words before and after the concorded word. Otherwise, the book would be too large.

And then there is all the information in the back of the exhaustive concordance. The *Strongest Strong's* has the best set of tools, I think, of all the concordances. In the back you will find Greek, Hebrew, and Aramaic dictionaries, and among a few other features an updated version of *Naves Topical Bible*. This is an especially valuable tool for Bible study because it lists verses based on topic and not just word. For example, here is the entry on "love."

There is one other type of concordance, traditionally called the "Englishman's concordance." Instead of showing you every place an English word occurs, it shows you every verse in which a specific Greek or Hebrew word occurs, but it lists the verses in English. We will look at this type of concordance in chapter 24.

Dictionaries

Let me spend a few pages covering the other types of books that you may find helpful. I hesitate to give any specific recommendations, because new books are always coming in print, but I will tell you my favorites. The books that I mention are not geared toward the specialist and scholar. I will reserve comment on books related to word studies until chapter 24.

Single volume Bible or theology dictionaries discuss key topics. Every one of you must have one of these, and my favorite is the *Evangelical Dictionary of Theology*, edited by Elwell and published by Baker. Time and time again I have found this volume helpful. The inital articles are "Abaddon, Abba, Abelard, Abide, Abolitionism, Abomination of Desolation, Abortion, Abraham, Abraham's Bosom, Absolution, Abstinence, Accommodation, Adam." Apart from the quality of the articles, what I appreciate is Elwell's wide selection of topics, much wider than most one-volume dictionaries.

Multi-volume dictionaries cover many more topics in much greater depth. *The International Standard Bible Encyclopedia*, edited by Bromiley (Eerdmans), has been the standard in evangelical circles for many years.

The best thing you can do is go down to your local Christan bookstore and page through these books. If they don't have a Bible dictionary, then shame on them and don't go back.

Commentaries

Commentaries are books that go through a biblical book, word by word, or verse by verse, or paragraph by paragraph. The author's goal is to help you see what the Bible means by telling you what he or she thinks it means. Commentaries fluctuate widely in what they cover and the depth of the discussion. There are some so shallow as to be worthless, and others are so detailed that for non-specialists they best serve as a door stop. I will spend chapter 29 on how to read a commentary and will include my listing of suggested commentaries at that time.

Other English Books

There are many other types of books that you might find helpful. *Nave's Topical Bible* lists verses by topic rather than simply by word, as a concordance does. Please check this one out. It is also included in the back of the *Strongest Strong's* concordance.

There is a field of study called "Introduction," and the books written for it deal with issues such as who wrote the biblical book, when, where, why. If you have technical questions about the background of any biblical book, this is the place to look. At the college level see *Encountering the New Testament* by Elwell and Yarbrough (Baker) and *A Survey of the New Testament* by Robert Gundry (Zondervan). At an advanced level see *New Testament Introduction* by Guthrie (InterVarsity Press) and *An Introduction to the New Testament* by Carson, Moo, and Morris (Zondervan).

Finally, every student should have a good theology reference book. The most important book of my life was *A Theology of the New Testament,* by George Ladd (Eerdmans). Professor Ladd laid out the meaning of the New Testament for me better than any other book. It technically belongs in the category called "Biblical Theology." When it comes to "Systematic Theology," I use Wayne Grudem's *Systematic Theology* (Zondervan). He condensed it into his *Bible Doctrine* (Zondervan), although the full-size book is understandable by most laypeople.

For the historical background to the New Testament see *New Testament History* by F. F. Bruce (Anchor Books) and *New Testament History* by Ben Witherington III (Baker). For additional lists of books see *Old Testament Exegesis* by Douglas Stuart (third edition, 2001, Westminster) and *New Testament Exegesis* by Gordon Fee (revised edition, 1993, Westminster/John Knox).

What Else Is in a Verb?

Last week we learned a lot about the Greek verbal system in the indicative. This week we are going to look at the nonindicative system. These are tremendously important elements of Greek grammar if we are going to know why translations are different and how to do exegesis properly. We will also cover what many of you have been waiting for, word studies.

CHAPTER 20

Participle

English

Present participles are formed by adding "-ing" to a verb. They are defined as "verbal adjectives."

> The man, *eating* by the window, is my Greek teacher.
> After *eating,* I will go to bed.

A participle can have an *adverbial* function.

> After *eating,* my Greek teacher gave us the final.

In this sentence, "eating" is a participle that tells us something in relationship to the verb "gave." The teacher gave us the final after he was done eating. ("After" is an adverb that emphasizes when the action of the participle occurred.)

A participle can also have an *adjectival* function.

> The woman, *sitting* by the window, is my Greek teacher.

In this example, "sitting" tells us something about the noun "woman."

When a participle has elements such as a direct object or an adverb, the participle and its accompanying elements form a **participial phrase**. In phrasing, it is important to identify the beginning and the end of the participial phrase, much like you do with a relative clause. The participial phrase is always dependent.

In a sentence like, "While eating, he saw her." English requires that "he" is the one who is eating, not "her," since "he" is closer in word order to the participle

Greek

Participles are widely used in the New Testament. You will find many examples on every page. But you will also discover that they have a much wider range of usage in Greek than in English, and this flexibility presents certain difficulties to the translator.

Aspect. The key to understanding participles is to recognize that their significance is primarily one of aspect, i.e., type of action. This is the genius, the essence, of participles, as it is of all the nonindicative verbal forms (subjunctive, infinitive, imperative; to be discussed in later chapters). A participle does not necessarily indicate when an action occurs ("time": past, present, future). Because there are three aspects, there are three types of participles.

- The *present* participle describes a continuous action.
- The *aorist* participle describes an action without commenting on the nature of the action (undefined).
- The *perfect* participle describes a completed action with present effects.

You will see that the translations often are not able to bring this significance of aspect into English.

(The terms "present," "aorist," and "perfect" do not refer to the meaning but to the form of the participle. The present participle is built on the present tense stem of the verb, but it does not necessarily denote an event occurring in the present time.)

Adjectival Participle

Adjectival. Because a participle is a verbal adjective, it can behave as an adjective. The participle will modify some other noun or pronoun in the sentence and will agree with that word in case, number, and gender, just like an adjective. In Rom 12:1, both ζῶσαν and θυσίαν are accusative singular feminine.

to	offer	your	bodies		as	living	sacrifices,	holy
→	παραστῆσαι	ὑμῶν	⌞τὰ	σώματα⌟		ζῶσαν	θυσίαν	ἁγίαν
	f.aa	r.gp.2	d.apn	n.apn		pt.pa.asf	n.asf	a.asf
	4225	7007	3836	5393		2409	2602	41

Substantival. Since an adjective can also function as a noun, so also can a participle. (Technically, when an "-ing" word is used as a noun, in English it is called a "gerund.") Remember: a participle is a verbal adjective, and anything an adjective can do a participle can do, usually better.

> *Mark 9:23*   πάντα   δυνατὰ   τῷ   πιστεύοντι.
> all things possible to the   *believing*
> NIV: Everything is possible for *him who believes.*
> ESV: All things are possible for *one who believes.*

Notice that once again we had to add words to say the same thing in English that is being said in Greek, just as we do with substantival adjectives.

The translation of the Greek participle is often idiomatic," i.e., not word-for-word.

Adverbial Participle

The adverbial participle tells us something about the finite verb. In many cases the translator will add words to bring out the significance of the participle, and this explains why translations are different in places.

1. The aorist participle can describe an action occurring *before* the time of the finite verb, while the present participle can describe something happening *at the same time* as the action of the main verb (*temporal*). "After" and "when/while" are often added to this type of participle.

> *Matt 4:2*   νηστεύσας ...   ὕστερον   ἐπείνασεν
> *fasting*   then   he was hungry
> ESV: *After fasting* ... he was hungry.
> NRSV: He *fasted* ... and afterwards he was famished.

> *Acts 1:4*   συναλιζόμενος   παρήγγειλεν   αὐτοῖς
> *staying with*   he charged   them
> RSV: *While staying with* them he charged them
> NET: *While he was with* them, he ordered them

> *Eph 1:20*   ἐνήργησεν   ἐν   τῷ Χριστῷ   ἐγείρας   αὐτὸν   ἐκ   νεκρῶν
> he worked   in   Christ   *raising*   him   from   dead
> NIV: which he exerted in Christ *when he raised* him from the dead

2. The participle can indicate the manner in which the action of the finite verb occurs (*manner*).

> *Matt 19:22*   ἀκούσας   δὲ   ὁ νεανίσκος   τὸν λόγον   ἀπῆλθεν   λυπούμενος
> hearing   and   the youth   the word   he went away   *grieving*
> NIV: When the young man heard this, he went away *sad*.
> NRSV: When the young man heard this word, he went away *grieving*.

3. The participle can indicate the means by which the action of the finite verb occurs (*means*).

> *1 Cor 4:12*   κοπιῶμεν   ἐργαζόμενοι   ταῖς   ἰδίαις   χερσίν
> we toil   *working*   with the   own   hands
> We toil *by working* with our own hands.
> NIV: We *work* hard with our own hands.
> ESV: We labor, *working* with our own hands.

4. The participle can indicate the cause or reason or ground of the action of the finite verb (*cause*).

Acts 16:34   ἠγαλλιάσατο πανοικεὶ   πεπιστευκὼς τῷ θεῷ

he rejoiced   with his whole house *having believed* in God

NIV: He was filled with joy *because he had come to believe* in God.

NASB: and rejoiced greatly, *having believed* in God

5. The participle can indicate a condition that must be fulfilled if the action of the finite verb is to be accomplished (*conditional*).

Matt 21:22 πάντα ὅσα ἂν   αἰτήσητε ...   πιστεύοντες λήμψεσθε

all   whatever you might ask *believing*   you will receive

RSV: And whatever you ask in prayer, you will receive, *if you have faith.*

NASB: And all things you ask in prayer, *believing,* you will receive.

6. The participle can indicate that the action of the finite verb is true despite the action of the participle (*concessive*).

Eph 2:1   Καὶ ὑμᾶς ὄντας νεκροὺς τοῖς παραπτώμασιν

and you   *being*   dead   the tresspasses

NET: And *although you were* dead in your transgressions

NIV: You *were* dead in your transgressions.

RSV: And you he made alive, *when you were* dead through the trespasses. (The RSV sees it as temporal.)

7. The participle can indicate the purpose of the finite verb (*purpose*). These are often translated as infinitives.

Matt 27:49 εἰ ἔρχεται   Ἡλίας σώσων αὐτόν

if he comes Elijah *saving* him

NIV: Let's see if Elijah comes *to save* him.

NLT: Let's see whether Elijah *will* come and *save* him.

8. The participle can indicate the result of the finite verb (*result*). This is close to the participle of purpose; the difference is whether the force of the particple is on the intention or the result.

Eph 2:15   τοὺς δύο κτίσῃ   ἐν αὐτῷ εἰς ἕνα καινὸν ἄνθρωπον ποιῶν εἰρήνην

the two he create in him into one new man   *making* peace

NIV: His purpose was to create in himself one new man out of the two, *thus making* peace.

Translated as Indicative Verbs

Often participles are translated as indicative verbs. This may create a problem for exegesis, because you can't distinguish between the main verb—which is normally indicative and normally contains the main thought—and the dependent participle, which normally contains a modifying thought. Translators do this for several reasons.

1. When Greek sentences get too long for English translations, it is often easiest to treat a long participial phrase as an independent sentence. Ephesians 1:3-14 is one sentence. V. 5 begins with a participial phrase, and many translations start a new English sentence by turning the participle into a finite verb, supply a subject, and hence turn a participial phrase into an independent sentence. The NET adds, "He did this," and the NRSV adds "He."

Eph 1:5	προορίσας	ἡμᾶς	εἰς	υἱοθεσίαν	διὰ	Ἰησοῦ	Χριστοῦ
	predestining	us	to	adoption	through	Jesus	Christ

NET: *He did this by predestining* us to adoption as his sons through Jesus Christ.

NRSV: *He destined* us for adoption as his children through Jesus Christ.

KJV: *Having predestinated* us unto the adoption of children by Jesus Christ to himself.

2. Greek likes to have an aorist participle before the main verb, but in English we use two finite verbs.

Mark 1:18	εὐθὺς	ἀφέντες	τὰ δίκτυα	ἠκολούθησαν	αὐτῷ.
	immediately	*leaving*	the nets	they followed	him

NASB. Immediately *they left* their nets and followed Him.

For the Curious

*λυ is the verbal root meaning "to destroy." The σα is a tense formative for the aorist.

Present active participle (singular)

	masc	*fem*	*neut*
nom sg	λύων	λύουσα	λῦον
gen sg	λύοντος	λυούσης	λύοντος
dat sg	λύοντι	λυούσῃ	λύοντι
acc sg	λύοντα	λύουσαν	λῦον

Aorist active participle (singular)

	masc	fem	neuter
nom sg	λύσας	λύσασα	λῦσαν
gen sg	λύσαντος	λυσάσης	λύσαντος
dat sg	λύσαντι	λυσάσῃ	λύσαντι
acc sg	λύσαντα	λύσασαν	λῦσαν

Advanced Information

A **genitive absolute** is a noun or pronoun and a participle in the genitive that are not grammatically connected to the rest of the sentence. In other words, there will be no word in the remaining part of the sentence that the noun, pronoun, or participle modifies.

These are common constructions especially in narrative passages. They usually occur at the beginning of the sentence and are usually temporal. Translation is often idiomatic.

Mark 14:43 αὐτοῦ   λαλοῦντος   παραγίνεται   Ἰούδας
　　　　　　he   speaking   comes   Judas
　　　　　　NASB: *While He was still speaking,* Judas … came up.
　　　　　　NIV: *Just as he was speaking,* Judas … appeared.

John 5:13 ὁ Ἰησοῦς   ἐξένευσεν   ὄχλου   ὄντος   ἐν   τῷ   τόπῳ
　　　　　　Jesus   he departed   *crowd*   *being*   in   the   place
　　　　　　NASB: Jesus had slipped away *while there was a crowd* in that place.
　　　　　　ESV: Jesus had withdrawn, *as there was a crowd* in the place.
　　　　　　NET: Jesus had slipped out *since there was a crowd* in that place.
　　　　　　NRSV: Jesus had disappeared *in the crowd* that was there.

Notice how αὐτοῦ ("he") in the first example functions as the "subject" of the participle, even though technically a participle cannot have a subject. The genitive absolute is often used when the noun or pronoun doing the action of the participle is different from the subject of the sentence.

Voice. A participle can be active, middle, or passive. If the verb is deponent, its corresponding participle will be deponent. Greek uses different participle morphemes for the different voices.

　　　　ἀκούων   (active)   hearing
　　　　ἀκουόμενος   (passive)   being heard

A "morpheme" is the smallest part of a word that conveys meaning. In the case of ἀκουόμενος, the morphemes are the stem (*ἀκου), connecting vowel (ο), participle morpheme (μενο), and the case ending (ς).

Relative time. This is quite an advanced topic, so be warned. Participles do not indicate *absolute* time. In other words, the present participle does not indicate an action occuring in the present time. The aorist participle does not indicate an action occuring in the past time.

However, participles do indicate *relative* time. In other words, they indicate time relative to the time of the main verb. The participle built on the *present tense stem* indicates an action occuring at the *same time* as the main verb. If the main verb is present time, then the present participle also indicates an action occurring in the present time.

Matt 3:1	παραγίνεται	Ἰωάννης	ὁ βαπτιστὴς	κηρύσσων	ἐν	τῇ ἐρήμῳ
	he came	John	the baptizer	*preaching*	in	the wilderness

ESV: John the Baptist *came preaching* in the wilderness.

But if the main verb is past time, then the present participle also indicates an action occurring in the past time.

Eph 2:13	ὑμεῖς	οἵ	ποτε	ὄντες	μακρὰν	ἐγενήθητε	ἐγγὺς
	you	the	once	*being*	far	*you have become*	near

NIV: You who *once were* far away *have been brought* near.
NET: You who *used to be* far away *have been brought* near.

It get trickier with the aorist participle, because it usually (but not always) indicates an action that occurs *before* the time of the main verb. Therefore, if the main verb is present time, then the aorist participle indicates an action occurring in the past time.

Matt 2:2	ποῦ	ἐστιν	ὁ τεχθεὶς	βασιλεὺς	τῶν Ἰουδαίων;
	where	*is*	*the one born*	king	of the Jews?

ESV: Where *is he who has been born* king of the Jews?
NET: Where *is the one who is born* king of the Jews?

If the main verb is past time, then the aorist participle indicates an action occurring prior to the past time of the main verb.

Matt 2:9   οἱ ... ἀκούσαντες   τοῦ βασιλέως   ἐπορεύθησαν
                the   *hearing*   the king   *they went on their way*
                NIV: *After they had heard* the king, *they went on their way.*
                RSV: *When they had heard* the king *they went their way.*
                ESV: *After listening to* the king, *they went on their way.*

The perfect participle almost always indicates an action that occurs *prior to* that of the main verb.

Matt 22:29   πλανᾶσθε   μὴ   εἰδότες   τὰς γραφὰς
                you are misled not   *knowing* the Scripture
                NET: You are misled, *because you don't know* the scriptures.
                NIV: You are in error *because you do not know* the Scriptures.

As you might imagine, all this can get a bit tricky and the fine distinctions are often passed over in translations as, for example, in the NIV of Matthew 22:29 above.

CHAPTER 21

Subjunctive

English

So far we have studied only the indicative mood. (Participles technically are not a different mood.) If a verb is making a statement or asking a factual question, the verb is in the indicative. As it is normally stated, the indicative is the mood of reality. The speaker presents something as a statement of what is.

> Greek *is* fun.
> Hebrew *requires* more study.
> Why *am* I procrastinating?

The subjunctive does not describe what is but what may (or might) be. In other words, it is the mood not of reality but of possibility (or probability).

> I *might learn* Hebrew.
> If we *were wealthy,* we would buy more Greek Bibles.

A common use of the subjunctive in English is in an "if" clause. "If I were a rich man, I would hire a Greek tutor." If in fact the speaker were rich, he would not have used the subjunctive "were" but the indicative: "I *am* rich and therefore I will hire a tutor." This would be a statement of fact, the mood being one of reality. However, if he were not rich, the speaker would use the subjunctive form "were": "If I *were* rich ...."

Because the action described by a verb in the subjunctive is unfulfilled, it often refers to a future event.

Greek

The basic definitions of the subjunctive and indicative moods in Greek are the same as in English. There are, however, several significant differences.

Aspect. A Greek verb has time significance only in the indicative. The only significance that a verb in the subjunctive has is one of aspect. This is the same as with the participle.

A verb in the present subjunctive indicates a continuous action; a verb in the aorist subjunctive indicates an undefined action. There is no concept of absolute past or absolute present time in the subjunctive.

It is difficult to bring out the aspect in translation. Sometimes translators will add in words like "continue" with the present subjunctive, but only rarely.

Uses of the Subjunctive

1. The subjunctive is frequently used in statements of *purpose*. The clause is often introduced with ἵνα.

> Matt 12:10 ἐπηρώτησαν   αὐτὸν ...   ἵνα   κατηγορήσωσιν   αὐτοῦ
>   they questioned   him   in order that *they might accuse*   him
>   NET: They asked him ... so that *they could accuse* him.
>   NIV: *Looking for a reason to accuse* Jesus, they asked him.

2. A *conditional statement* is an "if ... then ...." sentence. "If I were smart, I would have taken Hebrew." I discussed conditional sentences in chapter 12. Suffice it to say here that when a conditional sentence is introduced with ἐάν, the verb in the "if" clause will be in the subjunctive. And these break down into two categories that are important for exegesis.

The writer may be thinking of a *specific possible event in the future*.

> Matt 4:9   ταῦτά σοι   πάντα δώσω,   ἐὰν πεσὼν   προσκυνήσῃς μοι.
>   these to you all   I will give if   falling down *you worship*   me
>   ESV: All these I will give you, if you will fall down and *worship* me.

The writer may also be thinking not so much of a specific event but rather is stating a *general truth*.

> John 11:9   ἐάν τις   περιπατῇ ἐν τῇ ἡμέρᾳ,   οὐ   προσκόπτει.
>   if   anyone   *he walks* in   the day   not   he stumbles
>   ESV: If anyone *walks* in the day, he does not stumble.

How would you deal with these different categories in a Bible study?

3. In Greek there are different ways to state a *prohibition*, to tell someone not to do something. One way is to use μή and the subjunctive.

> Matt 1:20   μὴ   φοβηθῇς   παραλαβεῖν Μαρίαν τὴν γυναῖκά σου
>   *not you be afraid* to take   Mary   the woman   your
>   NIV: *Do not be afraid* to take Mary home as your wife.

If the writer uses οὐ μή and the aorist subjunctive, the prohibition is exceptionally strong. Often the translator will add a word like "never" to make the prohibition more emphatic.

> *Matt 24:35*   οἱ λόγοι   μου   οὐ   μὴ   παρέλθωσιν
>   the words   my   not   not   *they will pass away*
>   NIV: My words *will never pass away.*
>   NRSV: My words *will not pass away.*

"Never" is really an over-translation, because the construction is only an emphatic negation; it is not a statement about "forever." But English does not have a construction equal to the strength of this strong negation, so perhaps this is as close as we can get to the Greek.

4. A subjunctive in the first person (singular or plural) can be used as an exhortation (*hortatory*). The translator will usually have added words such as "let us."

> *Mark 4:35*   Διέλθωμεν   εἰς τὸ πέραν
>   *let us go across*   to   the other side
>   ESV: *Let us go across* to the other side.

5. When a person asks a question and expects the audience to think about the answer, the verb in the question is put in the subjunctive (*deliberative*).

> *Matt 6:31*   τί   φάγωμεν; ἤ· τί   πίωμεν; ἤ· τί   περιβαλώμεθα;
>   what *we eat*   or   what *we drink*   or what *we wear*
>   "What *should we eat?"*or "What *should we drink?"* or "What *should we wear?"*
>   ESV: "What *shall we eat?"* or "What *shall we drink?"* or "What *shall we wear?"*

6. When the word ἄν (by itself or in combination with another word) makes a statement more general, the verb will be in the subjunctive.

> *Mark 3:29*   ὃ ἂν   βλασφημήσῃ   εἰς   τὸ πνεῦμα τὸ ἅγιον,
>   *whoever* he blasphemes   against   the spirit   the holy
>   οὐκ ἔχει   ἄφεσιν   εἰς τὸν αἰῶνα
>   not he has   forgiveness forever
>   NET: *Whoever* blasphemes against the Holy Spirit will never be forgiven.

Advanced Information

There is another mood called the **optative**. If the subjunctive describes an action one step removed from reality (uncertain but possible), the optative describes an action two steps removed. It is sometimes called the mood of "wish."

Since the days of Classical Greek, the optative has been falling out of use. There are only 68 uses of the optative in the New Testament, and 15 are the expression μὴ γένοιτο (e.g., Rom 6:2), "may it not be," sometimes translated idiomatically as, "God forbid." "May it not even be a wish, much less a possibility." Beware of any pastor or lay teacher placing too much weight on the optative; its nuanced meaning is often difficult to pin down.

CHAPTER 22

Infinitive

English

An infinitive is a verbal noun, much like the participle is a verbal adjective. It is most easily recognized as a verb preceded by the word "to." "To study is my highest aspiration." In this case, the infinitive "to study" is the subject of the sentence. "I began to sweat when I realized finals were three weeks away." In this sentence, the infinitive "to sweat" is completing the action of the verb "began."

Greek

The same is true of the infinitive in Greek, although here it is capable of somewhat wider use. The infinitive is always indeclinable (which means it has no case—we will finalize our discussion of "case" next week). When it is preceded by a definite article, the article is always neuter singular and is declined according to the function of the infinitive. For example, if the infinitive is the subject, the article will be in the nominative case.

An infinitive can have a direct object and adverbial modifiers. "To study for a long time brings one into a state of ecstasy." In this silly illustration, the prepositional phrase "for a long time" modifies the infinitive "to study." An infinitive also has tense and voice, but this will be discussed below.

The infinitive has no person and no number!

Subject. Because an infinitive is not a finite verbal form (which have subjects), it technically cannot have a subject. However, there is often a noun in the accusative case that acts as if it were the subject of the infinitive.

Heb 5:12	χρείαν	ἔχετε	τοῦ	διδάσκειν	ὑμᾶς	τινά
	need	you have	the	*to teach*	you	*someone*

NIV: You need *someone to teach* you.

Aspect. As is the case with the participle and subjunctive, the infinitive has no time significance whatsoever. The only difference between the infinitive built on the present stem and that built on the aorist stem is one of aspect. The infinitive built on the present stem indicates a continuous action; the infinitive built on the aorist stem indicates an undefined action; the infinitive built on the perfect stem indicates a completed action with ongoing implications.

Due to the limitations of English, it is usually impossible to carry this significance across into English. Translators generally use the present punctiliar form of the verb (e.g., "to see," "to eat").

Adverbial Uses of the Infinitive

1. A finite verb's meaning may be incomplete apart from some additional information. An infinitive is often used to complete that meaning (*complementary*).

Acts 2:4	ἤρξαντο	λαλεῖν	ἑτέραις	γλώσσαις
	they began	*to speak*	other	tongues

NIV: They began *to speak* in other tongues.

2. **Articular infinitive and preposition**. When the infinitive is preceded by a preposition and the article, there are specific rules of translation. This is the most difficult use of the infinitive and the most idiomatic. Any attempt to translate word for word must be abandoned because we have no construction like it in English. The translator must see what the phrase means in Greek and then say the same thing in English.

Below we have listed the preposition and have italicized the word in the translation that translates the preposition. All of the pronouns below that act as the subject of the infinitive are accusative.

μετά indicating *antecedent time* (i.e., the infinitive happened *before* the main verb)

μετὰ τὸ βλέψαι τὸν Ἰησοῦν τοὺς ἁμαρτωλούς, ἔκλαυσεν.
After Jesus saw the sinners, he wept.

ἐν indicating *contemporaneous time*

ὁ κύριος κρινεῖ ἡμᾶς ἐν τῷ ἔρχεσθαι αὐτὸν πάλιν.
The Lord will judge us *when he comes* again.

πρό indicating *prior time* (i.e., the infinitive happened *after* the main verb)

> ὁ ᾽Ιησοῦς ἠγάπησεν ἡμᾶς *πρὸ τοῦ γνῶναι* ἡμᾶς αὐτόν.
> Jesus loved us *before we knew* him.

διά indicating *reason* or *cause*

> ὁ ᾽Ιησοῦς χαρήσεται *διὰ τὸ βλέπειν* αὐτὸν ὅτι ἀγαπῶμεν αὐτόν.
> Jesus will rejoice *because he sees* that we love him.

εἰς indicating *purpose*

> καθίζω ἐν τῷ ναῷ *εἰς τὸ ἀκούειν* με τὸν λόγον τοῦ θεοῦ.
> I sit in the temple *in order that I might hear* the word of God.

πρός indicating *purpose*

> κηρύσσομεν τὸν εὐαγγέλιον *πρὸς τὸ βλέψαι* ὑμᾶς τὴν ἀλήθειαν.
> We proclaim the gospel *so that you may see* the truth.

You can imagine how awkward it is to lay out this construction in an interlinear. *IRU* does it this way:

Before	certain	men	came		from	James,	he	used	to
πρὸ	τινας	←	⌐τοῦ	ἐλθεῖν⌐	ἀπὸ	᾽Ιακώβου	→	→	→
p.g	r.apm		d.gsn	f.aa	p.g	n.gsm			
4574	5516		3836	2262	608	2610			

3. Another function of the infinitive is to express purpose, "in order that" (*purpose*).

a. Purpose can be expressed using the articular infinitive preceded by εἰς or πρός (discussed above).

b. The articular infinitive with the article in the genitive case (no preposition) can also express purpose.

> ὁ ᾽Ιησοῦς ἀπέθανον *τοῦ εἶναι* ἡμᾶς σὺν αὐτῷ εἰς τὸν αἰώνιον.
> Jesus died *in order that we may be* with him forever.

c. The infinitive all by itself (without a preposition or the article) can express purpose.

> *Matt 5:17* Μὴ   νομίσητε   ὅτι   ἦλθον καταλῦσαι τὸν νόμον
>   not   do not think that   I came *to abolish* the law
>   NASB: Do not think that I came *to abolish* the law.

Rev 13:7	ἐδόθη	αὐτῷ	ποιῆσαι	πόλεμον
	it was given	to him	*to make*	war

NIV: He was given power *to make* war.

4. A common way of indicating the *result* of some action is to use a clause introduced by ὥστε. In this case ὥστε will not be followed by a finite verb as is the case in English but by an infinitive. Because we do not have a similar use of the infinitive in English, we must translate this infinitive with a finite verb.

Luke 5:7	ἔπλησαν	ἀμφότερα	τὰ πλοῖα	ὥστε	βυθίζεσθαι	αὐτά
	they filled	both	the boats	*so that*	*to sink*	them

NIV: They … filled both boats so full *that* they *began to sink.*
NASB: They … filled both of the boats, *so that* they *began to sink.*

Substantival Uses of the Infinitive

Because the infinitive is a verbal noun, it can perform any function that a substantive can. When used as a substantive, it will usually be preceded by the definite article. This construction can be translated with "to" and the verb, although normally the translators use another way to say it. This is a common construction.

Phil 1:21	ἐμοὶ	τὸ	ζῆν	Χριστὸς	καὶ	τὸ	ἀποθανεῖν	κέρδος.
	to me	*the*	*to live*	Christ	and	*the*	*to die*	gain

NASB: For to me, *to live* is Christ and *to die* is gain.

Mark 12:33	τὸ	ἀγαπᾶν	τὸν πλησίον	ὡς	ἑαυτὸν	περισσότερόν	ἐστιν …
	the	*to love*	the neighbor	as	yourself	more	it is

ESV: *to love* one's neighbor as oneself is much more …

For the Curious

*πιστευ is the verbal root meaning "to believe."

present active	πιστεύειν	*to believe*
present passive	πιστεύεσθαι	*to be believed*
aorist active	πιστεῦσαι	*to believe*
aorist passive	πιστευθῆναι	*to be believed*
perfect active	πεπιστευκέναι	*to have believed*
perfect passive	πεπιστεῦσθαι	*to have been believed*

CHAPTER 23

Imperative

English

The verb is in the imperative mood when it is making a command. In English, it is the second person form of the indicative, sometimes with an exclamation mark as the sentence's punctuation. "Study!" The understood subject of this sentence is "You" (singular).

The English imperative is usually not inflected, but we do add words to strengthen or further define the intent of the imperative. "Go quickly!"

Greek

The imperative is basically the same in Greek as it is in English. It is the mood of command. However, as is the case with participles and infinitives, the imperative has a greater range of meaning in Greek. It has second and third person, and its aspect is significant. However, it does not indicate time.

Person. In English all imperatives are second person; in Greek there are second and third person imperatives. Because there is no English equivalent to a third person imperative, the translation must be a little idiomatic. βλέπε (second person singular) means "(You) look!" βλεπέτω (third person singular) means "Let him look!" or "He must look!" The words "let" or "must," and a pronoun supplied from the person of the verb ("him"), can be added to convey the correct meaning.

Aspect. The imperative built on the present tense stem is called the "present imperative" and indicates a continuous action. The imperative built on the aorist tense stem is called the "aorist imperative" and indicates an undefined action. There is no time significance with the imperative.

Sometimes, to get the significance of the aspect into English, the translator may use the key word "continually" in the translation of the present imperative, although this is somewhat stilted English: "continually eat."

Uses of the Imperative

1. The imperative mood is used when a verb expresses a command (*command*).

Mark 2:14   ἀκολούθει   μοι
            you follow   me
            NASB: *Follow* me!

Mark 6:37   δότε   αὐτοῖς   ὑμεῖς   φαγεῖν
            you give   to them   you   to eat
            NET: *You give* them something to eat.

2. The imperative may also forbid an action (*prohibition*).

Matt 6:3   μὴ   γνώτω   ἡ ἀριστερά σου   τί   ποιεῖ   ἡ δεξιά   σου
          not   *you let know*   the left   your   what   it does   the right   your
          ESV: *Do* not *let* your left hand *know* what your right hand is doing.

3. The imperative may also express a request, as is appropriate when addressing a superior such as God (*entreaty*).

Luke 11:1   κύριε,   δίδαξον   ἡμᾶς   προσεύχεσθαι
          Lord   *you teach*   us   to pray
          ESV: Lord, *teach* us to pray.

Matt 6:10   ἐλθέτω   ἡ βασιλεία   σου·   γενηθήτω   τὸ θέλημά   σου
          you let come   the kingdom   your   *you let be*   the will   your
          NASB and most: Your kingdom *come*, your will *be done*.
          NET: *May* your kingdom *come, may* your will *be done*.
          NLT: *May* your Kingdom *come* soon. *May* your will *be done*.

Matt 6:10 gives what I think is an unfortunate example of compromised translation. I would guess that virually no one who prays the Lord's Prayer with the traditional "Your kingdom come" knows that they are using an imperative to call on God to send his kingdom. The NET and NLT bravely make an attempt to convey the clear meaning of the Greek, placing clarity of translation above tradition.

Exercises for Chapters 20-23

Identify the grammatical category of each bolded verb below and explain the different translations.

Matt 1:19 NASB. And Joseph her husband, **being** a righteous man and not wanting to disgrace her, planned to send her away secretly. NIV. Because Joseph her husband was a righteous man and did not want to expose her to public disgrace, he had in mind to divorce her quietly.

Luke 1:45 Where does the "she" come from? NIV. Blessed is **she who has believed** that what the Lord has said to her will be accomplished!

Luke 8:47 NASB. **When** the woman saw that she had not escaped notice, she came trembling and fell down before Him. NIV. Then the woman, seeing that she could not go unnoticed, came trembling and fell at his feet.

Rom 1:21 NLT. **Yes**, they knew God, but they wouldn't worship him as God or even give him thanks. NIV. For although they knew God, they neither glorified him as God nor gave thanks to him.

Gal 6:9 Where does the "if" come from? NIV. Let us not become weary in doing good, for at the proper time we will reap a harvest **if** we do not give up.

Eph 1:19 NLT. **I pray that** you will begin to understand the incredible greatness of his power for us who believe him. NIV. and his incomparably great power for us who believe

Eph 2:15 NIV. **by** abolishing in his flesh the law with its commandments and regulations. NRSV. He has abolished the law with its commandments and ordinances.

Eph 5:20-21 Use a traditional interlinear, look at the verbal forms, punctuation, and especially the use of a new paragraph and English headings, and then paraphrase Ephesians 5:20-22, emphasizing the flow of thought.

Phil 2:6 NIV. Who, **being** in very nature God, did not consider equality with God something to be grasped. NASB. who, although He existed in the form of God, did not regard equality with God a thing to be grasped

1 Peter 5:7 How does "casting" relate to 1 Peter 5:6? NIV. **Cast** all your anxiety on him because he cares for you. ESV. casting all your anxieties on him, because he cares for you.

Advanced Information

Sometimes the indicative and imperative are identical in form. In John 14:1 Jesus says,

πιστεύετε	εἰς	τὸν θεὸν	καὶ	εἰς	ἐμὲ	πιστεύετε.
you believe	in	the God	and	in	me	you believe

πιστεύετε can be either indicative or imperative. The translator will have made a decision, but you can see how this passage is difficult to exegete, especially when you add in that the indicative is used for statements and questions. There are several possibilities.

> Do you believe in God? Believe in me!
> Believe in God! Believe in me!

For many years it was believed that a prohibition (an imperative with a negation) using the present tense was a prohibition to stop something currently in progress. A prohibition using the aorist was a prohibition to not even start an action. Although you will find this distinction throughout the commentaries, grammarians today are for the most part agreed that this distinction is invalid. I comment in *BBG* (p. 310):

> This has tremendously important ramifications for exegesis. For example, Paul tells Timothy to have nothing to do with silly myths, using a present imperative (παραιτοῦ; 1 Tim 4:7). If the present imperative commands cessation from an action currently under way, this means Timothy was participating in the myths. This creates a picture of Timothy that is irreconcilable with his mission at Ephesus and what we know of him elsewhere. But if a present imperative does not carry this meaning, then Paul is stating a command regarding a "general precept" that is continuous in nature–continually stay away from the myths–and is saying nothing about Timothy's current involvement, or noninvolvement, in the Ephesian myths.

If someone wants the technical discussion, they can read it in *Verbal Aspect in New Testament Greek* by Buist Fanning (Oxford, pp. 325-388).

For the Curious

	present	*aorist*	*translation*
2 sg	λῦε	λῦσον	(You) Loose!
3 sg	λυέτω	λυσάτω	Let him loose!
2 pl	λύετε	λύσατε	(You) loose!
3 pl	λυέτωσαν	λυσάτωσαν	Let them loose!

CHAPTER 24

What Are Word Studies?

Words have a "semantic range." "Semantic" refers to a word's meaning; "semantic range" refers to the range of possible meanings a word possesses. Think of all the ways we use the word "run."

> I scored six runs today.
> Could you run that by me again?
> My computer runs faster than yours!
> He runs off at the mouth.
> I left the water running all night.
> He ran to the store.
> The car ran out of gas.
> The clock ran down.
> Duane ran for senate.
> Her nose ran.
> I ran up the bill.

In describing this concept to students I preferred the phrase "bundle of meanings." A word usually does not possess just one meaning; a word has different meanings, hence "bundle."

This is true in any language. For example, the semantic range of the preposition ἐν is quite large. Just look at how it is used in the following verses. (All translations are from the RSV.)

Matt 1:20   τὸ   γὰρ ἐν αὐτῇ γεννηθὲν ἐκ πνεύματός ἐστιν ἁγίου.
             the   for *in* her   conceived of spirit   is   holy
             for that which is conceived *in* her is of the Holy Spirit

Matt 2:1   Τοῦ ... Ἰησοῦ γεννηθέντος ἐν Βηθλέεμ ... ἐν ἡμέραις Ἡρῴδου
             the   Jesus was born   *in* Bethlehem *in* days   of Herod
             Jesus was born *in* Bethlehem ... *in* the days of Herod.

Matt 3:9   καὶ   μὴ   δόξητε   λέγειν   ἐν   ἑαυτοῖς
and   not   presume   to say   *in*   yourselves
and do not presume to say *to* yourselves

Matt 3:11   Ἐγὼ ... ὑμᾶς   βαπτίζω   ἐν   ὕδατι
I   you   baptize   *in*   water
I baptize you *with* water.

Matt 4:23   θεραπεύων πᾶσαν νόσον καὶ πᾶσαν μαλακίαν ἐν τῷ λαῷ.
healing   every   disease and every   infirmity   *in* the people
healing every disease and every infirmity *among* the people

Matt 5:34   μὴ ὀμόσαι ὅλως· μήτε ἐν τῷ οὐρανῷ, ὅτι θρόνος ἐστὶν τοῦ θεοῦ
not swear   at all   either *in* the heaven   for throne   it is   of the God
Do not swear at all, either *by* heaven, for it is the throne of God.

When we first looked at the nature of language and translations (chapter 4), we learned that languages are not codes. There is not a one–to–one correspondence between languages, and this applies especially to vocabulary. Rarely if ever can you find one word in one language that corresponds exactly to another word in another language, especially in its semantic range. English has no single word that matches the range of meanings for ἐν. The semantic domains of a Greek and English word may overlap, but they are not identical.

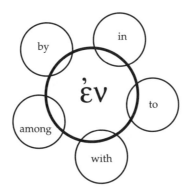

So how do we translate the Bible when we do not have English words that correspond exactly to the Greek? We have to interpret. All translation is interpretive. Translators are Traitors. For example, in 1 Timothy 6:13-14 Paul writes,

> In the presence of God who gives life to all things, and of Christ Jesus who in his testimony before Pontius Pilate made the good confession, I *charge* you to keep the commandment unstained and free from reproach until the appearing of our Lord Jesus Christ. (RSV)

The Greek word behind "charge" is παραγγέλλω, which means "to command, insist, instruct, urge." Quite a wide range of meanings for which there is no single counterpart in English. The translator must decide whether Paul is "commanding" Timothy (who is a member of his inner circle, fully trusted, and probably his best friend) or "urging" him. This is an interpretive decision that must be made by the translator. The RSV chose "charge,"the NLT "command," and the NKJV rightly (in my opinion) selected "urge."

But let's say that you want to know what Paul means when he "charges" Timothy to keep the commandment unstained. It doesn't do any good to look up the English word "charge," because "charge" can't mean "urge" (and "urge" can't mean " charge"). If you really want to decide for yourself what Paul is saying, if you want to know why the translations are different, you have to know the Greek word behind the English, learn its semantic range, and see the decision faced by the translators.

How do you do this? There are four steps. 1. Decide what word to study. 2. Identify the Greek word. 3. Discover its semantic range. 4. Look for something in the context that helps determine what the biblical author meant by this word in this particular verse.

Step 1. Choose the English Word

I annoyed many people for many years asking what I think is an extremely important question: "What is the minimum it takes to become a Christian?" You are at the dorm in college and a freshman walks up to you and says, "You're a graduate student in divinity, aren't you?" ("Divinity" is the word they use in Scotland for Biblical Studies.) You say, "Yes." She says, "What is a Christian anyway?" Go! You have two minutes to tell her. What are you going to say? You want to tell her enough of the gospel, so that if she responds she will truly have become a Christian. If you don't tell her enough and she responds, will she really have become a Christian? If you add to the basic gospel message, will it drive her away unnecessarily?

Sound hypothetical? No, it happened to me, and I didn't have an answer. I promised myself that would never happen again, so I started searching out all the short and succinct statements about becoming a Christian, because I wanted to have a two-minute answer the next time I was asked that question.

Romans 10:9-10 is one of the succinct and most crucial passages on the nature of salvation.

> If you confess with your mouth that Jesus is Lord and believe in your
> heart that God raised him from the dead, you will be saved. For with the

> heart one believes and is justified, and with the mouth one confesses and
> is saved.

The key term in the entire passage is what? It's "Lord," isn't it. The essence of salvation is the confession, "Jesus is Lord," accompanied with the acceptance of the resurrection. So what does "Lord" mean? Its meaning is crucial to the salvation of people.

This is actually the first step in doing a Greek word study: you've decided on a significant word. If you try to do word studies on every word you read, not only will you run out of time, but you'll get bored. So how do you pick the right words? There is not a clear-cut answer to this question, but here are some suggestions.

- Look for *repeated* words. This normally indicates a recurring theme, and perhaps the central theme in the passage. This includes the use of synonyms.

- Look for *theological* terms. This will be more obvious in teaching passages (e.g., in Paul) than in narrative (e.g., in the Gospels).

- Sometimes a verse will "hang" on a word. It is a word that is central to the meaning of the verse, and without it the sentence will not make sense. In Romans 10:9 it is "Lord."

- As you compare translations, you may find a significant word that is translated *differently* among the different translations.

What do you think "Lord" means? Let's find out.

2. Identify the Greek Word

Your next step is to find the Greek word behind the English. We have already talked about this in chapter 19. You can use your software program or an exhaustive concordance. You can also look up Romans 10:9 in *EGNT*.

9	That	if	you	confess		with	your	mouth,		"Jesus is
	ὅτι	ἐὰν	→	ὁμολογήσῃς		ἐν	σου	⸤τῷ στόματι⸥		Ἰησοῦν
	cj	cj		v.aas.2s		p.d	r.gs.2	d.dsn n.dsn		n.asm
	4022	1569		3933		1877	5148	3836 5125		2652

Lord,"	and	believe	in	your	heart		that	God		raised	him
κύριον	καὶ	πιστεύσῃς	ἐν	σου	⸤τῇ καρδίᾳ⸥		ὅτι	⸤ὁ	θεὸς⸥	ἤγειρεν	αὐτὸν
n.asm	cj	v.aas.2s	p.d	r.gs.2	d.dsf n.dsf		cj	d.nsm	n.nsm	v.aai.3s	r.asm.3
3261	2779	4409	1877 5148		3836 2840		4022	3836	2536	1586	899

The inflected form is κύριον, it is a noun, and its GK number is *#3261*. The conversion chart at the back of *IRU* tells you its Strong's number is *#2962*.

If your word study book does not use one of the two numbering systems, you will need to find the word's lexical form. If you have the *NIV Exhaustive Concordance*, look up word #3261 in the *Greek to English Lexicon* in the back. You will see that the lexical form is κύριος, transliterated *kyrios*. If you have the right software program, you can call up the verse, move your mouse over the appropriate word, and see the lexical form.

(If you want to do a word study and you are not thinking of any one particular verse, you can still find one verse that uses the word and follow this process.)

If you use the KJV, there are several alternatives. The exhaustive concordance by Strong lists the word's number just like the *NIV Exhaustive*. If you use Young's *Analytical Concordance*, he groups verses by the Greek/Hebrew original.

Step 3. Discover its Semantic Range

Before you can discover what the word means in a particular context, you have to learn its range of meaning, its "semantic range." As I have been saying, we are looking for the semantic range of the Greek, not the English, since they are almost always (if not always) different. So we are going to learn the semantic range of the Greek word κύριος.

(a) You already have a hint as to the word's semantic range, if you are using the *NIV Exhaustive Concordance*. When you look up the word in the *Greek to English Lexicon* in the back of the concordance, it shows you all the ways in which the NIV has translated the Greek word (see to the right). Quite a wide range of meanings, isn't it? "Sir" to "master" to the idea of "majesty."

(b) If you are using *The Strongest Strong's*, you can look the word up in its *Greek Dictionary-Index*. Here you learn even more, most importantly that κύριος is the name of God in the Old Testament. (sample to the right).

(c) You could also check other translations to see how they translate the term. For our case, they all use "Lord." But if we were looking up another word, you might see more variety. For example, the RSV translates 1 Corinthians 7:1 as, "It is well for a man not to *touch* a woman." (The Greek word behind "touch" is ἅπτω, #721.) But the NIV translates, "It is good for a man not to *marry*," and the NLT writes, "Yes, it is good to *live a celibate life*." Right there you can see the range of the word's meaning. If you use different translations to discover the word's semantic range, be sure to chose different types of translations, both formal and dynamic.

(d) Let me introduce you to another marvelous tool. It used to be called an "Englishman's Concordance." The new one by John Kohlenberger is titled, *The Greek-English Concordance to the New Testament*, and especially if you read the NIV, this is the one to use. With this text you look

3261   κύριος *kyrios* (720)
    Lord (600)
    master (35)
    Lord's (32)
    sir (23)
    master's (6)
    masters (6)
    owner (6)
    lords (3)
    owners (3)
    belong to Lord (1) + *1639*
    he (1) + *3836*
    his majesty (1)
    masters' (1)
    owns (1) + *1639*
    sirs (1)

NIV Exhaustive Concordance

2962 κύριος, *kyrios*, n. GK: *3261* [→ *2634, 2959, 2960, 2961, 2963; cf. 2964*]. lord, master. This can be a title of address to a person of higher status, "lord, sir"; a master of property or slaves; or a NT translation of the Hebrew 151 "Lord" or 3378 "LORD," that is "Yahweh," the proper name of God in the OT:—Lord/lord [703], Lord's/lord's [15], sir [11], masters [8], master [4], lords[3], God [1], masters' [1], owners [1], sirs [1]

The Strongest Strong's

up a Greek word based on its lexical form (or GK number), and you can see every place the Greek word occurs in the New Testament, *but the verses are listed in English* (sample on the next page).

There is a considerable difference between this type of concordance and others. In a regular concordance, if you look up "Lord," the entries list all the places where the English word "Lord" occurs. However, there may be several different Greek words that are translated "Lord," and κύριος may not always be translated with "Lord"; these are the limitations of a regular concordance. For example, σάρξ is translated in Galatians by the NIV as "body" (1 time), "flesh" (1), "human effort" (1), "illness" (2), "man" (1), "no one" (1), "ordinary way" (2), "outwardly" (1), "sinful

Mt	1: 20	an angel *of* the **Lord** appeared to him in a dream and said,
	1: 22	All this took place to fulfill what the **Lord** had said through the
	1: 24	he did what the angel *of* the **Lord** had commanded him and took
	2: 13	they had gone, an angel *of* the **Lord** appeared to Joseph in a dream.
	2: 15	so was fulfilled what the **Lord** had said through the prophet:
	2: 19	an angel *of* the **Lord** appeared in a dream to Joseph in Egypt
	3: 3	'Prepare the way *for* the **Lord**, make straight paths for him.' "
	4: 7	"t is also written: 'Do not put the **Lord** your God to the test.' "
	4: 10	it is written: 'Worship the **Lord** your God, and serve him only.' "
	5: 33	break your oath, but keep the oaths you have made *to* the **Lord**.'
	6: 24	"No one can serve two **masters**. Either he will hate the one
	7: 21	"Not everyone who says to me, '**Lord**, Lord,' will enter the
	7: 21	"Not everyone who says to me, 'Lord, **Lord**,' will enter the
	7: 22	Many will say to me on that day, '**Lord**, Lord, did we not prophesy
	7: 22	Many will say to me on that day, 'Lord, **Lord**, did we not prophesy
	8: 2	A man with leprosy came and knelt before him and said, "**Lord**,
	8: 6	"**Lord**," he said, "my servant lies at home paralyzed and in terrible
	8: 8	The centurion replied, "**Lord**, I do not deserve to have you come
	8: 21	disciple said to him, "**Lord**, first let me go and bury my father."
	8: 25	The disciples went and woke him, saying, "**Lord**, save us!
	9: 28	you believe that I am able to do this?" "Yes, **Lord**," they replied.
	9: 38	Ask the **Lord** of the harvest, therefore, to send out workers into his

. . . . .

	18: 25	the **master** ordered that he and his wife and his children and all
	18: 27	The servant's **master** took pity on him, canceled the debt
	18: 31	and went and told their **master** everything that had happened.
	18: 32	"Then the **master** called the servant in. 'You wicked servant,'
	18: 34	In anger his **master** turned him over to the jailers to be tortured,
	20: 8	the **owner** of the vineyard said to his foreman, 'Call the workers
	20: 30	going by, they shouted, "**Lord**, Son of David, have mercy on us!"
	20: 31	shouted all the louder, "**Lord**, Son of David, have mercy on us!"
	20: 33	"**Lord**," they answered, "we want our sight."
	21: 3	If anyone says anything to you, tell him that the **Lord** needs them,
	21: 9	"Blessed is he who comes in the name *of* the **Lord**!" "Hosanna in
	21: 30	to the other son and said the same thing. He answered, 'I will, **sir**,'
	21: 40	"Therefore, when the **owner** of the vineyard comes, what will he do
	21: 42	the **Lord** has done this, and it is marvelous in our eyes'?
	22: 37	" 'Love the **Lord** your God with all your heart and with all your
	22: 43	then that David, speaking by the Spirit, calls him '**Lord**'?
	22: 44	" 'The **Lord** said to my Lord: "Sit at my right hand until I put your
	22: 44	" 'The Lord said *to* my **Lord**: "Sit at my right hand until I put your
	22: 45	If then David calls him '**Lord**,' how can he be his son?"
	23: 39	until you say, 'Blessed is he who comes in the name *of* the **Lord**.' "
	24: 42	because you do not know on what day your **Lord** will come.
	24: 45	whom the **master** has put in charge of the servants in his
	24: 46	It will be good for that servant whose **master** finds him doing

The Greek-English Concordance to the New Testament

nature" (7), and "that nature" (1). (In some of these occurrences, σάρξ was combined with another word when translating.)

But with an "Englishman's" concordance, you know you are looking at every place the same Greek word occurs, regardless of how it is translated; in contrast to a Greek concordance, the entries are in English and not Greek. As you scan through the entries, you can see how the NIV has translated κύριος.

(e) If you want to learn more about the semantic range, you can always go to a Greek lexicon. The standard one is *A Greek-English Lexicon of the New Testament and Other Early Christian Literature*, third edition edited by Frederick Danker (University of Chicago Press). The entries are listed alphabetically (based on Greek, of course), and on pp. 576-579 you will find the following basic entries for κύριος.

---

1. one who is in charge by virtue of possession, *owner*
2. one who is in a position of authority, *lord, master*
   a. of earthly beings, as a designation of any pers. of high position
   b. of transcendent beings
      α. as a designation of God
      β. Closely connected w. the custom of applying the term κ. to deities is that of honoring (deified) rulers with the same title
      γ. κύριος is also used in ref. to Jesus:
         א in OT quotations, where it is understood of the Lord of the new community
         ב Apart from OT quots., Mt and Mk speak of Jesus as κύριος only in one pass.... but they record that he was addressed as 'Lord' (κύριε), once in Mk (7:28) and more oft. in Mt .... Lk refers to Jesus much more frequently as ὁ κ.
         ג Even in the passages already mentioned the use of the word κ. raises Jesus above the human level
      δ. In some places it is not clear whether God or Christ is meant
      ε. of other transcendent beings

A two-volume set that is more affordable and supplements Danker's work is The *Greek-English Lexicon of the New Testament Based on Semantic Domains* by Louw and Nida (United Bible Society). Look up your word in their index first; the words are not listed alphabetically but by their basic meanings.

There are some older Greek lexicons that, in their day, were helpful and often groundbreaking, but because of their age you should not use them now. *The Vocabulary of the Greek New Testament*, by Moulton & Milligan (Eerdmans). *Biblico-Theological Lexicon of New Testament Greek*, by

Cremer (T. & T. Clark). *A Greek-English Lexicon of the New Testament*, by Thayer (Harper).

(f) There are specific books that help you see the semantic range of a word and, to a greater or lesser degree, will tell you more about the word, especially its usage throughout the Bible and other ancient writings. But be careful when using these books. Up to this point you have been reading and studying the Bible and learning for yourself what the word means. It is a lot more fun and much more rewarding to discover this information by yourself. The minute you turn to one of these books, much of the fun of self-exploration is gone; but more importantly, realize that you are reading a person's opinion about the word. The word study books, while good, are not inspired like Scripture.

My favorite one-volume word study book is Verlyn D. Verbrugge's *New International Dictionary of New Testament Theology: Abridged Edition*. It lists words alphabetically and by their GK number, and the discussion is excellent. I've included his article on κύριος at the end of this chapter. Verbrugge's work is an abridgment of the three-volume set, *New International Dictionary of New Testament Theology*, edited by Colin Brown. This too is an excellent discussion of the words in the New Testament that often moves, as the name implies, into the word's theological significance; however, it is generally too advanced for most people at the "baby Greek" level. Zondervan published a fourth volume that contains all the indexes. Be sure to find the word here first; the indexes in the individual volumes are indexed just to that single volume and not to the set. Also, words are often listed with similar words, so it can be hard to find a word if you try to look it up alphabetically.

Geoffrey W. Bromiley's one volume *Theological Dictionary of the New Testament: Abridged in One Volume* is, as the name says, an abridgment of the multi-volume *Theological Dictionary of the New Testament*, edited by Kittel and Friedrich. We affectionately call Bromiley's abridgment *Little Kittel* or *Kittelbits*. Whatever its name, Dr. Bromiley did a masterful job of cutting out discussion that is mostly irrelevant for you at the "baby Greek" level. It lists words alphabetically based on their transliteration. But be sure to use the index; it doesn't discuss every Greek word, and you could spend a long time looking for an entry that isn't included. The full multi-volume series of *TDNT*, while it looks good on your shelf, is of little value for you at your stage.

Vine's Expository Dictionary of Biblical Words has been widely used since its publication in 1939. But there have been many advances in our understanding of Greek words since then, and I know of no Greek teacher who will recommend this work. A much better work is (pardon my bias again) *Mounce's Complete Expository Dictionary of Old and New Testament Words*.

(g) You could look up your passage in a good commentary, and it might discuss the word's meaning. In chapter 29 I will show you which commentary series are more likely to cover word studies.

(h) If the word is an important theological term, it may be discussed in reference works like the *Evangelical Dictionary of Theology,* edited by Walter A. Elwell (Baker). This is a marvelous book, and everyone ought to have a copy of it for their study. (I don't say that very often.)

4. Context

It's time to make a decision. Once you have located the Greek word and learned its semantic range, it is time to decide what it means in the particular verse you are studying. The question is, how do you decide?

In short, the answer is "context." You look for something in the immediate context that gives a clue as to the precise meaning of the word. I like to think in terms of a series of concentric circles. The word in the verse is the smallest circle. The next circle out is the verse, then the paragraph, the book, etc. The point is that you look for something in the verse that will define the word. If there isn't anything, then look at the paragraph. If there is nothing to help you in the paragraph, go to the book as a whole. But you want to stop as soon as you can. The further you go out from the center, the less assuredness you have that you are defining the word properly. But if you have to keep going out from the center, then you have to.

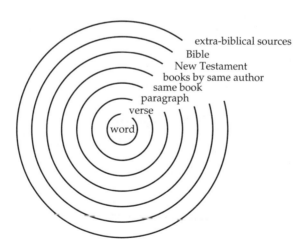

Why do you want to stop as soon as possible? Because different people can use the same word differently. Even the same person can use the same word differently in different contexts, as our previous example of σάρξ in Paul shows. Paul and James use "justify" in significantly different

ways, even though they both
mention Abraham and the same
verse in Habakkuk (discussed
later).

I saw this sign the other day:
"GO CHILDREN SLOW." One of
the sillier signs I have ever seen,
it seemed to me. What does it
mean? Does it mean, "Go, the
children are slow," or, "Go children, but slowly," or, "Go slow,
there are children." Obviously, it
is the latter, but why is it obvious? Because we understand the
sign within its *context* of being a

road sign, and we probably notice that we are driving through a neighbor-
hood full of children. And yet, in order to get to this understanding, we
had to alter the word order and recognize that there is a grammatical error
in the sign ("slow" should be "slowly" since it is an adverb).

Another good one is, "Speed radar controlled." Silly sign #2. The
radar doesn't control my speed. My foot does. (Of course, it could be
argued that the threat of a ticket proven by a radar gun is the ultimate
cause of my speed.) How about these signs? "Stop." Shouldn't it be "Stop
and then go"? "No parking here," when the sign is not in the parking lot

but on the curb. And my other favorites from New
England: "Lightly salted"; "Blind drive"; "Thickly
settled."

The point is that common sense tells us these
signs are to be understood within their context.
The same is true for word studies. How does the
context help us decided what a word means? Let's
look at some examples as we move out from the
center of the concentric circles.

Verse. 1 Thess 4:3. "For this is the *will* of God,
your sanctification." What is God's will for your
life? To be sanctified; to be holy.

Paragraph. 1 Tim 2:14-15. "and Adam was not
deceived, but the woman was deceived and
became a transgressor. Yet woman will be *saved*
through bearing children, if she continues in faith
and love and holiness, with modesty" (RSV). What
does "saved" mean? V 14 suggests we are dealing

with spiritual salvation ("transgression") and not physical safety.

Book. 1 Tim 1:10. At the end of a list of sins, Paul states that these are "contrary to *sound* doctrine." What is "*sound* doctrine"? Most translations miss the fact that the word is a medical metaphor meaning "healthy," and that it contrasts with the heresy being spread in Ephesus, which Paul elsewhere describes as sick and morbid (1 Tim 6:4), infectious abrasions (1 Tim 6:5) spreading like gangrene (2 Tim 2:17). Sound doctrine is that which is opposed to the false teaching.

New Testament. In Romans 4:2-3 (ESV) Paul says,

> For if Abraham was justified by works, he has something to boast about, but not before God. For what does the Scripture say? "Abraham believed God, and it was counted to him as righteousness."

("Justify" and "righteous" are the same concept.) What does "justification" mean? How are we justified? If you look at James 2:21-24 you will see that he says,

> Was not Abraham our father justified by works when he offered up his son Isaac upon the altar? You see that faith was active along with his works, and faith was completed by his works; and the Scripture was fulfilled that says, "Abraham believed God, and it was counted to him as righteousness"—and he was called a friend of God. You see that a person is justified by works and not by faith alone.

As you look at the whole of the New Testament a fuller picture emerges as to the meaning of "justification." Paul is discussing how justification is granted; James is discussing how justification is shown to have occurred. What at first appears to be a contradiction are actually complementary teachings.

Bible. Acts 4:8. "Then Peter, *filled* with the Holy Spirit, said to them, 'Rulers of the people and elders ....'" But I thought Peter was filled at Pentecost (Acts 2:4)? What does "filled" mean in v 8? If you look through Acts you will see this statement of "filling" repeated, always followed by mention of what the person said or did. But if you look at the book of

Judges in the Old Testament, you will see the same metaphor used the same way of the Spirit possessing the person in a powerful but temporary way in order to accomplish a specific task. While the Holy Spirit comes in his fulness at a believer's conversion, Luke uses the terminology of Judges to describe a work of the Holy Spirit in which he grips a person in a special way to enable them to say or do something special.

As you continue out to the outer circles, be careful. Once you get out of the Bible and are looking at how the word is used in secular thought, it becomes more and more likely that the words are going to be used differently. And especially if you are looking at how the word is used 500 years before the writing of the New Testament, you must recognize that words can totally change their meaning over this time span. For example, a century ago, if you were to "skim" a book, this meant you would read it carefully. "To prevent" was "to go before," which obscurs Paul's meaning in the KJV of 1 Thessalonians 4:15.

> For this we say unto you by the word of the Lord, that we which are alive and remain unto the coming of the Lord shall not *prevent* them which are asleep.

The dead in Christ will go *first*.

These extrabiblical references can sometimes give us helpful *illustrations*. For example, Paul tells Timothy not to become "entangled" in civilian affairs (2 Tim 2:4). The verb ἐμπλέκω (#1861) can mean much more than "to be involved" (contra the NIV), and this unfortunate translation has caused unnecessary grief for many pastors who were forced by their churches to have little or no contact with secular society, including a second job. (The blame for this does not lie with the NIV but with the unfortunate and unbiblical notion that a church must keep its pastor poor—but I digress.) ἐμπλέκω means "to be involuntarily interlaced to the point of immobility, be entangled; to become involved in an activity to the point of interference with other activity or objective" (BDAG, 324). The word is used by Hermes (*Similitudes*, 6.2.6-7) of a sheep and by Aesop (74) of hares caught in thorns. These make great illustrations, but it is dangerous to define a biblical word based on them since they are so far removed from the biblical writer.

Frankly, for those pursuing the "baby Greek" approach, it is probably too dangerous (exegetically) and too difficult to look at examples outside of the biblical canon. Extrabiblical texts may introduce problems with which you are not prepared to deal; best left alone at this stage I think.

So let's get back to our word study on "Lord" in Romans 10:9. Is there anything in the immediate context that will help us define the confession "Jesus is Lord" more precisely? The connection between the confession and belief in Jesus' resurrection suggests "Lord" means much more than "sir"; someone raised from the dead is more than a "sir."

As you move out into the paragraph, in v 12 Paul says that Jesus is "Lord of all," asserting his universal lordship. It is especially significant that in v 13 Paul quotes Joel 2:32, because in its Old Testament context Joel is speaking of Yahweh, God. Douglas Moo writes, "In the OT, of course, the one on whom people called for salvation was Yahweh; Paul reflects the high view of Christ common among the early church by identifying this one with Jesus Christ, the Lord" (*The Epistle to the Romans*, Eerdmans, p. 660).

In Romans 1:4 Paul states that Jesus "was declared to be the Son of God in power according to the Spirit of holiness by his resurrection from the dead, Jesus Christ our Lord,"connecting Jesus' Lordship with his resurrection as in 10:9 and with his identification as the Son of God. As we see who Jesus is as Lord, we see that he is also God's Son. As God's Son, the Old Testament references to God can be applicable to Jesus. It is a small step from this to agreeing with Thomas' confession: "My Lord and my God!" (John 20:28).

As you expand further out into the New Testament, we find similar confessions: "at the name of Jesus every knee should bow, in heaven and on earth and under the earth, and every tongue confess that Jesus Christ is Lord, to the glory of God the Father" (Phil 2:10-11; cf. 1 Cor 12:3).

The answer to my question with which I started this word study is much clearer. What is the minimum it takes to get into heaven? You must have a correct understanding of who Jesus is, and that understanding causes you to submit to his lordship. We must believe that Jesus was raised from the dead, that he was raised to a position of lordship over all, and in his lordship we see that he is in fact the Son of God. Christianity is grounded in the historical event of the incarnation, death, and resurrection of Jesus Christ. Who we are as disciples is intimately tied up with who he is as Lord, our Lord and our God.

Septuagint

As you get further into word studies, you will often see writers paying special attention to how a word is used in the Septuagint, often abbreviated LXX. This is the Greek translation of the Hebrew Scriptures that was probably started about 250 B.C. and finished somewhere around the time of Christ. There are certain words that are important in the Old Testament, especially theological words. When the Septuagint was translated, the translators chose a Greek word for each of these Hebrew words. When it comes to defining these Greek words in the New Testament, it is the word's background in the Old Testament via the Septuagint that is the most important background in defining the Greek word, not its general usage in the first century.

For example, how was the LXX to translate the Hebrew word חֶסֶד, which describes God's love for his covenantal people, when there is no such word in Greek? When the LXX translators finally settled on ἔλεος, ἔλεος automatically carried the specific meaning of חֶסֶד into the New Testament.

Given the fact that κύριος is used by the LXX to translate יהוה, "Yahweh," it is hard for me to imagine that the Jewish Paul meant anything less than confessing the deity of Christ in Romans 10:9.

Cognates

A cognate is a word that is related to another and actually shares the same root. In English, the words "prince" and "princess" share the same root, although their specific forms are altered because they are masculine and feminine gender, respectively.

Sometimes cognates have similar meanings. However, at other times there are definite nuance differences between cognates. For this reason it is important not to assume that all cognates have the same meaning, and when doing a word study try to stick to your specific lexical form. But if you can't get a clear meaning, then look at the cognates and see if they are used with the same or with different meanings as the word you are studying.

Common Mistakes

Before ending this discussion of word studies, I must cover common mistakes made in doing word studies. For a more detailed discussion of these issues you can read *Exegetical Fallacies* by D. A. Carson (Baker).

Anachronism

The first is the bad habit of defining a Greek word using an English word derived from that Greek word. My favorite example is when someone talks about the "power" of God, and adds that this word "power" is δύναμις, from which we get our word "dynamite," and then to say God's power is dynamite. This is totally backwards and totally wrong. English wasn't a language until the second millenium A.D. Regardless of where our words came from, the definitions don't work backwards. Supposedly there was a reason that a specific Greek word was used as the basis of an English word, but especially as the years go by that English word can take on a meaning totally different from its Greek origin. God's power is never pictured in Scripture as something that blows rocks apart. Despite the frequency of this mistake, this is not a controversial issue.

Etymological Fallacy

"Etymology" refers to how the word was originally created. What would you say if a pastor or Bible study leader told you that the "butter-fly" is an animal made of butter that can fly? Or perhaps that a pineapple is a type of apple grown on pine trees? After the laughter died down, and if the speaker were serious, you would point out that this is not what the word means. The etymology, the pieces that were originally used to make up the word, does not define the word today, any more than a butterfly is a milk by-product.

The worse example I know of is the Greek word for "repent," μετα-νοέω, which some people define as, "to change your mind," but not necessarily your behavior. They often base their position on the meaning of the two words that were used to create μετανοέω. "Repentance," they say, "involves an intellectual shift in understanding, but repentance does not require a change of action." This type of misuse of Greek etymology runs throughout *Vine's Expository Dictionary of Biblical Words,* and why it should not be recommended. Vine writes, "*meta,* 'after,' implying 'change,' ... *nous,* 'the mind,' ... hence signifies 'to change one's mind or purpose'" (Nelson, 1985, p. 525). Certainly, the word can mean "to regret" (cf. Luke 17:3-4; 2 Cor 7:9-10), but the New Testament's understanding of repentance is not drawn from the etymology of one word but from the biblical *concept* of repentance, especially from the background of conversion in the Old Testament. See the article on *metanoeō* in Bromiley's *Theological Dictionary of the New Testament: Abridged,* where he writes, "the concept of conversion stresses positively the fact that real penitence involves a new relation to God that embraces all spheres of life and claims the will in a way that no external rites can replace.... It means turning aside from everything that is ungodly" (pp. 640, 641).

Is it ever the case that a word carries the meaning of its parts? Sure. εἰσέρχομαι is made up of the preposition εἰς, meaning "into," and ἔρχομαι, meaning "to go." εἰσέρχομαι means "to go into." But it is not the word's etymology that determines its meaning. It is the fact that εἰσέρχομαι means "to go into" that we can see it has retained the meaning of its etymological parts.

It is also true that some prepositions (ἐκ, κατά, ἀπό, διά, σύν) have what is called a "perfective" function. When added to a word they can intensify its meaning. ἐσθίω means "I eat"; κατεσθίω means "I devour." Some perfective forms, however, have lost their intensified meaning, and the compound form has the same basic meaning as the simple word. For example, Paul tells Timothy that the teaching of the opponents in Ephesus produce only "speculations," ἐκζήτησις. It is difficult to determine whether Paul intended the intensified "extreme speculations" (or perhaps "useless speculations"), or just "speculations," which is the meaning of the simple ζήτησις ("investigation, controversy, debate"). As always, context is the guide as to whether or not the intensified meaning is present.

Connected to the etymological fallacy is the fact that words change their meaning over the years. Just think of the lyrics to the old song that ends, "We'll have a gay old time," or the KJV use of "prevent" in 1 Thessalonians 4:15 (cited above). What a word meant when it was first created, or what it meant 1,000 years ago, may be at best irrelevant today. A word's meaning today is seen in how it is used today, not in how it used to be used.

- "Hussy" is from the Middle English word "huswife," meaning "housewife."
- "Enthusiasm" meant to be inspired or possessed by a god.
- "Nice" originally meant "foolish" in Middle English (from the Latin *nescire*, "to be ignorant").
- "Gossip" is from *godsib*, a word that refered to godparents, and came to be used of the type of chatter that stereotypically occurs at christenings (see *God, Language and Scripture* by Moisés Silva, Zondervan). Today, when I preach about gossip, christenings are nowhere in my mind, and its etymology is irrelevant in an attempt to define the Bible's prohibition of slander.

Words have a range of meaning, but that range is not determined by the parts that made up the word or even by how it was used 1,000 years earlier.

A Few Other Errors

Don't put too much weight on a word, thinking that the word, all by itself, is full of meaning. Granted, there are a few technical terms that have a specific meaning in almost any context. But for the most part, we do not communicate with individual words but with phrases, sentences, and paragraphs. Focus your study on the larger unit, hesitating to place too much emphasis on an individual word. (This is connected to the technical concept of semantic "minimalism.")

Tied to this is the fact that theological concepts are larger than a word. Regardless of how many times you have heard the word ἀγάπη defined as the sacrificial love of the unlovely, the kind of love that is bestowed on the undeserving, that simply is not what the word in and of itself means. (I talk more about this on the lecture on this chapter contained on the CD-ROM.) It is not the word that conveys this meaning, but it is the concept of biblical love as illustrated by God that infuses ἀγάπη with this particular meaning in the biblical context.

Exercises

1. Do a word study on λόγος. Work hard to determine the semantic range of the word.

2. In Phil 4:21 Paul refers to the "brothers" who are with him. Do a word study on "brother," and be sure to include cognate forms. Find the range of meaning of the word in Paul, and then decide who is Paul referring to in this passage. Be sure to decide on the gender of this particular group.

3. σάρξ in Galatians.

4. "Grace," "mercy," and "peace."

5. "World" in the gospel of John

6. "Perfect" in 1 Cor 13:9-10.

7. παράκλητος.

8. How the Old Testament affects the meaning of "dwelt" in John 1:14.

9. The secular associations of "triumphing" in Colossians 2:15.

10. "Kiss" (Matt 26:48) and ψυχή (Jude 15) are especially good for working on the semantic range.

New International Dictionary of New Testament Theology: Abridged Edition

by Verlyn D. Verbrugge *(used with permission)*

3261   κύριος

κύριος (*kyrios*), lord, master, owner, Lord (3261); κυρία (*kyria*), lady, mistress (3257); κυριότης (*kyriotēs*), lordship, dominion (3262); κυριεύω (*kyrieuō*), be lord, master, rule (3259); κατακυριεύω (*katakyrieuō*), rule over, conquer, be master of (2894).

CL & OT   1. (a) In cl. Gk. *kyrios* is an adj., having power, authoritative, derived from the noun *to kyros*, power, might. As a subst. *kyrios* meant lord, ruler, one who has control. *kyrios* always contains the idea of legality and authority. Anyone occupying a superior position can be referred to as *kyrios* and be addressed as *kyrie* (fem. *kyria*).

(b) In early Gk. *kyrios* was not used as a divine title. Although the term was applied to the gods, there was no general belief in a personal creator Lord. The gods were not creators and lords of fate but were, like human beings, subject to fate. The Gks. of this period did not feel dependent on a god or personally responsible to the gods. Only insofar as the gods ruled over particular spheres in the world could they be called *kyrioi*.

(c) The situation was different in the East. The gods created humans who were personally answerable to them. They could intervene in human lives to save, punish, or judge. They also established justice and law, which they communicated to human beings, e.g., through the king. Therefore they were called lords.

(d) Instances of the title *kyrios* in Hel. times with reference to gods or rulers do not occur until the 1st cent. B.C. *kyrios basileus*, "lord and king," is found often between 64 and 50 B.C. In 12 B.C. Emperor Augustus was called *theos kai kyrios*, "god and lord," in Egypt. *kyrios* was also used of Herod the Great (ca. 73 – 4 B.C.), Agrippa I (ca. 10 B.C. – A.D. 44), and Agrippa II (A.D. 27 – ca. 100). Other high officials also received this title. *kyrios* was used of the gods who, in contemporary popular thought, were referred to as lords. Where *kyrios* was used of a god, the servant (→ *doulos*, 1528) using the term stood in a personal relationship of responsibility to the god. Individual gods were worshiped as lords of their cultic communities and of the separate members of the fellowship. The worship of other lords was not excluded, however, for no god was worshiped as universal lord.

(e) The Roman emperors Augustus (31 B.C. – A.D. 14) and Tiberius (A.D. 14 – 37) rejected the title *kyrios* and all that it meant. But Caligula (A.D. 37 – 41) found the title attractive. During and after the time of Nero (A.D. 54 – 68), who was described in an inscription as "lord of all the world," the title *kyrios* occurs more frequently (one of the oldest instances is Acts 25:26). In and of itself the title *kyrios* does not call the emperor god, but when he is worshiped as divine, the title *lord* also counts as a divine predicate. It was against such religious claims that the early Christians rejected the totalitarian attitudes of the state.

2. (a) *kyrios* occurs over 9,000x in the LXX. It translates *ʾādôn*, lord, which refers 190x to men as the responsible heads of groups (e.g., 1 Sam. 25:10). It is used only 15x for *baʿal*, which means the owner of a wife or a piece of land (e.g., Jdg. 19:22 – 23). Yahweh is rarely called owner (Hos. 2:16), but more frequently Lord of the community belonging to him (cf. Ps. 123:2). *kyrios* can also mean commander or ruler.

(b) In over 6,000 instances, however, *kyrios* replaces the Heb. proper name of God, the tetragrammaton *YHWH* (Yahweh). The LXX thus strengthened the tendency to avoid the utterance of God's name and finally to avoid its use altogether. Where *kyrios* stands for

ʾādôn or *ᵃdōnay* as a word relating to God, there is genuine translation; but where it stands for Yahweh, it is an interpretative circumlocution for all that the Heb. text implied by the use of the divine name: Yahweh is Creator and Lord of the whole universe, of humans, Lord of life and death. Above all he is the Lord God of Israel, his covenant people. By choosing *kyrios* for Yahweh the LXX also emphasizes legal authority. Because Yahweh saved his people from Egypt and chose them as his possession, he is the legitimate Lord of Israel. As Creator Yahweh is also the legitimate Lord of the entire universe, with unlimited control over it.

(c) *kyrieuō* occurs more than 50x in the LXX, generally with the meaning to rule.

3. In post-OT Jewish lit. *kyrios* appears as a term for God in Wis. (27x; e.g., 1:1, 7, 9; 2:13), then esp. often in Philo and Josephus. Philo seems to have been unaware that *kyrios* stood for the tetragrammaton, for he used *theos* ("God") to indicate the gracious power of God, while *kyrios* describes God's kingly power.

NT Of the 717x in which *kyrios* occurs in the NT, the majority are found in Luke's writings (210x) and Paul's letters (275x). This one-sidedness can be explained by the fact that Luke wrote for, and Paul wrote to, people who lived in areas dominated by Gk. culture and language. On the other hand, Mk., more firmly based in Jewish Christian tradition, uses the *kyrios* title only 18x, and these mostly in quotations. The remaining occurrences of *kyrios* are spread over the other NT books. The uses of *kyrios* accords with its varied use in the LXX.

1. *The secular use of* kyrios. The *kyrios* stands over against the slave (Matt. 10:24 – 25; 18:25, 27; 25:19; Lk. 12:36 – 37, 46; Eph. 6:5, 9; Col. 3:22). *kyrios* means owner (Matt. 15:27; Mk. 12:9; Lk. 19:33; Gal. 4:1) or employer (Lk. 16:3, 5). The husband faces his wife as *kyrios*, i.e., as superior (1 Pet. 3:6). *kyrios* used as a form of address can emphasize the power of a superior over an inferior, but it can also simply be politeness (Matt. 18:21 – 22; 25:20 – 26; 27:63; Lk. 13:8; Jn. 12:21; 20:15; Acts 16:30). The term is also used to address angels (10:4; Rev. 7:14) and the unknown in the heavenly vision outside Damascus (Acts 9:5; 22:8, 10; 26:15). A twice-repeated *kyrios* corresponds to Palestinian usage (Matt. 7:21 – 22; 25:11; Lk. 6:46).

2. *God as the* kyrios. God is frequently called *kyrios*, esp. in the many quotations from the OT in which *kyrios* stands for Yahweh, corresponding to the custom of pronouncing the title *kyrios* instead of the tetragrammaton in public reading (e.g., Rom. 4:8 = Ps. 32:2; Rom. 9:28 – 29 = Isa. 10:22 and 1:9; Rom. 10:16 = Isa. 53:1). In Lk.'s birth narratives *kyrios* frequently denotes God (e.g., 1:32; 2:9). In the gen. accompanying another word it corresponds to OT usage: e.g., the hand of the *kyrios* (1:66); the angel of the *kyrios* (Matt. 1:20); the name of the *kyrios* (Jas. 5:10); the Spirit of the *kyrios* (Acts 5:9); the word of the *kyrios* (Acts 8:25). The formula "says the *kyrios*" (e.g., Rom. 12:19 = Deut. 32:35) also comes from OT. The formula "our Lord and God" (Rev. 4:11) is reminiscent of the title adopted by Domitian.

Jesus is adopting Jewish forms of speech when he addresses God the Father as "*kyrios* of heaven and earth" (Matt. 11:25; Lk. 10:21). God is "the Lord of the harvest" (Matt. 9:38). He is the only ruler, the King of kings and the *kyrios* of lords (cf. Dan. 2:47), who will cause our *kyrios* Jesus Christ to appear (1 Tim. 6:15). God is the Creator and as such Lord of all (Acts 17:24). By acknowledging God as *kyrios*, the NT esp. confesses him as Creator—his power revealed in history and his just dominion over the universe.

3. *Jesus as the* kyrios. (a) The earthly Jesus as *kyrios*. This word applied to the earthly Jesus is first of all a polite form of address. This no doubt goes back to the title *Rabbi* (cf. Mk. 9:5 with Matt. 17:4; see also "sir" in Jn. 4:15; 5:7; 6:34). This address also implies recognition of Jesus as a leader and willingness to obey him (Matt. 7:21; 21:29 – 30). As Son of Man Jesus

is also *kyrios* of the Sabbath; he has control over the holy day of God's people (Mk. 2:28 – 29). Even after his death and resurrection the words of the earthly Jesus have authority for the Christian community. Paul appeals to words of the *kyrios* to decide a question (1 Cor. 7:10, cf. 25; 1 Thess. 4:15; cf. Acts 20:35).

(b) The exalted Jesus as *kyrios*. The confessional cry used in worship, *kyrios Iēsous* ("Jesus [is] Lord"), originated early in the Christian community. This confession is one of the oldest Christian creeds, if not the oldest. Note the Aramaic formula *Marana tha* (see 1 Cor. 16:22, NIV text note), which means "Lord, come," "Our Lord has come," or "The Lord will come"(cf. Rev. 22:20).

With this confession the NT community submitted itself to its Lord, but at the same time it also confessed him as ruler of the world (Rom. 10:9a; 1 Cor. 12:3; Phil. 2:11). God raised Jesus from the dead and "gave him the name that is above every name" (Phil. 2:9; cf. Isa. 45:23 – 24), i.e., the name *kyrios*, and with it the position corresponding to the name. The exalted *kyrios* rules over humanity (Rom. 14:9, *kyrieuō*). All powers and beings in the universe must bow before him. When that happens, God the Father will be worshiped (cf. Eph. 1:20 – 21; 1 Pet. 3:22).

Jesus Christ is called the ruler over all the kings of the earth, King of kings and Lord of lords (Rev. 17:14; 19:15 – 16). In this way he has received the same titles of honor as God himself (1 Tim. 6:15; cf. Dan. 2:47). According to contemporary Jewish thought, the different spheres of the world in nature and history were ruled by angelic powers. Since Christ has now been raised to the position of *kyrios*, all powers have been subjected to him and must serve him (Eph. 1:20 – 21; Col. 2:6, 10). When Christ has overcome every power (1 Cor. 15:25), he will submit himself to God the Father. Thus his lordship will have achieved its goal and God will be all in all (15:28). The one God and the one *kyrios* Jesus stand in opposition to the many gods and lords of the pagan world (8:5 – 6; Eph. 4:5 – 6).

Scriptural evidence for the exaltation of Jesus and for his installation as Lord was found in Ps. 110:1, the most quoted Ps. in the NT (cf., e.g., Matt. 22:44; 26:64; Acts 2:34; Eph. 1:20; Heb. 1:3, 13). The Jewish interpretation of this passage looked forward to the messianic future, but in the faith of the Christians this hope was transferred to the present. The lordship of the Messiah, Jesus, is a present reality. He is exercising in a hidden way God's authority and lordship over the world and will bring it to completion in the future. This faith was articulated in Thomas's confession (Jn. 20:28): "My Lord and my God." Early Christianity saw no infringement of monotheism in the installation of Jesus as Lord, but rather its confirmation (1 Cor. 8:6; Eph. 4:5; Phil. 2:11). It is God who exalted the Lord Jesus (Acts 2:36) and made him Lord of all things.

As far as we can establish, the NT church did not formally reflect on the relationship of the exalted Christ to God the Father as the church did later. Perhaps we can say that there is no developed doctrine of the Trinity in the NT, but that the writers thought in Trinitarian forms.

(c) *kyrios* and the Lord's Supper. *kyrios* figures frequently in expressions connected with the Lord's Supper. Note the phrases that are partly pre-Pauline: "the Lord's table" (1 Cor. 10:21), "the Lord's death" (11:26), "the cup of the Lord" (10:21; 11:27), "arouse the Lord's jealousy" (10:22), "the Lord's Supper" (11:20; → *kyriakos*, 3258), "judged by the Lord" (11:32), and "guilty of sinning against the body and blood of the Lord" (11:27). These expressions indicate that the Lord's Supper is the place where the Christian community submits itself in a special way to the saving work of the *kyrios* and receives a share in his body and power (see also *deipnon*, 1270).

(d) *kyrios* and Spirit. Paul taught the Christian community to distinguish between the one who is speaking in the Holy Spirit and the one who is not (1 Cor. 12:3). A person can only say "Jesus is Lord" if he or she is filled with the Holy Spirit. Anyone who, by acknowledging allegiance to Jesus as *kyrios*, belongs to the new covenant, belongs to the sphere of the Spirit and no longer to that of the old covenant and of the letter. Such a one stands in freedom: "Where the Spirit of the Lord is, there is freedom" (2 Cor. 3:17).

(e) *kyrios* in epistolary greetings. In the opening greetings of Paul's letters the "Lord Jesus Christ" is frequently mentioned beside God the Father (e.g., Rom. 1:7; 1 Cor. 1:3). The concluding greeting, with the phrase "the grace of the *kyrios* Jesus be with you," continued the pre-Pauline tradition that may have had its origin in the Lord's Supper (cf. 1 Cor. 16:23; 2 Cor. 13:14; Phlm. 25). The description of God as the "Father of our *kyrios* Jesus Christ" goes back to the early Christian community (Rom. 15:6; 2 Cor. 1:3; 11:31; cf. 1 Pet. 1:3). The formula was introduced into an originally Jewish context (the praise of God). Christian missionaries did not just call people to faith in God the Father but also to faith in the *kyrios* Jesus (Acts 5:14; 18:8).

4. *The lordship of the* kyrios. (a) The activity of the church before the *kyrios* Jesus. In every expression of its life the Christian community stands before the *kyrios* who has authority and exercises it over the community (1 Cor. 4:19; 14:37; 16:7). He causes the community to grow (1 Thess. 3:12 – 13), bestows authority on the apostles (2 Cor. 10:8; 13:10), and gives different ministries to the members of his body, the church (1 Cor. 3:5; 7:17; 12:5). The *kyrios* also gives visions and revelations (2 Cor. 12:1). The whole life of the Christian community is determined by its relationship to the *kyrios* (Rom. 14:8). The body, i.e., the complete earthly existence of the Christian, belongs to the *kyrios*; this precludes dealings with prostitutes (1 Cor. 6:13 – 17).

The *kyrios* gives to each one the measure of faith (1 Cor. 3:5; 7:17; Eph. 4:5). He is the *kyrios* of peace and gives peace (2 Thess. 3:16), mercy (2 Tim. 1:16), and insight (2:7). On the basis of faith in the *kyrios* Christ, even earthly relationships between masters and slaves take on a new aspect. Faithful service of earthly masters (*kyrioi*) is service of the *kyrios* of the church (Col. 3:22 – 24; cf. 1 Pet. 2:13).

(b) The formulae "through" and "in" the *kyrios*. The formula "through the [our] Lord Jesus [Christ]" occurs in the most varied contexts: e.g., thanksgiving (Rom. 7:25; 1 Cor. 15:57), praise (Rom. 5:11), and exhortation (15:30; 1 Thess. 4:2). In such phrases *kyrios* is used in order to claim the power of the exalted Lord for the life of the church and of the individual.

The phrase "in the Lord" occurs esp. in Paul and means the same as "in Jesus Christ," e.g., *in the Lord*: a door was opened for mission (2 Cor. 2:12), Paul affirms and exhorts (Eph. 4:17; 1 Thess. 4:1), Paul is convinced (Rom. 14:14), people are received (16:2; Phil. 2:29), and the church is to rejoice (3:1), stand firm (4:1), and greet one another (Rom. 16:22; 1 Cor. 16:19). Christians are to marry in the Lord (7:39), be strong in the Lord (Eph. 6:10), and walk in the Lord (Col. 2:6). People are chosen (Rom. 16:13) and loved (16:8; 1 Cor. 4:17) in the Lord; in him their work is not in vain (15:58). The whole of life, in both the present and the future, is determined by the fact of Christ expressed by this formula: Paul and his churches stand in the presence and under the power of the *kyrios*.

(c) Statements about the Parousia. At present Christians are separated from the *kyrios* and long to be with him (2 Cor. 5:6, 8). Those who are alive at the Second Coming will be caught up to meet the *kyrios* (1 Thess. 4:17). Thus, the NT church looks forward to the future, visible return of Christ and to a final union with the Lord of life and death. We read about the day of the Lord (1 Cor. 1:8; 5:5; 2 Cor. 1:14; 1 Thess. 5:2; 2 Thess. 2:2), "the coming [*parousia*] of our *kyrios*" (2 Thess. 2:1), and the "appearing [*epiphaneia*] of our *kyrios*" (1 Tim. 6:14). When he comes, the exalted *kyrios* is Judge (2 Thess. 1:9; 2:8) and Savior (Phil. 3:20).

5. *Derivatives of kyrios.* (a) *kyria* (fem. of *kyrios*) means lady, owner, mistress of the house. In the NT it occurs only in 2 Jn. 1, 5, where it refers to the church (cf. v. 13, where the churches are sisters and their members children). In addressing the church as "lady," the author is expressing his respect for it and honors it as a work of the *kyrios*.

(b) *kyriotēs*, lordly power or position, dominion. In the NT this word occurs in the pl. with reference to angelic powers (Eph. 1:20 – 21; Col. 1:16). The NT letters stress that the exalted Christ rules over these dominions. *kyriotēs* occurs in the sing. in Jude 8 and 2 Pet. 2:10, where the thought is not of angels but of God's dominion.

(c) *kyrieuō*, be a lord, act as master. In the NT this vb. occurs 7x. The rule of kings over their people is characterized by ambition (Lk. 22:25), because they misuse their power for selfish ends; the disciples are to seek rather to serve, as Jesus did (22:26 – 27). Paul uses *kyrieuō* to describe relationships of power. Because Christ has risen, death no longer has any power over him (Rom. 6:9). Christ died and rose in order that he might reign over the living and the dead (14:9). God is the ruler of those who rule (1 Tim. 6:15). Since Christians have been baptized into Jesus' death and have risen with him (Rom. 6:3 – 4), sin must not reign over them any longer (6:14). For they no longer stand under law but under grace (7:1, 6). Paul does not want to lord it over the faith of the Corinthians but to work with them for their joy (2 Cor. 1:24).

(d) *katakyrieuō*, rule over, conquer. The prefix *kata-* has a negative force. In the NT the word occurs 4x. It is a characteristic of Gentile rulers to exercise their rule to their own advantage and contrary to the interests and well-being of the people (Matt. 20:25; Mk. 10:42). The vb. also describes the man with an evil spirit who leaped on the seven sons of Sceva and "overpowered" them (Acts 19:16) as they attempted to imitate Christian exorcism. Finally, Peter exhorts elders not to exercise their office by lording it over the congregation, but to be examples to the flock (1 Pet. 5:2 – 3).

See also *theos*, God (2536); *Emmanouēl*, Immanuel (1842); *despotēs*, lord, master (of a house), owner (1305); *kyriakos*, belonging to the Lord, the Lord's (3258).

How do We Describe Things?

We are almost done with Greek grammar. The only major category left is that of nouns and their cases. Chapter 24 concludes our discussion on how to read a commentary. Chapter 25 discusses the history of how the Bible was transmitted in Greek and translated into Latin and English throughout the centuries.

CHAPTER 25

Nominative and Vocative

Introduction to Greek Noun Grammar

Stem. The basic form of a noun or adjective is called the "stem." For example, the stem of the Greek word for "God" is θεο. I'll put an asterisk before a stem to make this clear (*θεο).

Nominative. The Greek equivalent of the English subjective case is the nominative case. When a Greek word is the subject of a verb, it is in the nominative case.

Case endings. Unlike English, most Greek nouns and adjectives change their form depending on their function in the sentence. They do this by using case endings, which are suffixes added to the end of the stem.

If a word is the subject of a verb, the writer will put it into the nominative case by adding a nominative case ending onto the stem. ς can be used as a nominative case ending. In John 3:16, which word is the subject?

John 3:16	ἠγάπησεν	ὁ θεὸς	τὸν κόσμον
	he loved	the God	the world
	God loved the world.		

We see the ς case ending, recognize that this indicates the word is in the nominative case, and conclude that it is the subject of the verb.

This is how someone who actually reads Greek thinks. For our baby Greek approach, we just use the tools like *IRU*, and it tells us the word is in the nominative, but you still need to recognize the process.

Notice that word order does not identify the subject. In our example, θεός comes after the verb, but it is the case ending that tells us θεός is in the nominative and therefore is the subject of the verb.

Gender. A noun is either masculine, feminine, or neuter. It has only one gender and it never varies.

Most Greek nouns do not follow natural gender. ἁμαρτία is a feminine noun meaning "sin," although "sin" is not a female concept; ἁμαρτωλός is a masculine noun meaning "sinner," although "sinner" is not a masculine concept. However, you will see natural gender in pronouns (αὐτός, "he"; αὐτή, "she") and words like "brother" (ἀδελφός) and "sister" (ἀδελφή).

Number. Instead of adding an "s" to a word, Greek indicates singular or plural by using different case endings. The difference between the singular and plural here is indicated by the case endings ς and ι.

> ἀπόστολος ‣ apostle
> ἀπόστολοι ‣ apostles

Agreement. When a word like an adjective or article modifies another word, it will "agree" with that word in case, number, and gender. In other words, if the noun is nominative in case, singular in number, and masculine in gender, the modifying word will also be nominative singular, masculine.

Uninflected. Some words in Greek do not inflect, such as personal names and words borrowed from other languages. For example, Ἀβραάμ (Abraham) will always be Ἀβραάμ regardless of its function in the sentence.

Lexical form. The lexical form of a noun is its nominative singular form. If you found the inflected form ἀπόστολοι, which is nominative plural, it would be listed in the lexicon under ἀπόστολος.

This is important to know because if you want to do a word study, you will need to know the lexical form of the word (if you don't know its GK number). If you tried to look up the word ἀπόστολοι in a word study book, you would not find it.

Declensions. In Greek there are three basic inflectional patterns that a word can follow. Each of these patterns is called a "declension." Which pattern a word follows has no effect on its meaning, only its form.

For example, both ἀπόστολοι ("apostles") and πατέρες ("fathers") are nominative plural masculine. The two case endings ι and ς are both nominative plural case endings, but for different declensions.

The full language approach requires the memorization of these different patterns. For our part, we just need to recognize that different words will use different endings even though they may be in the same case, number, and gender.

Uses of the Nominative

1. The normal use of the nominative case is to designate the *subject* of a verb. It can be the main subject of a sentence, or the subject inside a clause.

Rom 10:9	ὁ θεὸς	αὐτὸν	ἤγειρεν	ἐκ	νεκρῶν
	the God	*him*	*he raised*	*from*	*dead*

NIV: *God* raised him from the dead.

Matt 24:2	οὐ	μὴ	ἀφεθῇ	ὧδε	λίθος	ἐπὶ	λίθον	ὃς		οὐ	καταλυθήσεται
	not	not	left	here	stone	upon	stone	*that*		not	thrown down

ESV: There will not be left here one stone upon another *that* will not be thrown down.

NIV: Not one stone here will be left on another; *every one* will be thrown down.

In phrasing and exegesis, it is necessary to identify the subject and main verb. That subject will be in the nominative.

2. The nominative is also used for a *predicate nominative*. In correct English we would say, "It is I," not, "It is me." Why? Because the verb "I am" in all its forms (e.g., "is," "was") is not followed by a direct object but by a predicate nominative. This means that the following word is in the subjective case. We have the same situation with the Greek verb εἰμί, which is always followed by a nominative. (ὁ χριστός is nominative.)

Matt 24:5	ἐγώ	εἰμι	ὁ	χριστός
	I	am	*the*	*Christ*

ESV: I am *the Christ*.

NRSV: I am *the Messiah*!

Vocative

There technically is a fifth case in Greek, although it is so similar to the nominative that we still speak of the "four" cases in Greek. The vocative is the case of *direct address*. The word used when speaking directly to a person is in the vocative.

Rev 22:20	ἔρχου	κύριε	Ἰησοῦ.
	come	*Lord*	*Jesus*

ESV: Come, *Lord Jesus*!

ὦ may be included if there is deep emotion.

Matt 15:28	ὁ Ἰησοῦς	εἶπεν	αὐτῇ,	ὦ	γύναι,	μεγάλη	σου	ἡ πίστις
	Jesus	said	to her	*O*	*woman*	great	your	the faith

ESV: Then Jesus answered her, "*O woman*, great is your faith!"

NET: Then Jesus answered her, "*Woman*, your faith is great!"

Word Order

The case endings, not the word order, are the key to knowing the function of a word. The only way to determine the subject of a Greek sentence is by the case endings since the subject can occur before or after the verb.

Take the following four sentences, for example. How do we know that they are all saying that God loves the world, and not that the world loves

God? (Remember, ς can be a nominative singular case ending.)

> ἀγαπᾷ   ὁ Θεὸς   τὸν κόσμον.
> loves   the God   the world
>
> ἀγαπᾷ τὸν κόσμον ὁ Θεός.
> τὸν κόσμον ὁ Θεὸς ἀγαπᾷ.
> ὁ Θεὸς ἀγαπᾷ τὸν κόσμον.

Although the order of the words is different, each example has the same basic meaning.

It is difficult to speak of "normal" Greek word order, since most Greek sentences do not follow it. But in a general sense, the normal word order is conjunction, verb, subject, and object.

Why would a Greek speaker alter the order? Mostly for emphasis. If they wanted to emphasize a word, they would tend to move it to an "unusual" location, normally forward in the sentence. Sometimes English can translate the nuance of the word order, but normally not. What is the point of the word order here?

> *1 Tim 2:4*   πάντας   ἀνθρώπους   θέλει   σωθῆναι
>   *all*   people   he wishes   to be saved
>   ESV: who desires *all* people to be saved

> *Eph 2:8*   Τῇ   γὰρ   χάριτί   ἐστε   σεσῳσμένοι
>   *by the* for   *grace*   you are   having been saved
>   NASB: For *by grace* you have been saved.
>   NIV: For *it is by grace* you have been saved.

Because Greek does not rely on word order, you will find that it often separates words we might expect to find in a different order.

> *Rom 5:8*   συνίστησιν δὲ   τὴν   ἑαυτοῦ   ἀγάπην   εἰς   ἡμᾶς   ὁ θεός
>   he shows   but   *the*   his own   *love*   for   us   the God
>   NET: But God demonstrates his own *love* for us.

Because *EGNT* alters the order of Greek to that of the English text, you cannot use it to determine the Greek word order. You will need to check with a regular Greek text or standard interlinear.

For the Curious

Here is the noun paradigm with the nominative.

	masculine	*feminine*	*neuter*
nom sg	λόγος	γραφή	ἔργον
nom pl	λόγοι	γραφαί	ἔργα

CHAPTER 26

Accusative

English

The direct object receives the action of the verb and is in the objective case. It is normally placed after the verb.

> John hit the *ball*.

Greek

The corresponding case in Greek to the English objective case is the accusative case. Remember, the case of the word and not word order tells you how the word is functioning in the sentence.

Uses of the Accusative

1. The primary use of the accusative is to indicate the *direct object*. For example, the stem of the Greek word for "apostle" is *ἀποστολο. If it is functioning as the direct object of a verb, it takes an accusative case ending such as ν.

John 3:16	ἠγάπησεν	ὁ θεὸς	τὸν κόσμον
	he loved	the God	*the world*

NET: God loved *the world*.

2. Some verbs require two objects to complete their meaning (*double accusative*).

John 14:26	ἐκεῖνος	ὑμᾶς	διδάξει	πάντα
	he	*you*	he will teach	*all*

ESV: He will teach *you all things*.

Sometimes a translation will add a word like "as" before the second accusative to help you understand its meaning.

1 John 4:10 ἀπέστειλεν τὸν υἱὸν αὐτοῦ ἱλασμὸν
He sent *the son* of him *propitiation*

NIV: he … sent his Son *as* an atoning sacrifice.

NASB: He … sent His Son *to be* the propitiation.

IRU will not place an arrow under that word (or words).

sent	his	Son		*as* an	atoning	sacrifice	for	our
ἀπέστειλεν	αὐτοῦ	⌊τὸν	υἱὸν⌋		ἱλασμὸν	←	περὶ	ἡμῶν
v.aai.3s	r.gsm.3	d.asm	n.asm		n.asm		p.g	r.gp.1
690	899	3836	5626		2662		4309	7005

3. The accusative can behave as an adverb, modifying the verb (*adverbial accusative; accusative of manner or measure*).

Matt 10:8 δωρεὰν ἐλάβετε, δωρεὰν δότε
free you received *free* give

NASB: *Freely* you received, *freely* give.

ESV: You received *without paying;* give *without pay.*

Matt 6:33 ζητεῖτε πρῶτον τὴν βασιλείαν τοῦ θεοῦ
seek *first* the kingdom of the God

ESV: Seek *first* the kingdom of God.

NET: Seek *first* his kingdom.

KJV: Seek ye *first* the kingdom of God.

4. Some prepositions like εἰς will take their objects in the accusative case.

Matt 2:11 ἐλθόντες εἰς τὴν οἰκίαν εἶδον τὸ παιδίον
going into *the house* they saw the child

NIV: On coming to the house, they saw the child.

For the Curious

Here is the noun paradigm with the nominative and accusative.

	masculine	*feminine*	*neuter*
nom sg	λόγος	γραφή	ἔργον
acc sg	λόγον	γραφήν	ἔργον
nom pl	λόγοι	γραφαί	ἔργα
acc pl	λόγους	γραφάς	ἔργα

CHAPTER 27

Dative

English

The indirect object, technically, is the person or thing that is "indirectly" affected by the action of the verb. This means that the indirect object is somehow involved in the action described by the verb, but not directly.

For example, "Karin threw Brad a ball." The direct object is "ball," since it is directly related to the action of the verb. It is what was thrown. But "Brad" is also related to the action of the verb, since the ball was thrown to him. "Brad" is the indirect object. If Karin threw Brad, then "Brad" would be the direct object.

One way to find the indirect object is to put the word "to" in front of the word and see if it makes sense.

> "Karin threw Brad a ball."
> "Karin threw to Brad a ball."

To whom did Karin throw the ball? To Brad. "Brad" is the indirect object.

English does not have a separate case for the indirect object. It uses the same form as the direct object (objective case).

Greek

The dative case is the third of the four Greek cases you will learn. As is true of the nominative and accusative, there are a series of dative singular and plural case endings that are attached to the end of the word when it needs to be in the dative case.

Many of the times when English uses prepositions, Greek uses the dative case (often without prepositions).

> τῷ ἐκκλησίᾳ ⋅ "to the church"

Since English does not have a dative case, the translator will often use an "extra" word in the translation of the dative such as "to" or "in." They are normally prepositions. In *IRU*, you will often see these little words with arrows under them. The arrow is pointing to the word in the dative case (or one of the other cases) that requires this helping word, such as "by" in Ephesians 2:8.

For	it	is	*by*	grace	you	have	been	saved,
γὰρ	→	ἐστε	→	⌐Τῇ χάριτι⌐	→	→	→	σεσωσμένοι
cj		v.pai.2p		d.dsf n.dsf				pt.rp.npm
1142		1639		3836 5921				5392

Is it wrong for a translator to "add" these words? Of course not. Because we do not have a dative case in English, we cannot say something in the same way as it is said in Greek. We have to use the tools our language gives us to say the same thing as is meant by Scripture.

There is a controversy in scholarship as to whether Greek has four or eight cases. Those who hold to an eight case system break what I am calling the dative case into three cases: dative, locative, and instrumental.

Uses of the Dative

Dative

1. The *indirect object* functions the same in Greek as it does in English, with the indirect object placed in the dative case.

John 5:27	καὶ	ἐξουσίαν	ἔδωκεν	αὐτῷ	κρίσιν	ποιεῖν,
	and	authority	he gave	*to him*	judgment	to make

NIV: And he has gave *him* authority to judge.
ESV: He has given *him* authority to execute judgment.

2. The dative can express the idea of "for" (*dative of interest*).

Luke 1:13	ἡ γυνή	σου	Ἐλισάβετ	γεννήσει	υἱόν	σοι
	wife	your	Elizabeth	she will bear	son	*to you*

Your wife Elizabeth will bear a son *for you.*
NET: Your wife Elizabeth will bear *you* a son.

When the idea is for the person's advantage, as in Luke 1:13 above, we call it a "dative of advantage." When context tells us that it is not for the person's advantage, we can call it a "dative of disadvantage" and often use a different preposition based on the meaning of the phrase.

Matt 23:31	μαρτυρεῖτε	ἑαυτοῖς
	you testify	*to yourselves*

NRSV: You testify *against yourselves.*
KJV: Ye be witnesses *unto* yourselves.

3. The dative can indicate what in English is awkwardly expressed by the phrase "with respect to" (*reference, respect*).

Rom 6:11   λογίζεσθε   ἑαυτοὺς   εἶναι νεκροὺ τῇ ἁμαρτίᾳ
              consider   yourselves to be   dead   *to the sin*
              ESV: Consider yourselves to be dead *to sin*.
              TEV: You are to think of yourselves as dead, *so far as sin is concerned*.

Locative

4. There is a little more nebulous use of the dative, indicating the sphere or realm in which something occurs (*sphere*).

Matt 5:8   μακάριοι   οἱ καθαροὶ τῇ καρδίᾳ
              Blessed   the pure   *in the heart*
              NIV: Blessed are the pure *in heart*.
              NLT: God blesses those whose hearts are pure.

5. A time designation in the dative specifies when something occurs (*time*).

Matt 17:23   τῇ   τρίτῃ   ἡμέρᾳ   ἐγερθήσεται
              to the   third   day   he will be raised.
              NET: *On the third day* he will be raised.
              NLT: *Three days later* he will be raised from the dead.

6. The dative can indicate the idea of "with" (*association*).

2 Cor 6:14   μὴ   γίνεσθε   ἑτεροζυγοῦντες   ἀπίστοις
              Not   you become   unequally yoked   *to unbelievers*
              ESV: Do not be unequally yoked *with unbelievers*.
              RSV: Do not be mismated *with unbelievers*.
              NRSV: Do not be mismatched *with unbelievers*.
              NLT: Don't team up *with those who are unbelievers*.

Instrumental

7. The dative can indicate the manner in which something is done (*manner*).

John 7:26   παρρησίᾳ   λαλεῖ
              in boldness he speaks
              NKJ: He speaks *boldly*.
              NASB: He is speaking *publicly*.

παρρησία can mean either "boldly" or "publicly."

8. The dative can also show the means (or the instrument) by which an action was accomplished (*means, instrument*).

Eph 2:8	Τῇ	γὰρ	χάριτί	ἐστε	σεσῳσμένοι
	the	for	*to grace*	you are	being saved

NIV: For it is *by grace* you have been saved.

With prepositions

9. Some prepositions like ἐν will take their objects in the dative case.

Matt 3:6	ἐβαπτίζοντο	ἐν	τῷ	Ἰορδάνῃ	ποταμῷ	ὑπ᾽	αὐτοῦ
	they were baptized	*in*		*the Jordan*	river	by	him

NRSV: They were baptized by him in *the river Jordan.*

Do you feel overwhelmed? Don't worry about it. All that I want you to see is the variety of meaning that can be expressed by the dative, why translators have to be interpreters, and hence why translations are different.

For the Curious

Here is the noun paradigm with the dative.

	masculine	*feminine*	*neuter*
nom sg	λόγος	γραφή	ἔργον
dat sg	λόγῳ	γραφῇ	ἔργῳ
acc sg	λόγον	γραφήν	ἔργον
nom pl	λόγοι	γραφαί	ἔργα
dat pl	λόγοις	γραφαῖς	ἔργοις
acc pl	λόγους	γραφάς	ἔργα

CHAPTER 28

Genitive

English

The possessive case in English is used to indicate possession. You can put "of" in front of the word ("The Word *of God* is true."), an apostrophe s after the word (*"God's* Word is true."), or just an apostrophe if the word ends in "s" ("The *apostles'* word was ignored.").

Make a list of all the ways you can use the word "of" in English. What does the expression "bowl of silver" mean? Is the bowl *made of* silver, or is it *full of* silver. This same type of ambiguity exists in the genitive case and often explains why translations are different.

Greek

Greek puts a word in the genitive case by adding genitive case endings onto the end of the word. The **head noun** is the word that the word in the genitive is modifying. In the phrase "love of God," "love" would be the head noun and "God" would be in the genitive.

Uses of the Genitive

1. The most common use of the genitive is when the word in the genitive gives some description of the head noun. You will often find "of" used to translate this use (*descriptive*).

> *Rom 13:12*   ἐνδυσώμεθα   τὰ ὅπλα   τοῦ φωτός
> Let us put on   the armor   *of the light*
> NKJV: Let us put on the armor *of light*.

2. The word in the genitive can be possessed by the head noun (*possessive*).

232

Matt 19:21 ὕπαγε   πώλησόν   σου   τὰ ὑπάρχοντα
              Go   sell   of you the things belonging
              NRSV: Go, sell *your* possessions.

In English the possessive case can be indicated by the apostrophe. "Everyone breaks God's laws." Greek, however, does not have the apostrophe, and so all Greek constructions are in the form "of ...."

3. In a general sense, if you have a noun that in some way equals the meaning of another noun, the writer can put the noun in the genitive, and it is said to be in *apposition* to the head noun. It is as if you drew an equals sign between the two words. The translations will often add a word or punctuation to help make this clear.

Acts 2:38 λήμψεσθε   τὴν δωρεὰν τοῦ ἁγίου πνεύματος.
          You will receive the gift   *of the Holy* *Spirit*
          You will receive the gift, *which is the Holy Spirit.*
          NIV: You will receive the gift *of the Holy Spirit.*
          TEV: You will receive God's gift, *the Holy Spirit.*

4. The word in the genitive can indicate something that is separate from the head noun or verb. It will often use the helping word "from" (*separation*).

Eph 2:12 ἀπηλλοτριωμένοι τῆς πολιτείας   τοῦ Ἰσραὴλ
        being alienated   *of the commonwealth* of the Israel
        ESV: alienated *from the commonwealth* of Israel
        NRSV: being aliens *from the commonwealth* of Israel
        NASB: excluded *from the commonwealth* of Israel
        NIV: excluded *from citizenship* in Israel

5. This category and the next two are extremely important. They occur with a head noun that expresses a verbal idea (i.e., the cognate noun can also occur as a verb). These three categories often present the translator with significantly different interpretations.

Sometimes the word in the genitive functions as if it were the subject of the verbal idea implicit in the head noun (*subjective*). You can use the helping word "produced" to help identify this usage. "The love produced by Christ."

Rom 8:35 τίς ἡμᾶς χωρίσει   ἀπὸ τῆς ἀγάπης τοῦ Χριστοῦ
        who us   he will separate from the love   *of the Christ*
        NIV: Who shall separate us from the love *of Christ*?
        NLT: Can anything ever separate us from *Christ's* love?

6. The word in the genitive functions as the direct object of the verbal idea implicit in the head noun (*objective*). This is the opposite of the subjective genitive. You can use the key word "receives." "The blasphemy received by the Spirit."

Matt 12:31 ἡ   τοῦ πνεύματος βλασφημία οὐκ ἀφεθήσεται
The *of the Spirit*   blasphemy   not it will be forgiven
The blasphemy *of the Spirit* will not be forgiven.
NIV: the blasphemy *against the Spirit* will not be forgiven.

7. Sometimes it appears that the word in the genitive is a combination of both the objective and subjective genitive (*plenary*).

2 Cor 5:14 ἡ ἀγάπη τοῦ Χριστοῦ συνέχει   ἡμᾶς
the love   *of the Christ* constrains us
NASB: The love *of Christ* controls us (i.e., both my love for Christ and his love for me).
NIV: For *Christ's* love compels us.
NLT: Whatever we do, it is because *Christ's* love controls us.

8. The genitive can indicate a familial relationship between a word and its head noun (*relationship*). Often the head noun is not expressed, so it is up to the translator's interpretive skills to determine the exact nature of the relationship.

John 21:15 Σίμων   Ἰωάννου
Simon, *of John*
NET: Simon, *son of John*

Simon son of John
Σίμων   →   Ἰωάννου
n.vsm   n.gsm
4981   2722

Luke 24:10 Μαρία ἡ   Ἰακώβου
Mary   the *of James*
NASB: Mary the *mother of James*

This was a particularly difficult construction to lay out in *IRU*. Here is how I did it.

Mary   the   mother of James,
Μαρία ἡ   →   Ἰακώβου
n.nsf   d.nsf   n.gsm
3451   3836   2610

9. Sometimes the noun in the genitive is a larger unit, while its head noun represents a smaller portion of it (*partitive*).

Rom 11:17   τινες   τῶν κλάδων
     some   *of the branches*
     NIV: some *of the branches*

See the detailed guidelines in *IRU* as to how we laid out this construction (p. 785).

10. Like the accusative and dative, some prepositions take their object in the genitive

Rom 7:6   νυνὶ   δὲ   κατηργήθημεν   ἀπὸ   τοῦ νόμου
    now   but   we were released   from   *the law*
    NASB: But now we have been released from *the Law.*
    ESV: But now we are released from *the law.*

Exercises for Chapters 25-28

Identify the grammatical category of each bolded verb below and explain the different translations.

John 20:13 NIV. They asked her, "**Woman**, why are you crying?" NLT. "Why are you crying?" the angels asked her.

Rom 1:5 ESV. through whom we have received grace and apostleship to bring about the obedience **of faith** for the sake of his name among all the nations NIV. Through him and for his name's sake, we received grace and apostleship to call people from among all the Gentiles to the obedience that comes from faith. NLT. Through Christ, God has given us the privilege and authority to tell Gentiles everywhere what God has done for them, so that they will believe and obey him, bringing glory to his name.

Rom 3:28 Explain where the "by" comes from. KJV. Therefore we conclude that a man is justified **by** faith without the deeds of the law.

Gal 5:5 ESV. For through the Spirit, by faith, we ourselves eagerly wait for the hope **of righteousness**. NIV. But by faith we eagerly await through the Spirit the righteousness for which we hope. NLT. But we who live by the Spirit eagerly wait to receive everything promised to us who are right with God through faith.

1 Thess 1:3 ESV. remembering before our God and Father your work **of faith** and labor **of love** and steadfastness **of hope**. NIV. We continually remember before our God and Father your work produced by faith, your labor prompted by love, and your endurance inspired by hope.

1 Thess 1:6 ESV. You received the word in much affliction, with the joy **of the Holy Spirit**. NIV. In spite of severe suffering, you welcomed the message with the joy given by the Holy Spirit.

2 Thess 3:5 NASB. May the Lord direct your hearts into the love of God and into the steadfastness **of Christ**. NIV. May the Lord direct your hearts into God's love and Christ's perseverance. NLT. May the Lord bring you into an ever deeper understanding of the love of God and the endurance that comes from Christ.

Philem 6 NRSV. I pray that the sharing **of your faith** may become effective when you perceive all the good that we may do for Christ. NIV. I pray that you may be active in sharing your faith, so that you will have a full understanding of every good thing we have in Christ. NLT. You are generous because of your faith. And I am praying that you will really put your generosity to work, for in so doing you will come to an understanding of all the good things we can do for Christ.

Use a traditional interlinear and paraphrase the following verses but emphasizing the Greek word order: 1 Corinthians 3:16-17; Galatians 5:25; Romans 12:9-13.

For the Curious

Here is the full paradigm of the four main cases. I threw in the definite article as well. Remember, however, that there are subpatterns; but you don't need to worry about them. We'll leave that to the "full" Greek approach.

	masculine	*feminine*	*neuter*
nom sg	ὁ λόγος	ἡ γραφή	τὸ ἔργον
gen sg	τοῦ λόγου	τῆς γραφῆς	τοῦ ἔργου
dat sg	τῷ λόγῳ	τῇ γραφῇ	τῷ ἔργῳ
acc sg	τὸν λόγον	τὴν γραφήν	τὸ ἔργον
nom pl	οἱ λόγοι	αἱ γραφαί	τὰ ἔργα
gen pl	τῶν λόγων	τῶν γραφῶν	τῶν ἔργων
dat pl	τοῖς λόγοις	ταῖς γραφαῖς	τοῖς ἔργοις
acc pl	τοὺς λόγους	τὰς γραφάς	τὰ ἔργα

CHAPTER 29

How to Read a Commentary

Congratulations. You have learned all the Greek grammar you need to know in order to accomplish our goals. However, one of our goals is to be able to read good commentaries. We have seen many of the bits and pieces necessary to do this, and it is time to pull them together.

What We Have Learned So Far

In many of the previous chapters, we have studied the same issues that a good commentary will discuss, and in so doing have been learning how to read commentaries. When looking at translation theory, we were learning about the nature of language and communication and about the necessity of interpretation. When looking at phrasing, we were learning to identify the main point(s) of the passage, how that point was modified, and how to discover the author's flow of thought. When we worked with word studies, we learned how words are ambiguous and open to different interpretations, how words have a range of meaning, and how it is the role of context to specify which specific meaning was intended in a particular context. We saw the flexibility and ambiguity of grammar in the tenses, moods, and cases. We have looked at some of the tools that will help us to interpret the Bible more accurately—translations, concordances, word study books, software. Now it is time to pull together what we have learned so that we can learn to use our final tool—commentaries. I want to do this by walking you through the basic process of what is called exegesis, a technical word for biblical interpretation, which is the primary task of a commentary.

But first I want to stress the proper role of a commentary. The best exegesis is begun with you and your Bible. I cannot emphasize this enough. Read the passage over and over. Do your phrasing. Pray that the Holy Spirit will show you things you normally would miss. This is the best kind of Bible study, and certainly the most rewarding. I don't know how many times I have been struggling with a passage for a sermon or a lecture, and I am not sure what phrase modifies what, or even what the main point is; and I read and reread the passage, move things around in my phrasing, and then, eventually, the light dawns and I see what the author is saying. This is the joy of independent exegesis.

However, you must not stop here. What if you are wrong? What if your interpretation sounds great to you but is really out-to-lunch? This is where commentaries come in. If you cannot find a major commentary to agree with your position, especially if they don't list it even as a possibility, then humility requires that you accept the error of your position and change your interpretation. It is a dangerous thing to say that you understand the passage correctly and all the people who have studied the passage for years totally missed its meaning. I guess it is possible you are right and everybody else is wrong, but it is highly unlikely. Even Luther had historical precedent for what he taught, even though he stood against the teaching of the current church.

I know there is a strong anti-intellectual bias out there. I have heard pastors tell their congregation not even to look at commentaries. Certainly there are commentaries from which I as a pastor want to protect my congregation. And certainly there are commentaries that major in the minutia and trivia and will bore a layperson into a coma (as well as a few seminary students). But don't think of a commentary as a book. Think of it as a chance to listen to a person who probably has substantially more formal training and experience than you have, a person who possibly has spent most of his or her life thinking about this one area. I spent fourteen years working on my commentary on the Pastoral Epistles. I know of people who have spent almost their entire careers working on just one biblical book or one area of theology. To have someone say that the fruit of a person's life's work should not even be read is—well, it is just wrong.

When you read a commentary, it will provide checks and balances against your possible mistakes. If you read more than one commentary, they provide checks and balances against each other as well. I am not saying that the commentary is automatically right. I have read many interpretations in commentaries that I believe to be totally wrong. But as I study the text for myself and then check myself with at least two commentaries, and especially when I find myself agreeing with the commentaries, then when I stand to preach before my church, I can preach with the full conviction of "thus saith the Lord."

But commentaries do more than provide checks and balances. They can answer questions that a reading of the text can never provide or ask questions you may never think of asking. They can give a depth to your study beyond phrasing as they fill in the holes, so to speak. So how do you read commentaries?

Hermeneutics

Hermeneutics has been defined as the science and art of biblical interpretation. Hermeneutics helps us understand the Bible. It is a science because there are specific rules the interpreter must follow. It is an art because it takes years of practice to develop the ability to employ those rules properly. There is a difference between a novice and a seasoned interpreter. Just look at how much better you handle Scripture now than you did when you were young in Christ. I could go to an art class and learn about colors, but if you put a paintbrush in my hand, I will only be able to produce the dabbling of a child. Hermeneutics is an art that takes years to develop.

Hermeneutics has two basic steps, finding what the text meant to its original audience, and then seeing how it applies to our current situation. As wise people who not only want to hear the words of the Lord but also put them into practice (Matt 7:24-27), we must be concerned with traveling the entire hermeneutical circle, of knowing what the text *meant* to its original audience and what it *means* to me today.

Step 1: Meant

The first step in hermeneutics is to learn what the author meant to convey to his original audience. This is the role of exegesis. The word "exegesis" was formed with the Greek preposition ἐκ, which means "out of"; exegesis is drawing the meaning out of the text, of learning what the author wanted to say. Exegesis is often contrasted with "eisegesis"; the Greek preposition εἰς means "into," and hence eisegesis means reading your own meaning into the text. Bible study is not reading your personal theology into some biblical passage. Bible study is letting the text talk to us; we are the listeners, not the talkers.

The commentary writer will therefore try to discover the meaning intended by the author. This is called "authorial intent." In a few places the author may have intended multiple meanings, as with a pun, or God may have intended a deeper meaning such as a prophecy. But the vast majority of the time the author meant something, one thing, and the goal is to find that one meaning.

Hard work

This can be hard work for both you and the commentary writer. It is easy to skim over a passage and then share with your Bible study group what the passage "means to me." But the cover on my Bible does not say "Bill's Holy Word." It says "God's Holy Word." If I have integrity, then I want to know what the biblical author meant, and through him what God meant. And this takes time and often hard work. The question you have to answer for yourself is, with your own view of Scripture, does it deserve the hard work. If you don't believe the Bible is God's Word, then perhaps all you think it deserves is a quick skim. But if Scripture did come from the very mouth of God (2 Tim 3:16), then I suspect it deserves more than a skim.

The Bible is not a novel. It is not a made-up story designed primarily to entertain, and hence it is not an easy read. While I enjoy reading the Bible, it was designed primarily to be life-changing, and this takes study. That is why we call it "Bible Study," not "Bible Skim."

Don't Skip This Step

Some people attending the proverbial Bible study want to skip this first step of exegesis. They want to know what the Bible "means to me." If you stop to think about it, this is impossible. We must do the hard work of learning the author's original meaning first, and without that we can't ever know "what it means to me." Fee and Stuart say, "A text cannot mean what it never meant" (*How to Read the Bible for All its Worth*, Zondervan, p. 26). A biblical passage can never carry a meaning for you that was not intended by the author (except perhaps prophecy)—if we have integrity in our interpretation. So one of the safeguards against reading our own ideas into the Bible, or against misunderstanding the Bible, is always to learn what it meant, and only after this to see what it means to me, today.

We do this automatically with every other kind of literature. If you read a Victorian novel, it is so full of English history and culture that you automatically understand what it is saying in its historical context, and only afterwards do you reapply its message in our own culture. Would anyone reading *Pride and Prejudice* think that Jane Austin is speaking directly to me, in 2002, in Spokane, Washington? The same is true of reading the Bible.

So the central goal of a good exegetical commentary is to learn the biblical author's intention, and only after that is done do we move into learning what it means to me today. How does the writer go about accomplishing this task?

Different Elements of Exegesis

Words, phrases, sentences, and paragraphs. People communicate with words, bound together into phrases, joined into sentences, that flow into paragraphs. The commentator's job is to look at each one of these components in order to learn the author's intent. In a sense, it is like the commentator is trying to restate what the author said in such as way that if the author were present, he would say, "Yes, that's what I meant."

Commentary writers will identify the main theme(s) in a passage and discuss the relationships among the phrases. They will discuss at least the major words, especially the theologically significant words. When you are done reading a good commentary, you should leave with a sense that you have spent time with the Biblical author and understand better the message he was trying to convey.

We sometimes talk about the "Grammatical-Historical Method" (spelled variously). This means that we use grammar and an understanding of the book's historical setting as the primary tool of exegesis. This method is sometimes set against the allegorical method of interpretation, which could make the Bible say almost anything the interpreter wanted it to say. One of the more famous examples is a typical allegorical interpretation of the parable of the Good Samaritan. Instead of being Jesus' answer to the question, "Who is my neighbor," it becomes an allegory of human creation (the man going down from Jerusalem to Jericho is Adam), the inability of the Law and Prophets to solve the human dilemma of sin (the priest and the Levite), and eventually of Jesus' coming (the "Good Samaritan") to care for sin, taking the robbery victim (you and me) to the Inn (the church) and paying the two denarii (baptism and the Lord's Supper). Let's not do this. Let's look at the words, phrases, sentences, and paragraphs and seek to learn what the biblical author meant.

Genres. A genre is a type of literature, like narrative, epistle, parable, prophecy, poetry, apocalyptic, etc. Each of these genres has its own specific rules of interpretation. For example, when the author of the Song of Songs says of his beloved, "your eyes are doves" (1:15), we don't imagine some grotesque science fiction type of genetically engineered monstrosity. We understand it as poetry, and that his beloved's eyes are *like* doves in their beauty. A commentary writer will take a passage's genre into consideration and apply the rules of interpretation appropriate for that genre. Any book on hermeneutics will discuss genre, but one of the best is *How to Read the Bible for All its Worth* by Gordon Fee and Douglas Stuart (Zondervan). Others are *A Basic Guide to Interpreting the Bible; Playing by the Rules* by Robert Stein (Baker), and *Grasping God's Word; A Hands-On Approach to Reading, Interpreting, and Applying the Bible* by J. Scott Duvall and J. Daniel Hays (Zondervan), the latter being a college textbook.

Setting. A good commentary will discuss the historical, cultural, geographic, and possibly theological setting of the passage. The point is to give the reader enough background information so as to understand the text. The biblical words do not exist in a vacuum. They were written to people who were as much a part of their world as you are a part of your world, and their meaning can only be understood when we read it within their ancient context.

Introduction. Almost every commentary has an introduction. Here the author is giving you the background necessary to understand the biblical book as a whole. He or she will discuss who the biblical author is, when he wrote, where he was in his life when he wrote, the occasion that prompted the writing, and his purposes in writing. The commentary writer will give an outline of the book and will summarize its basic themes, especially the theological themes. Trying to understand a biblical book without knowing something of these issues is like trying to understand a newspaper article written on September 12, 2002, without knowing what happened on September 11 in New York City. Without the background, much of the commentary (and biblical book) become nothing but disconnected pieces of information.

It is also in the introduction that the author may present arguments more geared for scholars than for most people. For example, in my commentary on the Pastorals I spend pages arguing that Paul wrote the Pastorals (1 and 2 Timothy, Titus) and more pages defending my understanding of the nature of the problems Paul is addressing and the basics of Paul's theological refutation of those problems. Much of what I wrote is of little consequence to a nonscholar who believes Paul wrote the Pastorals. But this is part of choosing the correct commentary for your needs; you have to match your needs with the commentary's purpose. But more about that below.

Analogy of Faith

One of the hermeneutical principles that came out of the Reformation is the "analogy of faith." It basically means that the biblical authors did not contradict themselves. In practice, this means that if you are having trouble interpreting one passage of Scripture, and the same biblical author writes on the same topic elsewhere, that you can use the second passage to help interpret the first.

Of course, if the commentator does not agree with this Reformation (and biblical) doctrine, then he or she will be free to claim that a biblical author contradicts himself. But as a general rule, most commentaries will compare the passage you are studying with other biblical discussions of the same topic.

Textual Issues

I will talk in more detail about this below, but suffice it to say here that some commentaries will talk about the differences that exist among the different Greek manuscripts of the Bible. For example, many Greek manuscripts of Ephesians lack the words "in Ephesus" in 1:1. It is important in the exegesis of Ephesians to know if Paul is writing to the church at Ephesus, or (if the words are not original) writing to the area of Asia Minor in general, of which Ephesus is a major city. Most commentaries do not go into detail on this issue; it is extremely complicated and very much the realm of the specialist.

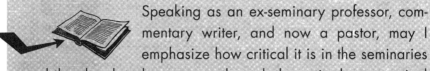

Speaking as an ex-seminary professor, commentary writer, and now a pastor, may I emphasize how critical it is in the seminaries and the church today to move through the entire hermeneutical circle, to always begin with what the text actually says and meant, and never stop short of the application of biblical truth in real-life situations. This is not an easy task. The series in which my commentary appears left application beyond its scope. And while I had many students in my class on the Pastorals who wanted to know the facts and the heart of the Bible so it could become real in their lives ("means"), I also had significant pressure from other students who wanted the "right answer" ("meant") so they could move on to graduate school. For many years much of seminary education has been concerned with the details and minutia of the Bible, without providing the synthesis necessary for effective pulpit ministry. As a reaction (to some degree), it is of little surprise that much of the fluff being passed off in church and preaching these days has little basis in biblical fact. Many pastors were never exposed to the relevancy of solid biblical exegesis, especially in the use of Greek and Hebrew, and so many pastors appear to have abandoned the meant stage and concentrate on application, but an application devoid of its exegetical foundation. If this book can play a small role in helping to reverse this trend, I will be gratified.

Between the Lines

In the advanced commentaries there will often be discussion about details that, for lack of a better expression, are between the lines. For example, commentaries on the Synoptic Gospels (Matthew, Mark, and Luke) will often compare the wording of one account with the wording of the same account in another gospel, and then ask why they are different. Commentaries on Paul's letters will often talk about the source of some of his statements; the assumption is that Paul borrowed bits and pieces, especially hymns and creeds, from other sources. Some commentaries on John will talk about the "community" that supposedly exerted pressure on the gospel and to some degree affected how it was written. These types of discussions often punctuate, and in some cases permeate, a commentary. For you at the "baby Greek" level, I recommend that if the commentary writer is more preoccupied with these types of issues rather than the meaning of the biblical text, don't use the commentary.

Step 2: Means

The second step of hermeneutics is to take what the passage meant and to see what it means today. Sometimes the word "hermeneutics" is used exclusively of this step. The idea is to bring the passage through the centuries, from the biblical culture to our culture, and to understand its meaning and application in our lives.

Few commentaries deal with this step. Most are content to work in the original context, and some writers even consider it wrong to try and apply the biblical message to today. The *NIV Application Commentary* series provides a welcomed relief to this practice. The volumes are written by true scholars and move through the issue of cultural context into the passages' contemporary significance. The *Preaching the Word* series is built around the expository preaching of Kent Hughes at College Church in Wheaton (Crossway Books) and likewise models the melding of authorial intent and application. Individual volumes sometimes move in this direction as well; Gordon Fee's commentary on 1 Corinthians, in an otherwise excellent but scholarly series, concludes each section with a discussion helping the reader move beyond meant into means. If you struggle with the issue of application, see *Applying the Bible,* a short book by Jack Kuhatschek (Zondervan).

How to Choose a Commentary

1. The best thing you can do is read several commentaries on a biblical passage. There is nothing like getting your "feet wet" to decide whether or not a commentary will be useful. Of course, in this day and age, many Christian bookstores are more concerned with inspirational writings and "Jesus Junk" (as one bookstore owner described it to me) than with books dealing with study and content, so you may not be able to check out different commentaries. Maybe there is a Christian school nearby or the library of a trained pastor.

2. You want to find a commentary whose philosophy matches your needs. Do you want to read the author's interaction with Greek and Hebrew? Do you want to walk through the author's reasoning process, or just hear her or his conclusions? Do you want to know about every word, or just the flow of thought and discussion of the difficult passages?

3. When you are done reading a passage in the commentary, do you know more about the biblical text or just things about it? This is a crucial distinction. Some commentaries appear to be written more for other commentary writers and scholars than for you. Many of the books lining my shelves have little to offer the pastor or Bible study leader who wants help preparing for the next week. Many of the discussions are technical and geared for scholarship. My suggestion for you is to avoid commentaries that enter into scholarly debate and concentrate on those that help you understand the text.

4. Does the author understand hermeneutics? Some commentaries, traditionally those considered more "devotional," spend little time with the meaning of the text and move quickly into application. But how do you know if the application is based on truth? Be careful of these.

5. Does the author argue fairly? Some authors are committed to presenting all interpretive decisions so fairly that even those with whom they disagree would appreciate the presentation. Dispensationalists used to compliment George Ladd in how fairly he presented the dispensational position, even though he argued against it.

But some writers skew the other positions, do not give all the counter-arguments, basically set up a "straw man" argument, and then shoot it down with ease. Some authors like to label those who hold another position and attack them as people, not dealing with the actual interpretation and the arguments. This might make for "fun" reading, but it is grostesquely unfair and un-Christian. Some authors like to make wide-sweeping claims that go far beyond the facts and give the appearance of wisdom. Beware also of someone using words like "clearly" and "obviously." If the answers to the questions raised by the text were truly "clear" and "obvious," then there wouldn't be much debate.

There is a tendency on the part of some people to think that the canons of Christian behavior—charity, fairness, kindness—have no relevance in book writing. But while it is true that commentary writing demands that you take a position and therefore disagree with another writer, it does not demand that we leave our Christian character at the door to the study and rationalize what can only be termed "cruel." These types of books should themselves be left at the door or simply discarded.

6. Does the author treat the biblical text with respect? It will be hard for you to tell this right away, but after a while you will probably be able to tell whether the commentary writer believes the Bible is worthy of respect. This is part of the difficulty for an evangelical in commentary writing. In a sense, you are standing over it and trying to understand it. But at the same time an evangelical will submit to its teaching. This is a difficult balance.

7. Does the commentary writer deal just with the text, or does he or she enter into scholarly debate? This happens at several levels. (a) In some commentaries all you read is the author's position. (b) In others the writer might show you different interpretations of the verse, and then associate different scholars with the appropriate interpretation. (c) The philosophy of other series requires the author to enter fully into scholarly debate. While many fine commentaries fall into this third category, it is these commentaries that will be the most difficult for you who are at the "baby Greek" level to understand.

Part of the problem is that the scholarly debate may be about a topic that is only remotely connected to the biblical passage you are studying. Without knowing the debate, it is generally not possible to understand the commentary writer's discussion. For example, many commentaries on the Pastorals talk about church structure (i.e., having elders and deacons) being a later development (by which they generally mean second century). This doesn't come from the text of the Pastorals; it comes from the writers' understanding of how the early church developed, that it originally was only Spirit-driven (like we supposedly see in Corinth) and only later developed administrative structures. I recommend that especially for those of you at the "baby Greek" level, read the commentaries that fit in levels (a) or (b). If you are reading a level (c) commentary, just skip over the scholarly debate.

8. We all see the Bible through a grid, usually through a theological grid. It is impossible to write a commentary that does not reflect your theological bias, and you should know your author's grid. Where was he trained? Where does he teach? Who published the book? If it is an academic work published by Zondervan, Baker, or Hendrickson, you can probably trust it. (I am speaking as an evangelical—that's my grid.)

One of the harder lessons I had to learn in college was that people considerably outside the orthodox definition of Christianity write books about the Bible. I remember one book that I simply could not understand, until I realized that the author did not believe in the physical resurrection.

The commentary series by William Barclay is wildly successful, if you judge by the number sold. He writes beautifully in ways that are easy to quote. But later in his life Barclay could be seen to be wondering about the possibility of the supernatural, specifically miracles. Be careful. And when you are reading his applications, make sure they actually come from the biblical text.

Some Bibles have notes along the bottom of the page. These are normally succinct but somewhat helpful. Just be aware that the notes are not part of the Bible, and each study Bible has its own theological bias. The *NIV Study Bible* is broadly evangelical. The *Scofield Reference Bible* is dispensational. The *Geneva Study Bible* is Calvinist.

9. Some people are impressed by length of pages, weight of the book, and the number of footnotes. I can still remember talking to someone at church who said that I must believe this one writer because there were so many footnotes in his book. Anybody can write with footnotes. Anybody can give the appearance of scholarship by listing long bibliographies. This has no necessary connection with truth.

My Favorite New Testament Commentaries

I hesitate to recommend any commentaries because the publishing houses are turning them out seemingly as fast as possible. I know some writers who have contracts for five of six commentaries over the next fifteen years. And I hesitate to list just two or three, because there are many good commentaries available. But as of 2002, here are the primary volumes I have found helpful. I would highly recommend *New Testament Commentary Survey* by D. A. Carson (Baker). It is in its fifth edition (2001) and I would assume he will keep it current. He discusses many more series and individual volmes than I will. For Old Testament commentaries see *A Guide to Selecting and Using Bible Commentaries* by Douglas Stuart (Word, 1987) or *Old Testament Commentary Survey* by Tremper Longmann III (Baker, 1995).

There are several good one- or two-volume commentaries on the New Testament or the entire Bible. These will paint the broad stroke of the biblical writer's teaching; they sometimes do not do as well with the difficult passages and aren't always concerned with showing you multiple interpretations. Here are my two favorites.

- *Evangelical Commentary on the Bible,* edited by Elwell (Baker).
- *Zondervan NIV Bible Commentary,* two volumes, edited by Barker and Kohlenberger (Zondervan). I used the New Testament volume in my seminary New Testament Survey class, and it worked well. It is an abridgment of the twelve volume *Expositor's Bible Commentary* (see below).

Commentaries that discuss just one (or sometimes two or three) biblical book are published either as independent books or as part of a series. Independent commentaries are unpredictable; there is no way to know if they will suit your purposes without reading through part of it, unless you know the author is reputable. Commentaries in series are a little more predictable because the series has a philiosophy of what it is trying to accomplish, and the editors should have made sure that each volume conforms to that philosophy. Some series are successful in doing this; others fail, and as a result the various volumes in the series differ significantly. Here are my recommended series, beginning with the easiest to the more scholarly, but none of these should be beyond your reach. Some of the books are published outside the United States; I have given the US publisher.

- *Preaching the Word*, edited by Kent Hughes (Crossway). Built around Kent Hughes' preaching (but includes others as well), the series will eventually cover the entire Bible and is primarily expositional (i.e., sermons).
- *The Expositor's Bible Commentary*, edited by Frank Gaebelein (Zondervan). An affordable series of generally consistent quality. It is being revised. This is a good series to purchase because it gives you at least one affordable explanation of both the New and Old Testaments. It is also available as a software module for Accordance and Zondervan's Bible search software.
- The *Tyndale New Testament Commentaries*, edited by Leon Morris (InterVarsity Press), has for many years been the standard commentary series for the evangelical layperson. The series is affordable, written by scholars, and is in the process of being updated.
- *New International Biblical Commentary*, edited by W. Ward Gasque (Hendrickson). A layman's commentary.
- *IVP New Testament Commentaries*.
- *The New American Commentary*, edited by David Dockery (Broadman & Holman), is a new series done by Baptist scholars that is generally of good quality and is understandable by pastor and layperson alike.
- *The NIV Application Commentary*, edited by Terry Muck (Zondervan). An excellent series written by competent scholars that goes further into hermeneutics than any other series. I think this is the best series overall for the studious layperson.
- Two other series that are approachable and have some worthwhile volumes are *Harper's New Testament Commentaries* (Harper & Row) and *New Century Bible* (Eerdmans).

The following series are written by scholars, most at the seminary level and above. At the "baby Greek" stage I would not recommend buying any of these sets as a whole, but individual volumes may prove themselves invaluable for indepth study. If you want to read word studies, these series are more likely to be helpful than those listed above.

- *Baker Exegetical Commentary on the New Testament*, edited by Moisés Silva (Baker). A new series of excellent works by competent scholars. Not yet completed.
- *The Pillar New Testament Commentary*, edited by D. A. Carson (Eerdmans). Another new series of excellent works by competent scholars. Not yet completed.

- *The New International Commentary on the New Testament*, edited by Gordon Fee (Eerdmans). These volmes are marvelous studies as a whole, but you are going to have to read through scholarly discussions that will often be irrelevant for you. The Greek is kept in the footnotes.
- *Word Biblical Commentary*, edited by David Hubbard, Bruce Metzger, and others (Thomas Nelson). I hesitate to list this series. Some of these volumes are excellent, but others are totally irrelevant for you. The theological and scholarly position of many of the Old Testament volumes is considerably different from most of the New Testament volumes. There is much heavy duty scholarly interaction, and they are often difficult to read because it does not use footnotes for the technical discussions and references. The Greek is throughout the text but with translation. My commentary on the Pastorals is in this series.

There are a few other series that have many excellent volumes, but they assume a working knowledge of Greek, Hebrew, and in some cases Latin. They are: *The International Critical* Commentary (T. & T. Clark); the *New International Greek Testament Commentary* (Eerdmans); *Hermeneia* (SCM/Fortress Press).

Here is my list of preferred commentaries for the New Testament with their series.

Book	Lay level	Advanced level
Matthew	Carson (EBC) Mounce, Robert (NIBC) Blomberg (NAC)	Keener Morris (PNTC) Hagner (WBC)
Mark	Garland (NIVAC)	Lane (NICNT) Edwards (PNTC)
Luke	Stein (NAC) Evans (NIBC)	Bock (BECNT)
John	Stott Burge (NIVAC)	Morris (NICNT) Carson (PNTC)
Acts	Marshall (TNTC) Fernando (NIVAC) Polhill (NAC)	Bruce (NICNT)
Romans	Stott Moo (NIVAC) Bruce (TNTC) Harrison (EBC)	Moo (NICNT) Schreiner (BECNT) Morris (PNTC)
1 Corinthians	Blomberg (NIVAC)	Fee (NICNT)
2 Corinthians	Barrett (HNTC)	Hafemann (NIVAC) Barnett (NIVNT)

Galatians	George (NAC)	Fung (NICNT)
Ephesians	Snodgrass (NIVAC)	Hoehner (Baker) Bruce (NICNT) O'Brien (PNTC)
Philippians	Thielman (NIVAC) Martin (TNTC)	Fee (NICNT) Hawthorne (WBC) Silva (BECNT)
Colossians/Philemon	Garland (NIVAC) Wright (TNTC)	O'Brien (WBC)
1/2 Thessalonians	Marshall (NCB) Holmes (NIVAC)	Morris (NICNT) Bruce (WBC)
Pastorals	Fee (NIBC) Guthrie, Donald (TNTC) Kelly*	Mounce, William (WBC)
Hebrews	Guthrie, George (NIVAC)	Lane (WBC) Bruce (NICNT)
James	Moo (TNTC)	Laws(HNTC)
1 Peter	Marshall (IVPNTC) Nystrom (NIVAC) Kelly** Grudem (TNTC) Schreiner (NAC)	Davids (NICNT)
2 Peter/Jude	Moo (NIVAC) Green (TNTC) Kelly** Schreiner (NAC)	Bauckham (WBC)***
1/2/3 John	Burge (NIVAC) Stott (TNTC)	Marshall (NICNT) Kruse (PNTC)
Revelation	Morris (TNTC) Johnson, Dennis Keener (NIVAC)	Mounce, Robert (NICNT)

* *Thornapple Commentaries* (Baker)
** *Black's New Testament Commentaries* (Adam & Charles Black)
*** Please note that Bauckham does not believe Peter wrote 2 Peter, but his handling of the text is still excellent.

CHAPTER 30

The History of the Bible and Textual Criticism

In my opening discussion, "What Would It Look Like If You Knew a Little Greek?" (p. xiii), I give two examples of different translations. The first was what the angels said to the shepherds, and I pointed out how these two are substantially different.

> Glory to God in the highest, and on earth *peace, goodwill toward men.* (KJV)

> Glory to God in the highest, and on earth *peace among men with whom he is pleased.* (RSV)

I also talked about how some translations stop at Mark 16:8 while others go on to verse 20, including v 18, which talks about Christians handling snakes and drinking poison.

These differences are not due to different translations of the same Greek words. The differences are due to the fact that there are variations among the many Greek manuscripts we have of the New Testament; some translations follow some manuscripts and other translations follow others. If you are going to know why translations are different, you need to have some awareness of this issue.

To put it another way, along the bottom of many Bibles you will see the constant mention of what "other manuscripts" say. These footnotes are talking about the differences that exist among the different Greek manuscripts. The easiest way to explain these differences is to walk through church history and see how the Bible comes down to us through the centuries. All Bible citations below are from the ESV unless otherwise stated.

Writing of the New Testament

The New Testament authors wrote for many different reasons. The gospels were written to slightly different audiences, and while they had the same basic message, they also had their own themes the authors wanted to stress. Matthew appears to have been written more for a Jewish audience as is seen, among other things, by his frequent assertion that a certain act fulfilled prophecy. Matthew wanted his audience to understand that Jesus was the Messiah. It is generally believed that Mark was written for a Roman audience and, among other things, wanted to show that Jesus was the Son of God. Luke, we believe, was written more for Gentiles; many of the passages that occur only in Luke address this specific audience. He also tells us that he wanted people (specifically Theophilus) to understand the "certainty" of the gospel story (Luke 1:4). John was written so that his audience "may believe that Jesus is the Christ, the Son of God, and that by believing you may have life in his name" (20:31). When these gospels were first written, they were probably sent to the author's specific audience.

The letters (or epistles) are another matter. Most of Paul's letters were written to a church. They were written to answer specific questions (e.g., 1 Corinthians, 1 and 2 Thessalonians), deal with specific problems (e.g.,

There are several books I will be citing. Each is worth reading if you want more information.

Paul Wegner, *The Journey from Texts to Translations* (Baker, 1999). A college-length textbook with many pictures and original citations. An excellent reference book as well as an enjoyable book just to read.

Philip Comfort, *Essential Guide to Bible Versions* (Tyndale, 2000). A lay-level discussion of the history of the Bible and its translations, written by the chair of the New Testament Committee for the New Living Bible.

Bruce Metzger, *The Bible in Translation* (Baker, 2001). An authoritative discussion by one of the preeminent translators and textual critics of our day, who was part of the translation team of the RSV and convener of the New Testament division for the NRSV. Prof. Metzger is a scholar and a gentleman.

Bruce Metzger, *The Text of the New Testament: Its Transmission, Corruption, and Restoration* (Oxford, 1992, third, enlarged edition). This is the best discussion of the history of the Greek text.

Galatians), thank the church (Philippians), or to prepare the way for future ministry (Romans). He also wrote letters to an old friend (Philemon) and two of his associates (1 and 2 Timothy, Titus). Some of the letters don't tell us much about to whom they were written (e.g., Hebrews, James, 1 and 2 Peter, 1 John). The short letters of 2 and 3 John were written to a specific church and to a friend, Gaius. Even more so than the gospels, these letters would have been sent to a specific audience.

These original writings, or what we call the "autographs," would have been written on papyrus (2 John 12) or possibly parchment (2 Timothy 4:13). They were then delivered to the churches/people to whom they were written, perhaps by friends traveling to the area or by people specifically sent (e.g., Eph 6:21-22; Col 4:7-9). When the New Testament was written, there were no printing presses, no photocopy machines, no Internet. They were not broadcast to the widest possible audience. They were written to specific audiences, and it was to each audience that the writing was first sent.

Spread of the Writings

So how were the writings spread? Obviously, when Paul's letter to a church arrived, it was read to all (e.g., 1 Thess 5:27). We can assume that different individuals wanted copies of the letters, either for their own reading or to share with other people in the city. It is also safe to assume that as people traveled, they wanted to take copies of these writings to people and churches in other cities, as well as obtain copies of the gospels/letters that perhaps had been written to the other church. In fact, Paul tells the Colossians to share their letter with the church at Laodicea, and to be sure to read the one he wrote the Laodiceans (Col 4:16). This type of sharing occurred throughout the ancient world.

So how were the copies made? It does not appear that the early church used professional scribes to make the copies, and the church was growing quickly and the word needed to get out. People either sat down and copied the letter/gospel, or sometimes, perhaps rarely, a person would read it aloud and a small group would write what they heard. As you might imagine, this is where a problem arose. If you were to sit down and copy the letter of Romans, or if you were to read it and have others write what they heard, you can imagine how many and what types of errors would creep into the copies. The fact of the matter is that no two manuscripts of the Greek New Testament are identical. There are differences among all of them.

This is not a made-up problem. This is not some problem created by a "liberal bias" against Scripture. These "mistakes," these differences among the copies of the New Testament writings, are real. You can look at them and see the differences.

It was merely a matter of time before the autographs, written as they were on biodegradable materials, would deteriorate, become unusable, and be discarded. All that the church had, then, were manuscript copies, with all their differences.

The Types of Differences Among the Manuscripts

If you sit down and look at the differences among the Greek manuscripts of the New Testament, they fall into one of two categories, unintentional and intentional. Many of the mistakes are **unintentional**, such as misspellings and transposition of words.

* The name John can be spelled Ἰωάνης or Ἰωάννης. While the shift from a double to a single ν is a difference, it is not that significant especially in terms of meaning. There are, likewise, multiple spellings of the names "Gerasenes" (Mark 5:1), "Bethesda" (John 5:2), and others.

Autograph. The original document written by the biblical author. **Manuscript**. Copies made of the autograph or other manuscripts. **Papyrus**. A writing material made of strips from papyrus reeds that were laid vertically, and another layer laid horizontally, and then pressed together. **Parchment** and **Vellum**. Writing materials made from animal hides, parchment from sheep and goats, and vellum from younger calves and kids. **Reading**. The word(s) used by a specific manuscript in a specific location. For example, I can talk about the reading "peace, goodwill toward men" and the reading "peace among men with whom he is pleased." **Textual Criticism**. The science of studying the differences among the manuscripts and deciding which reading is most likely to be original. **Translation**. Moving what was written from one language to another. Also called versions. The obvious bears repeating: no translation is inspired; all translations are interpretive. **Lectionary**. Biblical texts prepared for church reading in the liturgy. **Codex**. As opposed to a single piece of writing material or a scroll, the codex is like our modern books. Individual leaves were folded and then sewed together.

Mistakes include the omission of a word, transposing letters, or even transposing words.

- In several places we are not sure whether the author wrote "Jesus Christ" or "Christ Jesus" (e.g., 1 Tim 1:16).
- In some places we are not sure whether the author included the definite article or not (e.g., "the resurrection" in 2 Tim 2:18).

Some of these differences can be traced to similar sounding letters.

- Romans 5:1 says either "we have peace" (ἔχομεν) or "let us have peace" (ἔχωμεν); the difference in pronunciation between ο and ω was slight to negligible.
- Does John write "And we are writing these things so that our (ἡμῶν) joy may be complete" or "so that your (ὑμῶν) joy may be complete" (1 John 1:4)? Again, the difference in sound between η and υ is so slight, especially in medieval manuscripts, that they could easily be mistaken.

These types of differences constitute the bulk of the differences among manuscripts. Rarely do they affect the theological meaning of the verse; the last two examples constitute two of the more significant differences. For an excellent chart of these types of mistakes see Wegner, p. 225.

Intentional changes can be more difficult to detect, and just because a change appears to be intentional does not mean that the change was necessarily ill-intentioned. Sometimes we see a scribe changing what evidently he thought was an error. Either he was right, or in changing the text he introduced an error. Sometimes we see scribes trying to improve grammar, using a fancier word to dress-up the verse, or using a simpler word to make the verse more understandable. Sometimes words are added to help explain the text. (These additions may originally have been written in the margins and in later centuries moved into the text itself.) When the same account appears in more than one gospel, we can see the scribes trying to make sure the gospels do not contradict each other (i.e., "harmonization"). They do the same with harmonizing Old Testament citations in the New Testament with the Old Testament itself, as well as harmonizing similar statements in different New Testament passages. Scribes tended to add to the name of Jesus (e.g., changing "Jesus" to "Jesus Christ the Lord") out of reverence.

- Matt 9:17 reads, "But new wine is put into fresh wineskins, and so both are preserved." The parallel in Luke 5:38 reads, "But new wine must be put into fresh wineskins." Some Lukan manuscripts add, "and so both are preserved" to harmonize the saying.

- The manuscripts of Matthew 16:20 read "the Christ," "Jesus Christ," or "Christ Jesus" (cf. Gal 6:17).
- Matthew 15:8 reads,

> "This people honors me with their lips,
>   but their heart is far from me."

It is a citation of Isaiah 29:13, which reads,

> "Because this people draw near with their mouth
>   and honor me with their lips,
>   while their hearts are far from me."

Some manuscripts of Matthew 15:8 begin, "This people draws near to me with their mouth," to make the citations closer.

- Matthew 9:13 reads, "Go and learn what this means, 'I desire mercy, and not sacrifice.' For I came not to call the righteous, but sinners." Some manuscripts add "to repentance" after "sinners" for clarity's sake.
- John 5 contains the account of Jesus healing the paralytic in the pool of Bethesda. Vv 3, 5 read, "³In these lay a multitude of invalids—blind, lame, and paralyzed. ⁵One man was there who had been an invalid for thirty-eight years." Where did v 4 go that talks about the angel stirring the water? It doesn't exist in the oldest and best manuscripts; and in about twenty manuscripts that include v 4, the scribes indicated that the words are an addition to the original text. It is easy to imagine a scribe reading v 3 and v 5, knowing that readers will wonder why the paralytic was lying there for so long, and perhaps at first adding a comment in the margin, and then eventually the marginal note being added to the text. Vv 3b- 4 read, "waiting for the moving of the water, ⁴for an angel of the Lord went down at certain seasons into the pool, and stirred the water: whoever stepped in first after the stirring of the water was healed of whatever disease he had."

All of these scribal tendencies are natural and not necessarily the result of a desire to pervert Scriptures. Granted, there was some of this. The heretic Marcion tried to remove all the Jewishness from Jesus and the New Testament. But usually the changes appear to be well-intentioned.

Do scribes always add to Scripture? Couldn't they also drop out? It certainly is a possibility, but it appears that they rarely did; when they did omit, it was almost always due to accidental oversight. It is sometimes said today that the scribes tended to omit words and verses because of their heretical belief, but that is an unsubstantiated claim. It appears that the vast majority of the time scribes changed or added to the text.

If nothing else, this should help you understand many of the footnotes in your Bible. When the translators are not sure of the original reading

Why didn't God superintend the process? Why didn't God's providence control the copying process so that mistakes didn't creep into the copies? This is an interesting question, especially for those who hold to a high view of Scripture. There are several answers. (1) Regardless of one's theological position on Scripture, it is in fact remarkable how well the copies of the New Testament made it through the centuries. As we will see below, we have over 5,600 Greek manuscripts of the New Testament (most of them only partial), which is significantly more than any other writing from antiquity. It is because we have so many manuscripts that it is possible to look at all of them and come to a relatively comfortable conclusion as to what was originally written. (2) The vast majority of the differences are inconsequential (misspellings, a word left out), and no cardinal doctrine is brought into question by any viable variant. (3) From this I would conclude that God did superintend the process of copying the gospels/letters of the New Testament. For whatever reason he chose to allow mistakes to creep in, but he evidently did make sure that the basic message of the New Testament was never corrupted.

they will sometimes list the other reading(s) in the footnotes. Jude 5 reads, "Now I want to remind you, although you once fully knew it, that Jesus, who saved a people out of the land of Egypt," an amazing statement missed in some manuscripts, because it means the God of the Exodus was Jesus. The footnote on "Jesus" in the ESV reads, "Some manuscripts *although you fully knew it, that the Lord who once saved*." Footnotes are sometimes included when the translators are confident of the correct Greek reading, but out of deference to the KJV and the familiarity of the verse they list an alternate reading. For example, most modern translations recognize that the Lord's prayer ends, "but deliver us from evil" (Matthew 6:13). But they add the footnote, "some manuscripts add *For yours is the kingdom and the power and the glory forever. Amen*." While this ending of the prayer is well known, beloved by most, and without it the prayer "feels" incomplete, there is little question that it was added centuries after Christ said the prayer.

Uncials are a form of capital letters used in the 2nd through the 9th century. The script was written with more curves than the previous form of the alphabet, curves that make it easier to write. **Cursive** script was used from the 9th through the 16th century. It is like our handwriting where the letters are connected. **Lectionaries** are biblical texts prepared for church reading in the liturgy. **Papyri** refers to the type of writing material. (All extant Greek New Testament papyri use uncial script.)

Historical Events

There are several major events in the early history of the church that had a significant impact on the spread of the Greek manuscripts. The first is persecution. Christians have been persecuted from the earliest days, and their writings were often destroyed. During the persecution by the Roman emperors, many Christians were martyred and their sacred writings destroyed. In 303 Diocletian ordered the destruction of all Christian Scriptures. Fortunately, a few years later the emperor Constantine guaranteed the safety of religion, specifically Christianity, throughout the Roman empire, and the mass destruction of the Bible ceased.

The church grew publicly, and the need for Bibles increased greatly. The copying of manuscripts continued, more now by monks. Not only did they copy the text but they embellished it cosmetically with color and fancy edging. The fracture between the Eastern and the Western Church was also becoming significant. The Eastern Church was based in Constantinople and used Greek. The Western Church was centered in Rome, and Latin was becoming its official language.

The other major event had to do with a man named Lucian of Antioch. Before the Diocletian persecution, Lucian produced an edited version of the Greek New Testament (Jerome, *Patrologia Latina* 29, column 527). This means that he looked at different Greek manuscripts, and instead of simply copying one he merged all the manuscripts into one. In the process he smoothed over difficult readings, modified grammar, harmonized passages, and the such. When the Diocletian persecution began, many of the Bibles were destroyed, both some of Lucian's as well as the manuscripts he used. When Constantine reversed the policy and actually asked Eusebius to have fifty copies of the Bible made for the church at Constantinople, it was the remaining copies of Lucian's work that evidently were copied. (See Metzger, *Text*, for more details; this account is simplified.) Because the Eastern Church used Greek, it became the primary source of Greek manuscripts, and many copies were made. Despite their number, they were an altered text, significantly different from the citations of the New Testament that we read in the early Greek Church Fathers.

Latin Translations

In the Western Church, the Bible was translated into Latin. As early as 160 Tertullian evidently used a Latin Bible. By the end of the fourth century, there were so many versions of the Bible in Latin that Pope Damasus I (366-384) commissioned Jerome (c. 345-420) to standardize the Latin Bible. He began his work in Rome and finished many years later in Bethlehem. The New Testament was a revision of the older Latin versions as Jerome compared them to the Greek. The gospels were published in 383. However, he translated the Old Testament afresh into Latin from the Hebrew (390-405). He was severely criticized for doing so because, in the eyes of many, the Septuagint was the "inspired translation" and therefore of abiding authority. It appears that many people of all times have struggled with a new translation of the Bible, preferring the more familiar. Jerome called his opponents "two-legged asses" (F. F. Bruce, *The Books and the Parchments*, p. 205).

Jerome expressed his concern to Damasus about the nature of translating in the preface to his work:

> You urge me to revise the old Latin version, and, as it were, to sit in judgment on the copies of the Scriptures which are now scattered throughout the whole world; and, inasmuch as they differ from one another, you would have me decide which of them agree with the Greek original. The labour is one of love, but at the same time both perilous and presumptuous; for in judging others I must be content to be judged by all; and how can I dare to change the language of the world in its hoary old age, and carry it back to the early days of its infancy? Is there a man, learned or unlearned, who will not, when he takes the volume into his hands, and perceives that what he reads does not suit his settled tastes, break out immediately into violent language, and call me a forger and a profane person for having the audacity to add anything to the ancient books, or to make any changes or corrections therein? (in Wegner, p. 255)

Eventually Jerome's translation became the dominant translation in the West for 1,000 years. It is called the Latin Vulgate, "Vulgate" meaning "common" or "plain," the standard Bible of the church. It was a revised edition of Jerome's Vulgate that Wycliffe translated into English (see below). When Gutenberg (c. 1398-1468) adapted the Chinese invention of printing with moveable type to the much simpler Latin alphabet, the face of publication—both quantity and quality—was changed forever. Gutenberg's first printed book was a two-volume Vulgate. It was not until the Council of Trent (1546-1563) that the Catholic Church officially made it their authorized Bible and pronounced an anathema on anyone using any other translation.

Greek Texts

There were many forces at work in the world that had an effect on the Bible. The Eastern and Western Church continued to divide. With the downfall of the Byzantine Empire and the conquering of Constantinople (1453), the Greek scholars fled with their ancient manuscripts to the West. The Renaissance (14th - 16th centuries) and Reformation fostered a new interest in the Greek and Hebrew texts lying beneath the Latin.

The Complutensian Polyglot Bible was begun in 1502, with four columns of Hebrew, Aramaic, Greek, and Latin. The Greek manuscripts upon which it was based were evidently quite good (and a little different from Erasmus' text), and the project had significant funding. The New Testament was finished in 1514 and the Old Testament in 1517, but it was not published until 1522.

However, in 1515 a Swiss printer named Froben wanted to get a Greek Bible to market before the Complutensian Polyglot. He contacted the Dutch scholar Desiderius Erasmus (1469-1536), who then came to Basel, Switzerland, in July to begin his work. Metzger describes Erasmus' work as follows.

> For most of the text he relied on two rather inferior manuscripts from a monastic library at Basle, one of the Gospels … and one of the Acts and Epistles, both dating from about the twelfth century. Erasmus compared them with two or three others of the same books and entered occasional corrections for the printer in the margins or between the lines of the Greek script. For the Book of Revelation he had but one manuscript, dating from the twelfth century, which he had borrowed from his friend Reuchlin. Unfortunately, this manuscript lacked the final leaf, which had contained the last six verses of the book. For these verses, as well as a few other passages throughout the book where the Greek text of the Apocalypse and the adjoining Greek commentary with which the manuscript was supplied are so mixed up as to be almost indistinguishable, Erasmus depended upon the Latin Vulgate, translating this text into Greek. (*Text*, 99-100)

The three manuscripts are Codex 1, 2, and 2814 (earlier named 1^r).

Erasmus' work was very hurried and quite poor in many cases. Not only were there hundreds of typographical errors, but he added words that could not be found in any current Greek manuscripts. The most famous was his inclusion of Paul's question, "What shall I do, Lord?" in Acts 9:6, copied from the parallel account in Acts 22:10. His translation from Latin to Greek in Revelation includes words that do not exist in the Greek language (see Metzger, *Text*, p. 100n1). But Erasmus finished his work in ten months and beat the Complutensian Polyglot to market on March 1, 1516.

It was published as a diglot, with a parallel translation in Latin that Erasmus had been working on for several years. At first it was not well-received. Because his Latin translation was different from the more familiar Vulgate, he was viewed with suspicion, and the typographical errors brought him ridicule from many quarters. The Greek was also suspect because Latin had been the language of the Western Church for a thousand years, and many could not believe that the Greek texts were more reliable than the Latin translations. Strange but true (although the Greek texts Jerome used were evidently superior to those Erasmus used, and consequently his overall resultant translation was better, too). But the fact that it was published first, combined with the fact that it was smaller and cheaper than the Complutensian Polyglot, were major forces in its eventual acceptance and dominance in the market.

Erasmus's text went through five editions. The second (1519) was used by Luther as the basis for his German translation in 1522. The third edition (1522) was used by Tyndale. The fourth edition (1527) became the standard, an edition corrected by comparisons with the now-published and superior Complutensian Polyglot (about 90 changes in Revelation alone). Future editions by Stephanus and Beza were based on this fourth edition. The King James translators (1611) used Beza's editions of 1588-1589 and 1598. In 1633 two relatives, Bonaventure and Abraham Elzevir, printed a copy of Beza's 1565 edition with the following advertisement: "[The reader has] the text which is now received by all, in which we give nothing changed or corrupted" (Metzger, *Text*, 106). The Latin behind "text … received" is "textum … receptum," from which the phrase "Textus Receptus," or the "Received Text," came. This became the dominant Greek text for the next two and a half centuries. Yet, even by 1550 variants began to be noted. The TR was used, after a while, out of attrition. Variants to it were listed in footnotes.

Metzger concludes, "So superstitious has been the reverence accorded the Textus Receptus that in some cases attempts to criticize or emend it have been regarded as akin to sacrilege. Yet its textual basis is essentially a handful of late and haphazardly collected minuscule manuscripts, and in a dozen passages its reading is supported by no known Greek witness." (*Text*, 106)

As of today, there are 5,713 Greek New Testament manuscripts: 116 papyri; 310 uncials; 2,867 minuscules; 2,420 lectionaries. However, a few of these are actually parts of the same document. But taking these into consideration, there are more than 5,600 manuscripts. The most recent numbers can be found at the website for Institut für neutestamentliche Textforschung, at:

www.uni-muenster.de/NTTextforschung/INTF.html

English Translations

Over the centuries most people did not know how to read Latin or Greek, and it unfortunately became the teaching of the church that only the clergy were able to read and interpret the Bible. John Wycliffe (c. 1329-1384) was a pastor and a scholar who was highly critical of the current church, opposing its corruption and much of its teaching. As such Wycliffe has earned the title "Morning Star of the Reformation." Wycliffe believed that the Bible, not the Pope, had the right to determine biblical doctrine, and therefore he translated the Vulgate into English, along with the help of his students. Then his students and other people, nicknamed the Lollards, carried his translation and teaching throughout England. For his efforts Wycliffe was branded a heretic, anyone caught reading his translation was excommunicated, and some of his students were burned at the stake. Wegner (p. 282) writes,

> Archbishop Arundel denounces Wycliffe in a letter to Pope John XXIII in 1411: "This pestilent and wretched John Wyclif, of cursed memory, that son of the old serpent ... endeavored by every means to attack the very faith and sacred doctrine of the Holy Church, devising—to fill up the measure of his malice—the expedient of a new translation of the Scriptures into the mother tongue."

Even after Wycliffe's death, his work was continued by his followers. John Purvey produced a second edition (1388), which became the main English Bible until the time of Tyndale. In 1428 Pope Martin V had Wycliffe's body exhumed, burned, and the ashes thrown into the local river. Metzger poetically concludes, "But just as his ashes were carried by that river to multiple points, so his message went far and wide during the following centuries." (*Translation*, 57)

William Tyndale (c. 1494-1536) produced the first English translation from the Greek and Hebrew. One of the more famous quotations comes from his debate with a cleric.

> Not long after, Tindall happened to be in the company of a certain divine, recounted for a learned man, and in disputing with him drave him to that issue, that the great doctor burst out into these blasphemous words: "We are better to be without God's law than the Pope's." Master Tindall, replied, "I defy the Pope and all his laws," and added that if God spared him life, ere many years he would cause a boy that driveth the plough to know more of the Scripture than he did. (from *Foxe's Book of Martyrs,* in Wegner, pp. 285-286)

Tyndale was required to obtain ecclesiastical permission to write a new translation. Unable to do so, he went to London and for six months, supported by a wealthy cloth merchant, started his translation. Eventually he fled to Europe to finish. He translated the New Testament from the Textus Receptus and published it in 1526, with a second edition in 1534. In 1536 he was kidnapped, tried, killed by strangulation, and burned at the stake. His final words were, "Lord, open the King of England's eyes."

All this happened while King Henry VIII was married and without a male heir. The King eventually broke with the Roman Catholic Church, divorced his wife to marry Anne Boleyn, and within one year of Tyndale's death allowed the printing of an English Bible based largely on Tyndale's work. In fact, the long line of English translations that followed (Coverdale, Great Bible, Bishops' Bible) were all heavily indebted to Tyndale's work. It is estimated that over 80 percent of the English Bible, from the King James Version through the Revised Version (1881), was the work of Tyndale. It is fascinating to read about the opposition mounted toward these translations, how they were condemned as perversions written by "damnable" men who sought to destroy the faith. History is a record of entrenched thought preferring the comfortable to anything new, regardless of the quality of the new.

When Catholic persecution under Mary made Bible translation nearly impossible in England, many Protestant scholars fled to Geneva, Switzerland, for safety. The Geneva Bible was due primarily to the work of William Whittingham, brother-in-law to John Calvin. (The New Testament was published in 1557, the Old Testament in 1560.) Its margins were covered in notes, some doctrinal (Calvinist obviously), others political (e.g., the pope was identified with "the angel of the bottomless pit" [Rev 9:11]). It was the first English Bible with numbered verses, and continued the practice of italicizing English words not in the Greek. Its smaller size and cheaper price aided its popularity, dominating the market from 1560 through 1666. This was the Bible of Shakespeare, John Bunyan, the Puritan pilgrims, and the young King James.

In 1604 King James I held a conference at Hampton Court in an attempt to reconcile religious differences between the Church of England and the Puritans. It was there that the suggestion came for a revision of the Bishops' Bible. The revision was to stay as close to the Bishops' Bible as the Greek and Hebrew would allow, and the translators were to pay special attention to previous translations (except the Geneva Bible), ecclesiastical terminology was to be kept, and no notes critical of the church were to be included. The translation team was comprised of most of the best scholars of the day, and their work became the most dominating force in the history of English literature. The original title page reads,

> The Holy Bible, Conteyning the Old Testament, and the New: Newly Translated out of the Originall tongues: & with the former Translations diligently compared and revised, by his Maiesties speciall Commandment. Appointed to be read in Churches. Anno Dom. 1611. (in Metzger, *Translation*, 75)

The Greek, of course, was basically that of Beza (Erasmus; Textus Receptus), and the translation became known in America as the King James Version, in England as the Authorized Version.

Textual Criticism

So why is the King James Version of the Bible (and its most recent American revision, the New King James Bible) different in so many places from all other modern translations? I have been working slowly through history (actually, it was a sprint) so you can understand the issues in the following discussion.

Erasmus had very few Greek manuscripts from which to work, and they were quite late. Regardless of how many Greek manuscripts might have been available in 1611—and the number is considerably less than we now possess—the King James translators slavishly followed just Beza's edition. However, since that time thousands of additional Greek New Testament manuscripts (most containing only part of the New Testament) have been found in libraries and monasteries, and by archaeologists.

There are more than 5,600 Greek manuscripts of the New Testament. Most of them are parts of the New Testament; only about 50 are of the entire New Testament, only one of those being an uncial (Sinaiticus). Along with these manuscripts we also have about 10,000 manuscripts of the Bible in different languages (such as Coptic, Syriac, Armenian, Georgian, and Latin) as well over one million citations in the Church Fathers in Latin alone.

When we consider these manuscripts, especially the uncials and papyri, which were written centuries before the minuscules used by Erasmus, the question then becomes which of the readings are most likely to be original. The science of textual criticism was born in order to answer this question.

Basic to the science is the concept of "text-types." As the manuscripts were studied, it was found that they fall into four basic groupings. Manuscripts that showed the same types of changes, corrections, readings, and physical location were said to belong to a text-type. Four text-types are hypothesized: Alexandrian, Caesarean, Western, and Byzantine. The basic conclusion of textual criticism is that the manuscripts that belong to the Alexandrian text-type are most likely to consistently contain the original wording. They show less willingness on the scribes' part to change, add to, harmonize, or otherwise alter the text. They are also some of the oldest manuscripts, having been written as far back as the second century. Two of the more famous Alexandrian manuscripts are Sinaiticus, written about 350-375, and Vaticanus, also 4th century. On the other hand, textual critics are nearly unanimous that the Byzantine text-type is the least reliable, showing the greatest willingness on the part of the scribes to amend the text. These manuscripts stem, it is hypothesized, from the creative work of Lucian that I discussed above.

So convincing is the work of textual critics that all modern translations give significantly greater weight to the readings of the Alexandrian manuscripts. Erasmus, on the other hand, and therefore the King James translators had access only to a few manuscripts that stem from the Byzantine text-type. Because the Alexandrian and the Byzantine manuscripts are so different in places, because the King James Version is based on Byzantine manuscripts, and because all translations in the last century are based primarily on the Alexandrian manuscripts, you can see why recent translations are often different from the KJV.

Now here is the interesting point. There is little debate among scholars, whether they are on the evangelical or liberal side of the theological spectrum, as to the superiority of the Alexandrian text-type and the overall findings of textual criticism. However, in certain circles, what is called the "King James Debate" rages on, and the debate can often turn ugly. It is not my purpose here to defend my position. I primarily wanted to show you why there are manuscript differences and how those differences are reflected in the KJV and other translations. I would simply refer you to D. A. Carson, *The King James Version Debate* (Baker, 1979), for further reading. The basic contention of the minority view is that the Byzantine text-type is the best witness.

I will make one point, however. The science of textual criticism is unbelievably difficult. Very few world-class textual critics do anything but text criticism, and it is a lifelong endeavor. Their knowledge of Greek and the biblical texts is staggering. Many people who can read Greek with proficiency will quickly admit that they are not competent to enter into detailed debate on the topic. Of course, that doesn't always stop a person who lacks proficiency from jumping in. My encouragement is, if you find yourself embroiled in this debate, unless you have committed your life to Greek and have earned a proficiency in the field, defer to the experts and walk away.

Principles of Textual Criticism

1. **Manuscripts are not to be counted but weighed**. In other words, a simple counting of how many manuscripts support one reading as opposed to another does not arrive at the original. Let's say that two copies were made of an autograph. Scribe "A" was concerned to be as faithful as possible. Scribe "B," while perhaps well intentioned, wanted to make his copy more readable, more understandable, and more consistent (in his mind) with other books of the New Testament, and so he altered the text at will. What if manuscript "A" was never recopied, but manuscript "B" was taken to a large city where Greek was still spoken and 100 copies were made? You now have 102 manuscripts, assuming the autograph has been lost. Are the 100 copies necessarily more reliable than the single manuscript A? Of course not. You can't simply count manuscripts.

Part of this "weighing" process looks at what text-type the manuscript is from. The reading of an Alexandrian manuscript is more likely to be original than a Byzantine, since the manuscript as a whole shows more restraint at changing the biblical text. A related principle is that the older the manuscript, the closer it is to the time of the original, and the less time has passed for errors to creep in.

But let's throw a monkey wrench into the mix. What if you have an eleventh-century minuscule that is an excellent copy of a third-century uncial, and you have another minuscule that was compiled in the ninth century. Which is to be preferred? The eleventh-century will be viewed as superior to the ninth-century one, even though it was written two centuries later. Textual criticism is a complicated field that lies in the realm of the specialist.

2. **The shorter reading is preferred.** In general, it is easier to believe that the scribe would add to the text rather than drop out parts. (The defenders of the Byzantine text argue that the scribal tendency was to omit words.) An example is the final part of the Lord's Prayer as found in the KJV. "For thine is the kingdom and the power and the glory forever.

Amen." The oldest manuscripts do not have the phrase, and it seems more likely that the words were added rather than subtracted from the text.

3. What reading best explains the other readings? When a textual critic compares two readings, he or she will ask which reading most likely gave rise to the other. For example, if you have the same story in Matthew and Luke, and in one manuscript the accounts are identical and in the other manuscript they are slightly different, which is to be preferred? The general assumption is that the manuscript that has slightly different accounts is original, since it is more believable that a scribe changed them to agree ("harmonization").

If you want to see textual criticism at work, you can read Bruce Metzger's *A Textual Commentary on the Greek New Testament* (second edition, 1994, American Bible Society). In it Metzger walks you through how the committee made its decisions in preparing their edition of the Greek New Testament.

There are two editions of the Greek New Testament used as the basis of most modern translations. The text is identical in both, although their discussion of the various readings are different and complementary: *Novum Testamentum Graece*, 27th edition revised, German Bible Society; *Greek New Testament*, 4th edition revised, American Bible Society. Zane Hodges and Arthur Farstad have done an excellent job collating the Byzantine manuscripts in *The Greek New Testament According to the Majority Text* (Thomas Nelson, 1985, 2nd edition, revised), so it is easy to see where the Byzantine text-type differs.

Conclusion

Thankfully, as I said earlier, no cardinal doctrine is brought into question by any viable variant. Despite claims to the contrary, the Alexandrian text has not dropped words because of the scribes' heretical beliefs.

The KJV is a beautiful translation written by the best scholars of their day, scholars who also had a command of the English language that has not since been paralleled. But the English language has changed substantially, superior Greek manuscripts have been found, and the purpose of translation is to convey the beautiful message of God's salvation in terms that the untrained person can understand. After all, the New Testament is written in "Koine" Greek—not the fancy Greek of previous centuries, but the language most familiar to Jesus, Paul, and their contemporaries. So should our translations be understandable.

Exercises for Chapter 30

Be sure to check the translations and, if necessary, the commentaries for the textual problems in each of the following verses.

1. What does John 1:18 tell us about God the Son?

2. Who is Mark quoting in 1:2, and why is there a difference?

3. To whom was the letter of the Ephesians written? Check 1:1 and a commentary.

4. Why do you think the KJV added "unworthily" in 1 Corinthians 11:29? Check the paragraph.

5. The ESV of 1 Corinthians13:3 reads, "If I give away all I have, and if I deliver up my body to be burned,* but have not love, I gain nothing." The asterisk after "burned" refers to the footnote that reads, "Some manuscripts *deliver up my body* [to death] *that I may boast.*" What is behind the change from "burn" to "boast"?

6. See how the different Bibles handle Mark 16:9-20 and John 7:53-8:11. How would you explain these differences to your Sunday School class, which has not yet read *Greek for the Rest of Us*?

Thank you

I have spent quite a bit of time walking you through the history of the Bible. It was partly so you could see why the KJV is different from more recent translations. But it was also to give you one final encouragement as we complete our study of Greek. The Bible is a precious book. Learned men and women have given their lives so we can read and understand it, in Greek, Hebrew, English, and many other languages. It is a message of truth and freedom, often opposed by the religious hierarchy currently in power. Throughout history people have been told that they are not able to read and understand the Bible, both in Catholicism as well as, ironically, in Protestantism. But when the Bible is made available in a form that we can study and from which we can learn, people can and do understand its basic message. I trust that after six weeks of study you now have the tools to better understand both your English and Greek Bibles. In the Appendix I will have a few comments on Hebrew and the Old Testament.

A P P E N D I X

Hebrew for the Rest of Us

Congratulations. You've made it through Greek. You've learned enough to handle many of the issues that will arise in the study of the New Testament. But what about the first three-fourths of the Bible, the Old Testament?

A companion volume, *Hebrew for the Rest of Us*™, would have significant overlap with this book. Lessons we learned on exegesis and word studies and many other areas would be repeated. But it would also include enough new material that it deserves its own book.

But because so many classes on Greek tools want to expose their students to some Hebrew, I have included this appendix. I am indebted to my good friends Gary Pratico and Miles Van Pelt for the following. At their suggestion, most of the following material is taken directly from their first-year Hebrew grammar, *Basics of Biblical Hebrew* (Zondervan, 2001).

Hebrew Alphabet

The Hebrew alphabet consists of twenty-three consonants or letters. For the "baby Hebrew" approach, you probably need to learn only the names of the letters and their transliteration.

Hebrew letter	Name	Pronunciation	Transliteration
א	Alef	silent	ʾ
ב	Bet	b as in boy	b
ג	Gimel	g as in God	g
ד	Dalet	d as in day	d
ה	He	h as in hay	h
ו	Waw	w as in way	w
ז	Zayin	z as in Zion	z
ח	Ḥet	ch as in Bach	ḥ
ט	Tet	t as in toy	ṭ
י	Yod	y as in yes	y
כ	Kaf	k as in king	k
ל	Lamed	l as in lion	l
מ	Mem	m as in mother	m
נ	Nun	n as in now	n
ס	Samek	s as in sin	s
ע	Ayin	silent	ʿ
פ	Pe	p as in pastor	p
צ	Tsade	ts as in boots	ṣ
ק	Qof	k as in king	q
ר	Resh	r as in run	r
שׂ	Sin	s as in sin	ś
שׁ	Shin	sh as in ship	š
ת	Taw	t as in toy	t

Final Forms. Five of the Hebrew letters have final forms. That is to say, when one of these letters occurs at the end of a word, it is written differently than when it appears at the beginning or in the middle of a word, like the Greek sigma. The changing of a letter's form, however, does not change its pronunciation or transliteration.

Regular form	Final form	Example	Transliteration	Translation
כ	ך	דרך	*drk*	road, way
מ	ם	עם	*ʿm*	nation, people
נ	ן	זקן	*zqn*	old man, elder
פ	ף	כסף	*ksp*	money, silver
צ	ץ	ארץ	*ʾrṣ*	earth, land

Transliteration. It is important to learn the system of transliteration, not for the purpose of pronouncing or reading biblical Hebrew, but for studying other books that refer to Hebrew words without using Hebrew characters. Many commentaries, word study books, theological dictionaries, and other language tools do not use Hebrew font characters but only their transliterations. In most instances, these books will list their system of transliteration somewhere at the beginning; be sure to check them out because different books follow slightly different transliteration schemes, especially the vowels.

Right to left. Hebrew is written right to left (but when it is transliterated it is written left to right). For example, the word "king" is written in Hebrew as מלך (read from right to left) but it is transliterated as *mlk* (read from left to right). Here is the alphabet written out right to left.

א ב ג ד ה ו ז ח ט י כ ל מ נ ס ע פ צ ק ר ש שׂ ת

Hebrew Vowels

You might be surprised to learn that originally the Hebrew language had no *written* system of vowels. This does not mean, however, that Hebrew vowels did not exist. While they did not exist in written form, they had always been present in the *spoken* form of the language. If we were to take the vowels out of the English writing system, these vowels would still be present in the spoken form.

Let's use the English translation of Deut 6:5 as an example: "Love the Lord your God with all your heart." Without the vowels, we are left with a series of consonants, much like the ancient written form of Hebrew:

Lv th Lrd yr Gd wth ll yr hrt.

In order to read this sentence out loud, you would need to rely on your knowledge of English and supply the necessary vowels. In the same way, when Joshua read the entire law of Moses to the Israelites (Joshua 8), he had before him a consonantal text with no vowels. This required Joshua to supply from memory the necessary vowels when reading.

Fortunately for us, this is not the case today. In the second half of the first millennium A.D., a group of dedicated scribes called *Masoretes* became concerned with preserving the spoken form of Hebrew. They developed an elaborate system of vowel notation called *pointing*. This pointing system was designed to preserve the spoken system of vowels in the written text. Because the masoretic scribes considered the biblical text to be sacred, their vowel symbols were designed in such a way as never to alter the original consonantal text. To do this, the Masoretes developed vowel symbols that were placed under, inside (to the left), or above the consonantal characters.

Let's look again at Deut 6:5 but this time in Hebrew. You will notice that the consonants are exactly the same in both examples. In the second example, however, the masoretic vowel pointing system has been added.

ואהבת את יהוה אלהיך בכל לבבך

וְאָהַבְתָּ אֵת יְהוָה אֱלֹהֶיךָ בְּכָל־לְבָבְךָ

First-year Hebrew students often struggle to understand how the consonants and vowels go together. Perhaps the following chart will help. מֶלֶךְ (*melek*) is formed like this:

ךְ ← ֶ ← ל ← ֶ ← מ

Because we are pursuing the "baby Hebrew" approach, all that you need to be aware of are the names of the vowels and how they are transliterated. The names of the vowel categories below are not important for you.

	Symbol	Vowel Name	Pronunciation	Transliteration
Short vowels				
a-type	בַ	Pathach	*a* as in *bat*	*a*
e-type	בֶ	Seghol	*e* as in *better*	*e*
i-type	בִ	Hireq	*i* as in *bitter*	*i*
o-type	בָ	Qamets Hatuf	*o* as in *bottle*	*o*
u-type	בֻ	Qibbuts	*u* as in *ruler*	*u*
Changeable long vowels				
a-type	בָ	Qamets	*a* as in *father*	*ā*
e-type	בֵ	Tsere	*e* as in *they*	*ē*
o-type	בֹ	Holem	*o* as in *role*	*ō*
Unchangeable long vowels				
a-type	בָה	Qamets He	a as in father	*â*
e-type	בֵי	Tsere Yod	e as in they	*ê*
	בֶי	Seghol Yod	e as in better	*ê*
i-type	בִי	Hireq Yod	*i* as in *machine*	*î*
o-type	בוֹ	Holem Waw	o as in role	*ô*
u-type	בוּ	Shureq	u as in ruler	*û*
Reduced vowels				
a-type	בֲ	Hateph Pathach	*a* as in *amuse*	*ă*
e-type	בֱ	Hateph Seghol	*a* as in *amuse*	*ě*
o-type	בֳ	Hateph Qamets	*a* as in *amuse*	*ŏ*

Shewa. You will notice in the last chart that each reduced vowel is joined with a pair of vertical dots on the right side of the vowel symbol. These vertical dots also occur without an accompanying vowel (בְ). This vowel sign is called *Shewa*. The Shewa is not listed separately in the above vowel charts because it is not like any other vowel.

There are two types of Shewa in Hebrew: *Silent Shewa* and *Vocal Shewa*. The Silent Shewa is never pronounced and never transliterated. The Vocal Shewa maintains a *hurried* pronunciation and sounds like the *a* in *amuse*. It is transliterated either as an upside-down *e* (בְ, *bə*) or as a superscript *e* (בְ, *bᵉ*).

Advanced Information on the Consonants

Easily confused letters. For the beginning student, certain groups of consonants can sometimes look alike and become confused (just as in English with the capital *I* and lowercase *l* in the word "Idol"). You have probably also observed that different Hebrew letters can sound alike (just as in English with the *c* in "cat" and the *k* in "kite"). In order to avoid any confusion, it is sometimes helpful to compare the following characters and carefully note the distinguishing features. However, their transliterated values are quite distinct.

1. בּ (*Bet*) and כּ (*Kaf*)
2. ג (*Gimel*) and נ (*Nun*)
3. ה (*He*) and ח (*Ḥet*) and ת (*Taw*)
4. שׂ (*Sin*) and שׁ (*Shin*)
5. ם (final *Mem*) and ס (*Samek*)
6. ד (*Dalet*) and ר (*Resh*)
7. צ (*Tsade*) and ע (*Ayin*)
8. ו (*Waw*) and ז (*Zayin*)
9. ן (final *Nun*) and ך (final *Kaf*)

Begadkephat letters. Six of the Hebrew consonants have two possible, but closely related, pronunciations. Collectively, these are known as the *begadkephat* consonants. This term is simply a mnemonic device allowing for the easy memorization of these six letters (ת פ כ ד ג ב). To distinguish between the two pronunciations, a dot called a Daghesh Lene was inserted into the consonantal character (תּ פּ כּ דּ גּ בּ). The presence of the Daghesh Lene indicates a hard pronunciation and its absence denotes a soft pronunciation. A Daghesh Lene will only appear in the *begadkephat* letters. Each letter without the Daghesh Lene is sometimes transliterated with a small horizontal line either above or below the English character.

Begadkephat letter	Pronunciation	Transliteration
בּ	*b* as in *boy*	*b*
ב	*v* as in *vine*	*ḇ*

בּ	g as in God	g
ג	gh as in aghast	ḡ
דּ	d as in day	d
ד	dh as in the	ḏ
כּ	k as in king	k
כ	ch as in Bach	ḵ
פּ	p as in pastor	p
פ	ph as in alphabet	p̄
תּ	t as in toy	t
ת	th as in thin	ṯ

Hebrew Words

Roots and stems. Many nouns and verbs share the same consonants. For example,

מֶלֶךְ	king	➤	מָלַךְ	to reign
דָּבָר	word	➤	דִּבֶּר	to speak
מִשְׁפָּט	judgment	➤	שָׁפַט	to judge

Notice how each pair shares a common set of consonants and related definitions. The reason for this relationship is due to the fact that they share a common root. It is important to understand the distinction between a root and those words derived from that root. It is a distinction between root and stem.

Hebrew roots are typically composed of three consonants (triconsonantal), occasionally two (biconsonantal). *A root represents the origin or simplest form from which any number of Hebrew words are derived.* From a root, therefore, any number of nouns or verbs may be derived. *A stem is the most basic form of any word derived from a root.*

For example, from the triconsonantal root מלך comes the noun stems מֶלֶךְ (king), מַלְכָּה (queen), מַלְכוּת (kingdom), and the verb stem מָלַךְ (to reign, be king). Once again, notice how each different word shares a common set of consonants and related definitions. This relationship is based upon the sharing of a common root.

Word studies, cognate words, and cognate languages. Word studies will often take these related forms into consideration. The meaning of most Hebrew words is quite clear. However, the meaning of some words is less clear, and writers will often turn to related Hebrew words to help determine the meaning of these words.

If related Hebrew words do not help, writers will often resort to looking at related or cognate languages (e.g., Akkadian, Arabic, Aramaic, Egyptian, Ugaritic) in order to determine what a particular Hebrew word may mean.

Lexical form for Hebrew verbs. The lexical form of any triconsonantal verb is the Qal Perfect third person masculine singular.

Person, gender, and number. In English, a verb by itself does not have person, gender, or number (e.g., "study"). (Greek verbs, likewise, do not designate gender.) It must be supplied by the addition of a personal pronoun (e.g., "she studied"). However, in Hebrew, most verbs have person, gender, and number. These verbal characteristics are indicated by certain patterns of inflection. For example, the verb כָּתַב means "he wrote" and the verb כָּתְבָה means "she wrote." The different ending indicates person, gender, and number.

Even though most Hebrew verbs are capable of indicating person, gender, and number by themselves, verbs may also occur with independent personal pronouns. For example, כָּתַבְתִּי and אֲנִי כָּתַבְתִּי are both translated "I wrote." Because Hebrew verbs by themselves indicate person, gender, and number, the addition of an independent personal pronoun typically expresses some type of emphasis.

With regard to person, Hebrew verbs can be first person (I, we), second person (you), or third person (he, she, it, they). With regard to number, Hebrew verbs will be either singular (I, you, he, she, it) or plural (we, you, they). And with regard to gender, Hebrew verbs will be either masculine (he), feminine (she), or common (I, we, they).

Software. If you are using a tool such as a software program like *Accordance* to look at a Hebrew word, you will quickly notice that when you move the cursor over what appears to be a single word, the software is telling you the one form is actually multiple words. In fact, a single cluster of Hebrew letters, something that looks like a single word to most of us, may in fact represent an entire clause consisting of multiple lexical items or words. For example, the single Hebrew construction וָאֹהֲבֶהָ

actually consists of three different lexical items. The initial letter (וֹ) is the Hebrew conjunction translated "and." The last letter (הּ) is a third person, feminine singular, pronominal suffix translated "her." The middle section of this Hebrew construction (יֶאֱהַב) contains a verb that we can translate as "he loved." When we put it all together, this single Hebrew construction represents an entire English clause translated "and he loved her." This example represents a common feature of the Hebrew language. That is, Hebrew nouns and verbs can take a number of prefixes (such as conjunctions, prepositions, or the definite article) and/or suffixes (such as pronominal suffixes with objective or possessive translation values) that have their own distinct lexical values.

Doing Hebrew Word Studies

John Kohlenberger has written an excellent interlinear, *The NIV Interlinear Hebrew-English Old Testament* (Zondervan, 1979). This can help you find the Hebrew word behind the English, but because of the issues I have been raising, this may not be the best choice for you.

You can use an exhaustive concordance that lists the number of the Hebrew word at the end of the entry. Some of the software programs also give you access to the Hebrew behind the English.

If you want to do serious word study, we are pleased to have the five-volume *New International Dictionary of Old Testament Theology and Exegesis*, edited by Willem A. VanGemeren (Zondervan, 1997). It is also available in software. VanGemeren organized the Hebrew words based on their GK number, so once you have the number it is easy to find the word. This is as advanced as you will need, and it is a trustworthy resource. You can also use Kohlenberger's *The English-Hebrew Concordance to the Old Testament* that, like its Greek counterpart, will list in English every verse that uses a specific Hebrew word, in order to discover the word's semantic range. *The Theological Wordbook of the Old Testament*, edited by R. Laird Harris, Gleason L. Archer Jr., and Bruce K. Waltke (Moody, 1980), is not as detailed but may be helpful. The *Theological Dictionary of the Old Testament*, a multi-volume word study edited by Botterweck and Ringgrem (Eerdmans), is considerably advanced for the "baby Hebrew" student.

Commentaries on the Old Testament are usually less than helpful. The more technical commentaries are often more concerned with "scholarly" issues (and less with the meaning of the biblical text) such as ancient Near

Eastern parallels and source criticism. *The Expositor's Bible Commentary* is worth purchasing, and it plus two good study Bibles are probably your best bet. You may also want to look at *The New American Commentary* (Broadman Press) and the *NIV Application Commentary* (Zondervan). If you want to work with biblical and theological teaching, you may want to pick up the commentaries by Calvin and Luther. For a helpful listing of Old Testament Commentaries see Douglas Stuart, *A Guide to Selecting and Using Bible Commentaries* (Word, 1990).

Advanced Word Studies: Choosing and Using a Hebrew Lexicon

It may be that you do not need a Hebrew lexicon. The information in *New International Dictionary of Old Testament Theology and Exegesis* will be easier for you to understand and probably more than you need. But if you want a Hebrew lexicon, there are two types of lexicons: *standard* and *analytical.* The most important is the standard lexicon.

The Standard Lexicon

For the beginning student, the choice of a standard lexicon is somewhat limited. For reasons of cost and quality, there are basically two possibilities. The standard lexicon is by F. Brown, S. R. Driver, and C. A. Briggs, *The New Brown-Driver-Briggs-Gesenius Hebrew and English Lexicon* (Hendrickson, 1979), referred to as *BDB*. An easier lexicon to use is by W. L. Holladay, *A Concise Hebrew and Aramaic Lexicon of the Old Testament* (Grand Rapids: Eerdmans, 1988).

BDB, unfortunately, has two significant liabilities: (1) It is seriously outdated and (2) despite a cross-referencing system, it is difficult for a beginning student to use because its entries are not arranged alphabetically but according to verbal root. For example, the noun מִצְוָה (command) is not entered alphabetically under מ but rather under צ because מִצְוָה is derived from the verbal root צָוָה (to command). For many words you may have little difficulty identifying the verbal root from which a word is derived, but the verbal root for many entries is difficult to identify. For example, the noun מוֹשָׁב is listed under יָשַׁב, and תּוֹרָה is listed under יָרָה. As you can see, the ordering of *BDB* by verbal root requires a fairly advanced understanding of the so-called weak verbal roots. All of this is certainly not to suggest that *BDB* is unusable by the beginning student. Just be aware that it can be difficult to find certain words in *BDB*.

There are two resources available that can help with navigating *BDB*. The first is an index arranged by chapter and verse: Bruce Einspahr, *Index to Brown, Driver & Briggs Hebrew Lexicon* (Chicago: Moody Press, 1976). The second resource is the electronic version of *BDB* available with Accordance and other software programs. With the electronic version, you can search *BDB* in a number of different ways (by entry, English gloss, English content, Hebrew content, Greek content). Additionally, the Hebrew text of *Accordance* is linked to the *BDB* lexicon. This means that you can seach *BDB* automatically by "triple-clicking" on a word in the Hebrew text.

For the beginning student, the Holladay lexicon is to be preferred over *BDB*. Though it is an abridged version of an earlier lexicon,* its great advantage over *BDB* is that it offers an alphabetical ordering of all entries rather than an arrangement by verbal root.

It takes time to learn how to use any lexicon effectively. While it is not our intention to provide exhaustive instructions on the use of the Holladay lexicon, a few suggestions and observations should be helpful.

1. Given that words are entered alphabetically in the Holladay lexicon, make sure that you have memorized the alphabet in its proper sequence. If you have not memorized the Hebrew alphabet in order, it will be difficult to look up words.

2. Remember that many consonants sound and look alike. Be certain that your search in the lexicon is conducted with the correct consonants and vowels. For example, the consonant שׂ precedes שׁ in the lexicon and your best efforts will not locate שַׂר (official, leader) under שׁ. Similarly, confusion between א and ע will produce difficulty as with אִם (if) and עִם (with). Imagine the awkwardness of a translation that confuses אֵימָה (terror, fear) with אָמָה (maidservant).

3. Holladay is both a Hebrew and an Aramaic lexicon. While there is much in common between the two languages, you must restrict your search to the Hebrew portion of the lexicon. The Aramaic entries are listed in the last few pages of the lexicon (396-425).

4. In the Holladay lexicon, words are located according to the sequence of consonants and not according to vowels. The one important

---

* L. Koehler and W. Baumgartner, *Lexicon in Veteris Testamenti Libros* (Leiden: E. J. Brill, 1958).

exception is that the unchangeable long vowels (vowel letters) are considered to be consonantal. For example, תְּהִלָּה (praise, glory) precedes תּוֹדָה (song of thanksgiving) because the Holem Waw of תּוֹדָה is treated as a consonant in terms of location in the lexicon.

5. Nouns are listed in a standard lexicon in their singular (lexical) form, such as דָּבָר (masculine singular) or תּוֹדָה (feminine singular). The entry is sometimes followed by gender identification and the frequency of occurrence in parentheses. Variant spellings of a noun (such as defective spelling) are sometimes provided immediately after the lexical form or after the frequency statistic. Before the range of a word's meaning is given, a number of additional forms are listed that generally include: the construct singular form, the singular noun with selected pronominal suffixes, the absolute plural form, the construct plural form, and the plural form with a selection of pronominal suffixes. This selection of forms is then followed by the range of meaning, often with specific biblical references. Remember, however, that the Holladay lexicon is an abridged lexicon and so the presentation of word meaning and biblical attestation is not comprehensive. In order to get a sense of the arrangement of noun entries, look over the entries for דָּבָר (word), תּוֹרָה (law), מַלְאָךְ (messenger), and אֶבֶן (stone). Remember too that in Hebrew, the definite article (הַ) is attached to a noun (e.g., הַשָּׁמַיִם), and you need to drop the letter to look up the Hebrew word.

6. Verbs are listed in a standard lexicon in their Qal Perfect third person masculine singular form, such as כָּתַב (to write) or בָּנָה (to build). The only exception to this practice is the listing of biconsonantal verbs in their Qal Infinitive Construct form. As with nouns, frequency statistics are sometimes provided for verbs. Entries are arranged according to a verb's attestation in the Qal and derived stems. For example, the verb אָכַל (to eat) is presented in the categories of Qal, Niphal, Pual and Hiphil because these are the stems in which this verb is attested. When looking up a verb in the lexicon, it is important that you correctly identify the verbal stem and consult the appropriate category for verbal meaning. In other words, when you are looking for the definition of a particular verb and that verb appears in the biblical text as a Niphal, you must be sure to check its meaning in the Niphal category.

After you have located the correct verb and identified the correct stem, you will encounter two basic types of information. First, you will see a selection of inflected forms (Perfect, Imperfect, Imperative, etc.). Next, the range of verbal meaning is given (with a small selection of biblical references). The Perfect and Imperfect selection will frequently include forms with pronominal suffixes. Sometimes suffixes are shown on the Imperative, Infinitive, and Participle. Note, however, that the person, gender, and number of the suffixes are not identified nor are the Infinitives labeled as Construct or Absolute.

7. The arrangement of entries for other parts of speech is similar to that of nouns and verbs. Familiarity with how all of the entries are arranged will come from your frequent use of the lexicon.

8. Unfortunately, the Holladay lexicon does not translate or give the meaning for most proper names. Masculine names of persons, places, and gentilics (Egyptian, Israelite, Moabite, etc.) are simply identified as "n.pers." and feminine forms are labeled "n.pers.f."

9. It is best to begin your exposure to the Holladay lexicon by reading the introduction and then familiarizing yourself with the list of abbreviations located in the beginning of the lexicon.

10. The effective use of any lexicon takes time, concentration, and a concern for painstaking detail. Be patient! With persistence, you will gradually acquire the ability to use a standard lexicon effectively.

The Analytical Lexicon

The comments above have focused on choosing and using a standard lexicon. As noted at the beginning of this discussion, there is another type of lexicon that is known as an "analytical lexicon." An analytical lexicon is basically a parsing guide. Unlike a standard lexicon, an analytical lexicon lists *inflected* forms with full parsing information. For example, if you were unable to identify a form like כְּתַבְתֶּם (an inflected verbal form), an analyti-

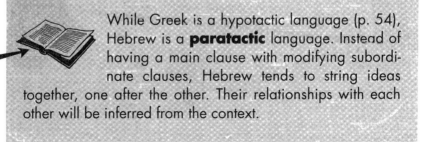

While Greek is a hypotactic language (p. 54), Hebrew is a **paratactic** language. Instead of having a main clause with modifying subordinate clauses, Hebrew tends to string ideas together, one after the other. Their relationships with each other will be inferred from the context.

cal lexicon will provide its full parsing information (Qal Perfect second person masculine singular from כָּתַב) with translation. Similarly, a noun or preposition with a pronominal suffix will be identified by its lexical form and the person, gender, and number of the suffix.

The same information is available more quickly from several of the software packages. As you move the cursor over the Hebrew word, its lexical form, parsing, and other information is shown.

The analytical lexicon that is the easiest to use is the work by J. J. Owens, *Analytical Key to the Old Testament* (Grand Rapids: Baker, 1989). These volumes are arranged according to the canonical ordering of the Old Testament in the Protestant tradition (Genesis-Malachi), progressing chapter by chapter and verse by verse. Every word or phrase in each verse is identified together with its page location in *BDB*. The translation of each word or phrase generally follows the RSV. Other analytical lexicons include those by B. Davidson, *Analytical Hebrew and Chaldee Lexicon* (New York: Harper & Brothers, 1956) and T. S. Beall and W. A. Banks, *Old Testament Parsing Guide* (Chicago: Moody Press, 1986).

Verbal Stems

In the Hebrew verbal system, there are seven major stems: the Qal, Niphal, Piel, Pual, Hiphil, Hophal, and Hithpael. The Qal stem is the basic or simple verbal stem. From the Qal stem all other verbal stems are formed. For this reason, the Niphal through Hithpael stems are called "derived stems" because their forms are derived or based on the Qal stem. Verbal stems tell us two things about the action or meaning of a verb: the type of verbal action and the voice of verbal action.

In Hebrew, there are three basic categories of verbal action: *simple* action (e.g., to break), *intensive* action (e.g., to smash into pieces) and *causative* action (e.g., to cause to break). There are also three basic categories of verbal voice: *active, passive,* and *reflexive.* The first two are the same distinction as found in Greek. With the reflexive voice (which is somewhat like the Greek middle voice), the subject of the verb is both doing and receiving the action of the verb. In the example "David dressed himself," David is both performing and receiving the verbal action.

Understanding the basic significance of a verbal stem is necessary if you are going to follow the discussion in a commentary.

1. Qal. The Qal is the simple or basic verbal stem. Qal verbs are active in voice, though a few passive forms do exist. The Qal stem also exhibits the simple or unnuanced type of action. For example, "he heard."

2. Niphal. The Niphal stem is used to express simple action with either a passive or reflexive voice. In other words, whatever a verb means in the Qal stem, it becomes passive or reflexive in the Niphal stem. An example of a translated Niphal verb is "he was heard" (passive) or "he heard himself " (reflexive).

3. Piel. The Piel stem is sometimes used to express an intensive type of action with an active voice. In other words, the simple action of the Qal stem will take on some type of intensive nuance in the Piel stem. For example, a verb meaning "he broke" in the Qal stem can mean "he smashed into pieces" in the Piel stem.

4. Pual. The Pual is the passive form of the Piel. The Pual stem, therefore, is used to express an intensive type of action with a passive voice. For example, the Piel verb meaning "he smashed into pieces would be translated in the Pual stem as "he (it) was smashed into pieces."

5. Hiphil. The Hiphil stem is used to express causative action with an active voice. For example, a Qal verb meaning "he was king" or "he reigned" would be translated "he caused to reign" or "he made (someone) king" in the Hiphil stem.

6. Hophal. The Hophal is the passive form of the Hiphil. The Hophal stem, therefore, is used to express causative action with a passive voice. For example, the Hiphil verb translated "he made (someone) king" would be translated "he was made king" in the Hophal stem.

7. Hithpael. The Hithpael stem is used to express an intensive type of action with a reflexive (or sometimes passive) voice. For example, a Qal verb meaning "he hid" would be translated "he hid himself" in the Hithpael stem.

	simple	*intensive*	*causative*
active	Qal	Piel	Hiphil
passive	Niphal	Pual	Hophal
reflexive	Niphal	Hithpael	

Verbal stems and verbal meaning. Many verbs in Hebrew are "regular." That is to say, their meanings follow the pattern summarized above when they appear in the different stems. For example, a Hebrew verb in

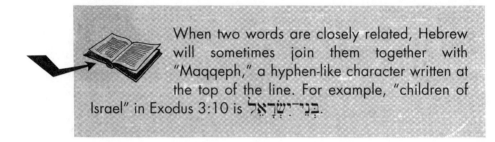

When two words are closely related, Hebrew will sometimes join them together with "Maqqeph," a hyphen-like character written at the top of the line. For example, "children of Israel" in Exodus 3:10 is בְּנֵי־יִשְׂרָאֵל.

the Qal meaning "to break" will mean "to smash into pieces" in the Piel stem. In this and many other instances, the relationship between the meanings of a verb in different stems is apparent in light of the discussion above.

However, the meaning of a verb in the Qal may be significantly different when that same verb appears in another stem. For example, the verb בָּרַךְ means "to kneel" in the Qal, but in the Piel stem it means "to bless." Always consult a lexicon to be certain of a verb's meaning in a given stem.

Verbal Conjugations

In English and Greek, verbs are conjugated in order to express different verbal functions such as tense. English verbs may also be conjugated as participles (studying), infinitives (to study), or imperatives (study!). Each English verb takes on a different form (study, studies, studied, studying, to study) in order to express a different verbal function.

In Hebrew, there are eight basic verbal conjugations: Perfect, Imperfect, Imperative, Cohortative, Jussive, Infinitive Construct, Infinitive Absolute, and Participle. This means that a verb in the Qal may be conjugated any one of eight different ways, depending on what verbal function the author intends. In most cases, the change in verbal function will be identifiable by a change in verbal form. Each of the derived stems (Niphal, Piel, Pual, etc.) may also be conjugated in any one of these eight different conjugations. In Hebrew, therefore, there are seven verbal stems (Qal and the derived stems) and eight verbal conjugations (Perfect, Imperfect, etc.).

1. **Perfect**. The Perfect conjugation is used to express a completed action or a state of being. When used to describe a completed action (either in reality or in the mind of the speaker), the Hebrew Perfect may be translated by the English past tense (he studied), present perfect (he has studied), past perfect (he had studied), or future perfect (he will have

studied). When used to describe a state of being (stative verbs), it will be translated with the English present tense (he is wise). The Hebrew Perfect may also be translated by the English present tense with verbs of perception or attitude (he knows, he loves). It must be emphasized that the Hebrew Perfect does not have tense (time of action) apart from context and issues of syntax. Rather, it signifies aspect (type of action). The Perfect aspect designates a verbal action with its conclusion envisioned in the mind of the speaker or writer. To state it differently, the Perfect aspect denotes completed action, whether in the past, present, or future.

2. Imperfect. The Imperfect conjugation is used to express incomplete action and is usually translated by the English present tense (I study) or future tense (I will study). The action of the verb occurs either at the time of speaking or after the time of speaking. The Hebrew Imperfect is also used to denote habitual or customary action, whether in the past, present, or future (he prays regularly, he used to pray). The Imperfect may also be rendered by one of several modal values (would, could, should, may, might, can, etc.). These modal translation values are suggested by various contextual considerations. It must also be emphasized that, like the Perfect, the Hebrew Imperfect does not have tense (time of action) apart from context and issues of syntax. It too signifies aspect (type of action). The Imperfect aspect designates a verbal action for which, in the mind of the speaker or writer, the conclusion is not in view. To state it differently, the Imperfect aspect denotes incomplete action, whether in the past, present, or future.

3. Imperative. The next three conjugations (Imperative, Cohortative, and Jussive) are volitional conjugations, meaning they are used to express some type of command, wish, or desire. The Imperative conjugation is used primarily to express direct commands, demanding immediate action from the one being addressed. It can also be used to request permission or communicate a request. The Hebrew Imperative occurs only in the second person. For example, "(You) defend the cause of the weak!"

4. Cohortative. This second volitional conjugation is used much like the Imperative, to express a wish, request, or command. It may also be used, however, to express purpose (in order to) or result (resulting in). The Cohortative conjugation occurs in the first person, for example, "Let me (first person singular) honor the Lord!" or "Let us (first person plural) honor the Lord!"

5. Jussive. The Jussive conjugation is also used to express either some type of mild command or strong wish. Strictly speaking, it occurs only in the third person, singular and plural. For example, "May the Lord (third person) give to me another son."

To sum up the volitional conjugations, all three are used to express some type of command, request, or desire. Context will help determine which volitional nuance is intended by the author. The Cohortative occurs in the first person (I, we), the Imperative in the second person (you), and the Jussive in the third person (he, she, it, they).

6. Infinitive Construct. An Infinitive is a verbal noun. In Hebrew, there are two Infinitive forms: the Infinitive Construct and the Infinitive Absolute. The Infinitive Construct may function much like an English Infinitive, usually translated with the preposition "to" plus a verb as in "to study" or "to learn." Like a noun, it can be used as the subject (To study is hard work.) or object of a verb (I want to study.). It may also be used in a number of other ways.

7. Infinitive Absolute. The Hebrew Infinitive Absolute has no real English counterpart. It may be used in conjunction with other verbs to emphasize or intensify the verbal action. It may also be used in the place of an Imperative to express a command. In special instances, it can be used with other verbs to express two verbal actions occurring at the same time, that is, contemporaneous action.

8. Participle. A Participle is a verbal adjective. As such, it has both verbal and adjectival characteristics. Verbally, it expresses some type of verbal action such as "studying" or "learning." Adjectivally, it is used much like a Hebrew adjective: attributively, predicatively, or substantively.

Word Order in the Hebrew Verbal Sentence

In English, the ordering of words in a sentence helps to identify the function of those words. For example, in the sentence "Jacob loved Rachel," Jacob is the subject of the verb because his name precedes the verb. Additionally, Rachel is the object of the verb because her name follows the verb. If the sentence was "Rachel loved Jacob," then Rachel would be the subject and Jacob the object because of their positions in the sentence. In English, normal word order is subject-verb-object. In Biblical Hebrew, however, normal word order for a verbal sentence is verb-subject-object. It must be acknowledged, however, that there are frequent variations and exceptions to this "normal" ordering of words. For example, it is common for the direct object to stand at the beginning of a Hebrew sentence for the purpose of emphasis.

Textual Criticism

Textual criticism in the Hebrew Bible shares many characteristics in common with that of the Greek Testament. Some books and sections of the Old Testament are relatively free of textual problems (the Pentateuch, Judges, Jonah). Other sections present the reader with an array of textual difficulties (Samuel-Kings, Psalms, Job, Ezekiel, Zechariah).

One of the uniquely Hebrew intentional errors is the altering of a text because the scribe deemed the wording to be disrespectful to God. We also see the substitution of a euphemism for a word or expression that the scribe deemed to be indelicate or offensive, and the introduction of glosses into the text for the purpose of clarification or explanation.

When doing Hebrew textual criticism, the textual critic uses different Hebrew manuscripts such as those from Qumran, the Targumim, and other translations such as the Septuagint, Coptic, Syriac, and Vulgate (the latter three being translations made from the Septuagint).

You will sometimes see modern writers "emending" the text. Because the vowels were added later, and because different vowels can produce a considerably different meaning for the three consonants, some writers emend or alter the vowels to produce a different meaning. Some also emend the consonants.

Hebrew Bible

The standard Hebrew Bible is *Biblia Hebraica Stuttgartensia* (*BHS*). A better and more affordable Hebrew Bible for beginning students is *Biblia Hebraica Lenningradensia*, edited by Aron Dotan (Peabody, MA: Hendrickson, 2001). For a listing of additional tools and resources, see *BBH* 36.8. While it is fun to look at these two books, at the "baby Hebrew" stage they would be overwhelming to try and use.

Like most English Bibles, the text of the Hebrew Bible is divided into chapters and verses. There was no such numbering system in the original Hebrew texts. This was the work of Christian scholars in the thirteenth century and later. You should also note that the chapter and verse divisions of the Hebrew Bible do not always correspond with the divisions of our English Bibles. This phenomenon is especially common in the book of Psalms. The elements of English punctuation (such as a comma, period, semicolon, question mark, exclamation point, etc.) do not appear in the Hebrew Bible. The end of each verse is marked, however, with what looks like a large colon (:). This symbol is called Sof Pasuq and means "end of verse" in Hebrew.

The Hebrew Bible is composed of twenty-four books arranged in three major divisions: the Law, the Prophets, and the Writings. The Hebrew Scriptures are sometimes referred to as the Tanak (also Tanach), an acronym derived from the initial letters of the Hebrew names of the three divisions. The Law is composed of the books of Genesis through Deuteronomy. The remaining two divisions of the Hebrew Bible have a different ordering and numbering of books compared to the various Christian Bibles. The Prophets comprise eight books: the former Prophets, consisting of Joshua, Judges, 1 and 2 Samuel (counted as one book), 1 and 2 Kings (also counted as one book); and the four Latter Prophets, containing Isaiah, Jeremiah, Ezekiel and the Twelve (the Minor Prophets counted as one). The Writings number eleven books that are ordered in various ways.

Advanced: The Masorah of *BHS*

One of the important and interesting contributions of the Masoretes was their system of marginal notes. These notes are called the Masorah and are traditionally categorized into two main groups: the *marginal Masorah* and the *final Masorah*. The category of marginal Masorah is further divided into the Masorah parva (small Masorah) in the outer side margins and the Masorah magna (large Masorah), traditionally located in the top and bottom margins of the text. The Masorah parva consists of word-use statistics, similar documentation for expressions or certain phraseology, observations on full or defective writing, references to the Kethiv-Qere readings, and more. Though some of this information seems trivial and inconsequential to the modern reader, these observations are the result of a passionate zeal to safeguard the accurate transmission of the sacred text. The Masorah magna, in measure, is an expanded Masorah parva. Oftentimes, the notations simply provide greater depth or specificity beyond those in the Masorah parva. Traditionally, the Masorah magna was recorded in the top and bottom margins of the text.

The final Masorah is located at the end of biblical books or after certain sections of the text, such as at the end of the Torah. The final Masorah contains information and statistics regarding the number of words in a book or section, the middle word of a book or even the middle consonant of a book. For example, after the conclusion of Deuteronomy, we learn that the book has 955 verses and that the precise midpoint falls in Deut 17:10. Additionally, we learn that the Torah has 5,845 verses, 79,856 words and 400,945 letters. The purpose for this statistical information was to ensure accuracy in the transmission of the text with the production of subsequent copies that were done by hand.

The Kethiv-Qere. The most important of the Masoretic notes are those that detail the Kethiv-Qere that are located in the Masorah parva in the outside margins of *BHS*. Given that the Masoretes would not alter the sacred consonantal text, the Kethiv-Qere notes were a way of "correcting" or commenting on the text for any number of reasons (grammatical, theological, aesthetic, etc.) deemed important by the copyist. The consonantal (uncorrected) wording of the text is the Kethiv, an Aramaic term meaning "what is written." The Kethiv is the reading that comes literally from the consonantal text. The reading that is suggested for "correction" by the Masorete is the Qere, an Aramaic term meaning "what is to be read." The Qere is signaled by a small circle that is written above the word in the text. This circle refers the reader to a marginal note where the consonants to be read are given. The vowel points of the Qere were placed under the consonants in the text. The consonants to be read with those vowels are printed in the margin. There are hundreds of Kethiv-Qere notations in the Hebrew Bible of varying significance.

Interlinear for the Rest of Us

The Reverse Interlinear for New Testament Word Studies

William D. Mounce

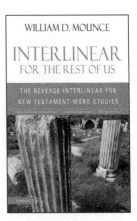

Most interlinear Bibles are superb resources for Greek students. But what about the rest of us who don't know Greek?

Here is the answer. While other interlinear Bibles assume that you know Greek. *Interlinear for the Rest of Us* assumes that you don't, or that you've forgotten much of what you once knew. Designed for busy pastors, Sunday school teachers, and anyone who wants a practical tool for studying the Scriptures, this interlinear makes reading easy by flip-flopping the usual order of appearance. It uses the English text as the main text rather than the Greek, so there is absolutely no confusion about the meaning of what you're reading. Discover the Greek words behind the English translation. Conduct your own word studies using Greek word study books—without knowing Greek.

Interlinear for the Rest of Us offers these features:

- Interlinear passages appear in a "staff" with four interrelated lines (see excerpt)

    From top to bottom, the lines are:
    English text in New International Version
    Corresponding Greek words
    Parsing information
    Goodrick-Kohlenberger numbers

- Greek text in normal Greek order at the bottom of the page, underneath the interlinear section
- Mounce's Greek-English Dictionary at the back of this volume, keyed to both Goodrick-Kohlenberger and Strong's numbering systems

Ideal for use with *Greek for the Rest of Us* and other Greek study tools.

Available in stores and online!

The Zondervan Greek and English Interlinear: New Testament (NASB/NIV)

William D. Mounce and
Robert H. Mounce, General Editors

This Zondervan interlinear Bible offers the following features:

- The new interlinear translation flows in beautiful English
- Greek words are grammatically explained and linked to the GK numbers
- Includes a comprehensive dictionary of the Greek words
- Unique Greek text depicts variations reflected in modern translations

The Zondervan Greek and English Interlinear: New Testament (KJV/NIV)

William D. Mounce and Robert H. Mounce, General Editors

Older interlinears have the interlinear text in an old typeface, sometimes hard to read, and are based on the Greek New Testament of 1952 (*Nestle-Aland 21st ed.*). The English is stilted and awkward. This new interlinear has Mounce's own formal equivalent translation as the interlinear English text, and by use of the GK numbers and a series of arrows and asterisks, relates the Greek words to the English text. The KJV and NIV text run in columns on either side of the interlinear text for easy comparison of the Greek text and modern translation. By careful spacing and with computer technology, both the interlinear text and the translation text run full length on the page.

Mounce's Complete Expository Dictionary of Old and New Testament Words

William D. Mounce

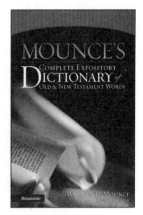

For years, *Vine's Expository Dictionary* has been the standard word study tool for pastors and laypeople, selling millions of copies. But sixty-plus years of scholarship have shed extensive new light on the use of biblical Greek and Hebrew, creating the need for a new, more accurate, more thorough dictionary of Bible words. William Mounce, whose Greek grammar has been used by more than 100,000 college and seminary students, is the editor of this new dictionary, which will become the layperson's gold standard for biblical word studies.

Mounce's is ideal for the reader with limited or no knowledge of Greek or Hebrew who wants greater insight into the meanings of biblical words to enhance Bible study. It is also the perfect reference for busy pastors needing to quickly get at the heart of a word's meaning without wading through more technical studies.

What makes *Mounce's* superior to *Vine's*?
- The most accurate, in-depth definitions based on the best of modern evangelical scholarship
- Both Greek and Hebrew words are found under each English entry (*Vine's* separates them)
- Employs both Strong's and G/K numbering systems (*Vine's* only uses Strong's)
- *Mounce's* accuracy is endorsed by leading scholars

Available in stores and online!

Basics of Biblical Greek Grammar
Third Edition

William D. Mounce

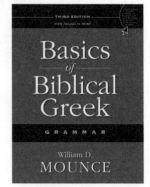

First published in 1993, *Basics of Biblical Greek* is the most popular introduction to the field, used in universities and seminaries around the world. Over 200,000 students have learned biblical Greek under its guidance. This significant third edition has been carefully developed in consultation with instructors, students, self-learners, and homeschoolers.

Users can now take advantage to the many improvements made at the book's website, www.Teknia.com, where they will find—for free—an online course, walking students through every chapter; vocabulary flashcards; video and audio helps; Greek fonts; quizzes for each chapter; fun songs and games; and much, much more.

Now in a larger size, with an attractive 2-color design, the third edition adds an element of fun, with encouragement, songs, and more, which appear in the margins. Chapter 35 has been split into two chapters, "half-time review" sections have been added to every chapter, and new exegesis sections are now included. These and other improvements serve to enhance the learning experience and will continue BBG's legacy as the premier introduction to biblical Greek.

Available in stores and online!

A Graded Reader of Biblical Greek

William D. Mounce

Making the leap from the *Basics of Biblical Greek* to its real-life application can be a frustrating challenge for students of intermediate Greek. *A Graded Reader of Biblical Greek* was developed to make the transition easier. It takes beginning exegetes from simple to progressively more difficult biblical texts. Students can now learn New Testament Greek the way they would any other language: through a graded program.

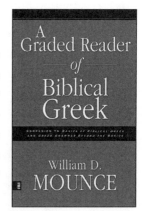

A Graded Reader of Biblical Greek applies an inductive method to learning intermediate Greek grammar. It provides a workable introduction to exegesis, word studies, and developing a large vocabulary; and it assists the student in preparing for class, allowing classroom time to be put to its most effective use.

- Twenty Greek passages are presented in graded order.
- Difficult and unfamiliar grammatical constructions are explained.
- All words that occur fewer than twenty times in the New Testament are defined.
- An Exegetical Discussion section helps the exegete gain a deeper understanding of the language.

A Graded Reader of Biblical Greek is the result of ten years of use and refinement by the author in an actual classroom setting.

Available in stores and online!

Greek Grammar Beyond the Basics
An Exegetical Syntax of the New Testament
Daniel B. Wallace

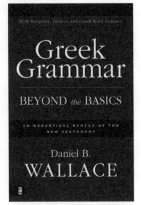

For seminary students, the goal of studying Greek grammar is the accurate exegesis of biblical texts. Sound exegesis requires that the exegete consider grammar within a larger framework that includes context, lexeme, and other linguistic features.

While the trend of some grammarians has been to take a purely grammatical approach to the language, *Greek Grammar Beyond the Basics* integrates the technical requirements for proper Greek interpretation with the actual interests and needs of Bible students. It is the first textbook to systematically link syntax and exegesis of the New Testament for second-year Greek students. It explores numerous syntactical categories, some of which have not previously been dealt with in print.

Greek Grammar Beyond the Basics is the most up-to-date Greek grammar available. It equips intermediate Greek students with the skills they need to do exegesis of biblical texts in a way that is faithful to their intended meaning. The expanded edition contains a subject index, a Greek word index, and page numbers in the Syntax Summary section.

Available in stores and online!

Biblical Greek Survival Kit

William D. Mounce

Equip your students for success in first-year Greek, and save them money! Assign the *Biblical Greek Survival Kit* as a supplemental "text" for your course and give your students the tools they need. This value-priced kit ($8 less than items purchased separately) includes:

- *Basics of Biblical Greek Vocabulary Cards* — this set contains all words occurring in the Greek New Testament more than fifteen times as well as all vocabulary from the book of 1 John.
- *Basics of Biblical Greek Vocabulary* audio CD (also in mp3 format) — with all the words contained in Basics of Biblical Greek, in chapter order.
- *Zondervan Get an A! Study Guides: Biblical Greek* — all the noun and verb paradigms they need to know in one handy place.

Available in stores and online!

New International Dictionary of New Testament Theology

Abridged Edition

Verlyn D. Verbrugge

This abridgment of Colin Brown's original four-volume work is arranged with its entries in Greek alphabetical order, which makes it easy to find the discussion of a particular word. All Greek words are transliterated into English and linked with their Goodrick/Kohlenberger numbers. This book was formerly titled *The NIV Theological Dictionary of New Testament Words*. Now it has been reset in double columns and wider margins.

Available in stores and online!

We want to hear from you. Please send your comments about this book to us in care of zreview@zondervan.com. Thank you.

ZONDERVAN.com/
AUTHORTRACKER
follow your favorite authors